'This impressive book is the most significant contribution thus far to the growing literature on "the spatial turn" in peace and conflict studies. Because conflict and peace take place in particular spaces, peacemaking is an inherently spatial project. Yet too often geography has been assumed as the inert stage for (supposedly) more fundamental processes. Drawing on fieldwork from around the world, Annika Björkdahl and Stefanie Kappler demonstrate how spatiality is crucial to understanding the role of agency in peacebuilding. Their sophisticated analysis of how this occurs at the intersections of space and place is required reading for anyone wanting to understand how violent places can be transformed into peaceful ones – and why attempts to do this so often fail.'

Nick Megoran, Newcastle University, UK

'Annika Björkdahl and Stefanie Kappler have made me look at the rebuilt historic bridge in Mostar afresh, so I now can see that it is a place that has been turned into a space for stoking on-going distrust. This book also, though, shows how even modest physical places can be transformed, by commitment and creativity, into spaces where post-war tensions can be reduced.'

Cynthia Enloe, Clark University, USA

Peacebuilding and Spatial Transformation

This book investigates peacebuilding in post-conflict scenarios by analysing the link between peace, space and place.

By focusing on the case studies of Cyprus, Kosovo, Bosnia-Herzegovina, Northern Ireland and South Africa, the book provides a spatial reading of agency in peacebuilding contexts. It conceptualises peacebuilding agency in post-conflict landscapes as situated between place (material locality) and space (the imaginary counterpart of place), analysing the ways in which peacebuilding agency can be read as a spatial practice. Investigating a number of post-conflict cases, this book outlines infrastructures of power and agency as they are manifested in spatial practice. It demonstrates how spatial agency can take the form of conflict and exclusion on the one hand, but also of transformation towards peace over time on the other hand. Against this background, the book argues that agency drives place-making and space-making processes. Therefore, transformative processes in post-conflict societies can be understood as materialising through the active use and transformation of space and place.

This book will be of interest to students of peacebuilding, peace and conflict studies, human geography and IR in general.

Annika Björkdahl is Professor of Political Science, Lund University, Sweden, and is author/editor of numerous titles, including *Peacebuilding and Friction* (Routledge 2016) and *Spatializing Peace and Conflict* (2015).

Stefanie Kappler is Lecturer in Conflict Resolution and Peace Building, Durham University, UK, and is author of *Local Agency and Peacebuilding* (2014).

Studies in Conflict, Development and Peacebuilding

Series Editors: Keith Krause, Thomas J. Biersteker and Riccardo Bocco, Graduate Institute of International and Development Studies, Geneva

This series publishes innovative research into the connections between insecurity and under-development in fragile states, and into situations of violence and insecurity more generally. It adopts a multidisciplinary approach to the study of a variety of issues, including the changing nature of contemporary armed violence (conflict), efforts to foster the conditions that prevent the outbreak or recurrence of such violence (development), and strategies to promote peaceful relations on the communal, societal and international level (peacebuilding).

Peacebuilding and Spatial Transformation
Peace, Space and Place

Annika Björkdahl and Stefanie Kappler

Foreword by Johan Galtung

Routledge
Taylor & Francis Group

LONDON AND NEW YORK

First published 2017 by Routledge

2 Park Square, Milton Park, Abingdon, Oxfordshire OX14 4RN
52 Vanderbilt Avenue, New York, NY 10017

Routledge is an imprint of the Taylor & Francis Group, an informa business

First issued in paperback 2018

British Library Cataloguing in Publication Data
A catalogue record for this book is available from the British Library

Library of Congress Cataloging in Publication Data
Names: Björkdahl, Annika, author. | Kappler, Stefanie, author.
Title: Peacebuilding and spatial transformation : peace, space and place /
Annika Björkdahl and Stefanie Kappler.
Description: Abingdon, Oxon ; New York, NY : Routledge, 2017. | Series:
Studies in conflict, development and peacebuilding | Includes bibliographical
references and index.
Identifiers: LCCN 2016053933 | ISBN 9781138924154 (hardback) |
ISBN 9781315684529 (ebook)
Subjects: LCSH: Peace-building--Case studies. | Space--Social aspects. |
Agent (Philosophy) | Place (Philosophy) | Peace-building--Cyprus. | Peace-
building--Kosovo (Republic) | Peace-building--Bosnia and Herzegovina. |
Peace-building--Northern Ireland. | Peace-building--South Africa.
Classification: LCC JZ5538 .B56 2017 | DDC 303.6/6--dc23
LC record available at https://lccn.loc.gov/2016053933

ISBN: 978-1-138-92415-4 (hbk)
ISBN: 978-0-367-07627-6 (pbk)

Typeset in Times New Roman
by Taylor & Francis Books

To Florian
&
To Olle, Ella and Erik

Contents

Figures

Acknowledgments

This book is the result of three years of intellectually stimulating collaboration, not only between us as authors, but also with people 'here and there'. These are people we met with in the different localities of our empirical research and people who gave us repeated feedback on our work at conferences, via e-mail and in private conversations. There are so many people who took time out of their busy schedules to meet with us and to give us the context and detail that has fed into our analysis and we would like to extend our collective thanks to all of them.

In addition, we would particularly like to thank people who talked and walked with us in the journey towards this book. They include Lejla Somun-Krupalija, Jasmin Ramović, Gëzim Visoka, Ivan Gusic, Maria Hadjipavlou, Ahmed Sözen, Brendan Murtagh, Mustafa Akıncı, Lellos Dimitriadis, Steven Kuo, Steven Leach and Laurence Piper. Thank you to David Ratford and Rahel Weldeab-Sebhatu for assisting the copy-editing process. We are also most grateful to Johan Galtung who provided a very inspirational foreword to this book.

Annika Björkdahl extends her gratitude to the Crafoord foundation for providing a travel grant necessary for the extensive fieldwork that went into this book, and to the Swedish Research Council, for a generous research grant that made this research possible. Stefanie Kappler would like to thank the Durham Global Security Institute, the Arts and Humanities Research Council as well as Liverpool Hope University for financially supporting this research.

Finally, we would like to thank our families, and most notably Olle, Ella and Erik and Florian to whom this book is dedicated, for supporting our research and the associated repeated absences from home.

Lund and Durham

Foreword

Space and Time, War and Peace

Space and time were among Immanuel Kant's primordial categories, together with causality; to be accepted as frameworks for thinking. But another German, Albert Einstein, coalesced them into 'spacetime'. The social sciences can learn from that. Our study objects also extend in time, not only in space; if not, they would have disappeared.

Being crucial for human unfolding space and time are used for the opposite, for punishment by depriving deviants of both. Space may be limited to a cell or a bed, free time to unfold may be taken away. A sentence limits space and free time; the legal code says for how long. Other civilisations limit the human body's ability to break laws by cutting off parts. And still others deprive them of togetherness.

The opposite of deprivation is enriching space and time; space by expanding or filling it with more variety, time by extending to longer lives, also filled with more variety. Spacetime offers little variety at several space points, more variety at one point, neither, both. Primitive-nomadic societies did the first, traditional-modern the second, the third is punishment, the fourth is post-modern nomadism, people moving many times, changing life-styles, careers.

Or, being stable at the same point, seeking spiritual variety in inner space. How fortunate we humans are with all these possibilities!

Two primordial sciences, geography dedicated to space and history to time, might also coalesce, into 'geo-story' or 'histo-graphy', for social spacetime. Space and time are two sides of the same coin. This fascinating book by Stefanie Kappler and Annika Björkdahl, *Peacebuilding and Spatial Transformation: Peace, Space and Place*, highlights space, but time is there. They have five case-(hi)stories: Cyprus, Kosovo, BiH, Northern Ireland, South Africa. Of course, space expands beyond those places to Greece-Turkey, USA-EU-Russia for the next two, London-Dublin-USA, Hague-London-Washington.

And time extends back to 1453 and 1389, the Orthodox Muslim fault-lines in the Eastern Mediterranean for the first three, to Oliver Cromwell and the 1690s for Northern Ireland, to 1652 for South Africa, the Dutch arrival. At least. And into the future, for images, visions. From five here-nows to past and future here-thens in time.

Let us explore Kant's categories modified by Einstein, and peace. Two models where space is concerned: tight borders protecting individual space as property and collective space as states, and open borders letting being good to each other flow unlimited. My peace, our peace, our joint peace. But how about time and peace? And how about spacetime and peace? Space is where events, processes, stability are located; time is where they unfold as processes. Location vs process. But, to unfold there must be free, uncluttered, open time.

Spacetime opens for more possibilities. We jump mentally in space at the same point in time, comparing; and we move in time at the same point in space, also comparing. Spacetime opens for both; comparing here, now with here, then, there, now and any there, then. Are South Africa in 1993 and Northern Ireland in 1998 sufficiently isomorphic (same structure) to tell us something about the first 3? And, beyond that, could isomorphism become causation? Could there be a causal flow from the two that obtained some kind of peace to the three that have not, by people acting or merely thinking, accordingly?

Draw spacetime. Put space North Europe–South Africa vertically, and time 1400–2100 horizontally. Locate the five case-points, and draw five parallel horizontal lines from past into future. They stand for five parallel processes identifying possible internal causal flows. Vertical lines connect five global system points at the same time.

But, diagonal lines may be more interesting, for instance between some there,now and a here,then in the future, exploring how something there,now may be mobilised to create a more peaceful here, then.

A basic point about spacetime is that it sensitises us to all combinations, not only the inner change here or there through time, or the possible causal flow within a global system now. Much more peace can be created in space-time than in space only or in time only.

Of course, the word 'spacetime' is not needed to arrive at that, but it helps. My metaphor is watching from a helicopter high up, seeing space-points flow in time like rivers, and seeing these rivers spilling into each other, or not. Descend low down, for details.

In European space power centres moved from South to North and in North, so also in Chinese space. What corresponded to what? Was there a connection, did the flows mix? Maybe today, imitating each other, also as defence, but further back less and less. Their vast regions kept them busy; today simultaneity make them parts of a global system.

The nationalists – Sun Yatsen, Chiang Kaishek – made China a state from a succession of dynasties with shifting power centres from 1910; the Europeanists did the same with Europe from 1950. But their use of 'China' for more than two thousand years' history confused a diverse region with a unified nation-state. Did Chinese see Europe that way?

However that may be, we have to see 'globalization' less as a system to be established and more as vast regions connecting in time. Rivers spilling into each other. The old Ubuntu, Zulu, truth, sabona, 'I am in you and you in me' becoming spacetime reality.

Johan Galtung

List of Abbreviations

ANC	African National Congress
BiH	Bosnia-Herzegovina
CHWB	Cultural Heritage Without Borders
CoE	Council of Europe
DPA	Dayton Peace Accord
ECHR	European Convention on Human Rights
EOKA	National Organisation of Cypriot Fighters
EU	European Union
EULEX	European Union Rule of Law Mission in Kosovo
GFA	Good Friday Agreement
H4C	Home for Cooperation
ICCT	International Centre for Conflict Transformation
ICO	International Civilian Office
ICTY	International Criminal Tribunal for the former Yugoslavia
IDPs	Internally Displaced Persons
INLA	Irish National Liberation Army
IRA	Irish Republican Army
JNA	Yugoslav National Army
KFOR	the Kosovo Force
KLA	Kosovo Liberation Army
MLK	The Maze/Long Kesh
MNC	Multinational corporation
NGO	Non-governmental organisation
NMP	Nicosia Master Plan
OBZ	Occupy Buffer Zone
OHR	Office of the High Representative
OSCE	Organisation for Security and Cooperation in Europe
PbCRC	Peacebuilding and Conflict Resolution Centre
SDA	Stranka demokratske akcije
TMT	Turkish Resistance Organisation
TRC	Truth and Reconciliation Commission
TRNC	Turkish Republic of Northern Cyprus
UDA	Ulster Defence Association

UN	United Nations
UNDP	United Nations Development Programme
UNFICYP	United Nations Peacekeeping Force in Cyprus
UNHCR	United Nations High Commission for Human Rights
UNMIK	United Nations Interim Administration Mission in Kosovo
UNPROFOR	United Nations Protection Force
UVF	Ulster Volunteer Force

Introduction

Space, Place and Agency – Mapping Peace Across Sites

Introduction

The abandoned Old Nicosia International Airport in the United Nations buffer zone in Cyprus is a space stuck in the past from which both Greek and Turkish Cypriots are barred. As UN guests we were driven in a white UN jeep along the runway towards the terminal hall. Our passing gaze caught the bombed airplane on flat tires on the side of the runway, before we could see the once so modern check in area with its waiting lounge chairs, the shattered glass and faded signs all carpeted with bird droppings abandoned in the debris of the Turkish invasion of 1974. We felt we entered a dead zone within which the Cyprus conflict has been emplaced and frozen. This place, we understand, has unintentionally become a contested heritage site. We find ourselves in this location, which is outside the purview of contemporary daily life of the Cypriots, yet it provides the structure on which the communities construct discourses of the past and of modernity. Leaving the site, we reflect how the legacy of the conflict is still shaping narratives about identity, otherness, remembering and forgetting, affecting the stumbling steps towards reconciliation and peace on this divided island.

Field notes, Nicosia, Cyprus, 2014.

What can places such as the abandoned Nicosia International Airport tell us about peace and peacebuilding? Places reveal the tangible and intangible legacy of conflict, ground transitions from conflict towards peace, and situate peacebuilding processes and actors. This book calls for a careful rethinking of the interconnectedness between peace, and space and place in order to understand where peace 'takes place' and peacebuilding agency unfolds. Our aim is to provide new insights into the transformation of war into peace by grounding the analysis of peace and peacebuilding agency in time and space, or 'spacetime' (Galtung, 2017: xii–xiii). We note that there has been no sustained inquiry into the relationship of peace with space and place. In general, space and place have been one of the 'silences' in the study of the contentious politics of peace. To investigate spaces and places of peace is a challenging research endeavour. Yet, we find that scholars are increasingly taking on this challenge, and spatial perspectives are slowly but steadily becoming part of Peace and Conflict Studies. To contribute to this spatial turn, we critically read, map and compare key post-conflict places and spaces in Cyprus, South

Africa, Northern Ireland, Bosnia-Herzegovina and Kosovo that foreground the legacy of conflict and processes of peacebuilding.

Thus, the overall ambition of this research endeavour is to emplace the analysis of peace, peacebuilding and agency in their appropriate spatial and temporal context. To do so, we raise critical questions, such as how can warscapes transform into peacescapes, i.e. how are spaces and places tainted by conflict transformed to represent and manifest peace? How can peace-building agents be captured spatially? By addressing these questions we hope to advance the critical peace research agenda. We suggest space and place as vehicles through which peace can be explored. Furthermore, we argue that the transformation of space and place can be approached through a focus on agency. Space, place and agency are useful concepts to re-theorise peace-building and we find that their analytical potential has not yet been fully exploited in Peace and Conflict Studies. In this vein, we develop a theoretical framework that provides a re-reading and conceptualisation of space, place and agency in order to capture their mutual constitution and, therefore, to understand agency in processes of space-making and place-making. To read peacebuilding agency through space-making and place-making endeavours is one way of investigating the interconnectedness between peace and space (an immaterial, imaginary phenomenon) and place (a material phenomenon). Our approach to space and place therefore emphasises their interrelationship. On being inhabited, space is appropriated, given meaning and interpreted and thus transformed into place. Furthermore, we are intrigued by the role of agency in space and how agency is placed. In this vein, we conceptualise agency as situated at the intersection between place- and space-making. We suggest that agency can be found in the capacity to transform place into space (through the (re-)creation of its meanings and possibilities) on the one hand, and the capacity to transform space into place (that is, the capacity to render ideas as material reality) on the other hand. Therefore, transitional processes in conflict-affected societies can be understood as materialising through the active use and transformation of space and place. Thus, this book will attempt to grapple with peace(s) as they are manifested in spatial practices, and in material and symbolic representation.

Our thinking is inspired by three strands of research that can be seen to make up the spatial turn in Peace and Conflict Studies, namely Critical Peace Studies to rethink what peace is, for whom and where it takes place; and Critical Human Geography to focus on the mutual constitution of space and place. In addition, we draw on the field of research which centres on the notion of agency in order to theorise the latter as situated in the transformation of space and place.

To investigate peacebuilding agency requires reflexive research methods. This book is a first attempt to rethink the methodologies of peace and conflict research and to advance critical and reflexive research methods based on ethnographic fieldwork. This research endeavour focuses on place as that is where people experience peacebuilding and conflict dynamics in their everyday. Thus, 'being in place', semi-structured in-depth interviews and participant observation, as well as walking, become key ethnographic tools to investigate where peace develops and to map peacebuilding agency. Intrigued by the everyday spaces and places in post-conflict landscapes we ask: How do people living in contested spaces and places narrate the particular locales and what spatial practices follow from those narratives? How can we as researchers read the spatial narratives of contested spaces and places? Our methodology is inspired by Marcus' (1995) idea of multi-site ethnography, through which we investigate spaces and place in transformation to manifest peace, such as for example the Maze/Long Kesh Prison in Northern Ireland, Robben Island in South Africa, the bridge that divides Mitrovica, the Sarajevo Roses, and the buffer zone in Nicosia.

Advancing the agenda

Peace and conflict research has traditionally paid more attention to conflict than to peace. It has often been assumed that peace is the opposite of war, and where war is present peace is assumed to be absent. Following from this is an understanding of peace as emerging when conflict abates. However, recent developments in Peace and Conflict Studies have come to question such a neat distinction between war and peace (Mac Ginty, 2006) as well as the assumed linear development of transitions from war to peace (Galtung, 2016; Browne, 2014: 7). War and peace seem to be intertwined and if there ever was a clear line between them, it has become increasingly blurred. Thus, in the midst of conflict there are islands of peace and in times of peace there are outbreaks of violence (Hancock & Mitchell, 2007). This means that peace and war often co-exist and that the binary of war and peace becomes unsustainable. This is reflected in the use of terms such as 'conflict-affected' societies or 'post-conflict' societies. The term post-conflict is useful, as it does not simply define the period after violent conflict, but rather denotes the continuation of violence in various forms, and of conflict by other means in societies in transition.

   Such societies are inherently unstable and run a great risk of relapsing into violent conflict. As, often, peace accords are born out of urgency and pragmatism, many collapse as the implementation of peace fails or reaches an impasse. Imposed or internationally brokered peace accords are often more prone to failure than locally constructed peace accords. Consequently, much research has thus conceptualised peace as precarious, turbulent, or fragile (Werner, 1999; Crocker et al., 2001; Debiel & Klien, 2002). Furthermore, most efforts to build peace entail a profound social transformation and are not least about spatial politics and the restructuring of power relations. Against this background, recent research has critically questioned the poor quality of the peace reached in many post-conflict societies and pointed out that peacebuilding interventions, well intended as they may be, do not seem to produce an everyday peace and allow for a peace dividend to materialise (Wallensteen, 2015; Pugh et al., 2008; Mac Ginty & Richmond, 2013).

Peace and conflict research has further raised the question of whether peacebuilding has to be seen as a primarily internationally driven endeavour that is culturally insensitive and fails to adapt to the local givens of the host societies (cf. Richmond, 2005). However, recent place-based approaches have tended to shy away from this critique of an 'international versus local' and instead focused on an 'international encountering the local' through an emphasis on the hybridity of peace (Mac Ginty, 2011; Richmond, 2014). This is based on the assumption that peacebuilding always consists of a process of encounter and fusion of different approaches, forms of agency and normative orders. Recent contributions to this debate focus, for instance, on the encounters between 'global' and 'local' actors, discourses and practices through the notion of friction. Such an approach views global and local spaces as relational and mutually constitutive, and finds that scales and relations between scales are fluid, contested and constantly reproduced through social and political processes of peacebuilding (Buckley-Zistel, 2016). Thus, it draws attention to the 'social construction of space and agency over time in a manner that unsettles the boundaries between the two' (Björkdahl et al., 2016: 4). Thus, recent research shows that peace, peacebuilding and agents can be located according to their scale of operation and this has implications for how we conceptualise where peace and peacebuilding agencies are emplaced.

In a similar vein yet challenging the often-static assumption of a hybrid cocktail of local and international approaches, peace and conflict research taking an interest in the question of 'the local' has increasingly come to question the assumed static nature of the local as the anti-pole to an international identity and instead argued that the two have to be seen as intricately linked, mutually intertwined and in constant flux (Kappler, 2015). It has further been suggested that, instead of focusing on hybridity as an outcome of politics, or on frictional encounters, we need to focus on the politics of scale through which diverse social forces move between difference scales of governance (Hameiri & Jones, forthcoming). In that sense, Peace and Conflict Studies have developed to include a critical reflection of what constitutes the local or the 'field' (Richmond et al., 2015) and put this in relation to the realities of peace as it plays out in post-conflict societies. At the same time, a clear spatial dimension as an entry point to analysing the fluid nature of peace as well as the subversive nature of the field has been lacking from such studies. From a spatial perspective, the local may be understood as a place in space, which has become a material location that can be marked geographically (Massey, 1994: 154) but is not fixed or essentialised in its identity. In contrast, the latter is in constant flux due to possible movements within and across spaces and places.

It seems that, like peace and conflict researchers, geographers have paid more scholarly attention to war than to peace (Agnew, 2009; Dodds & Ingram, 2009; Gregory, 2011; Flint, 2011). On war, Geography is 'authoritative and informed, eloquent, theoretical, and interdisciplinary' but it has 'a long and patchy history of geographical engagement with peace' (Megoran, 2010). Political Geography's disproportionate focus on war provides a negative framing of peace in which peace exists as an empty other (Williams & McConnell, 2011). To think in territorial terms has been widespread in military and security circles where frontlines, war zones, international borders are drawn onto maps. Maps clearly matter as they are instruments of geopolitical and geostrategic thinking and help to internalise an image of a geopolitical reality. 'Geographies of violence' have therefore been of central importance, mainly in the discipline of Geography (Korf & Raeymaekers, 2012; Springer & Le Billon, 2016). It is, against this background, particularly interesting to observe a tendency through which 'geographies of peace' are paid increasing attention and problematised in terms of the spatial contestations that are inherent not only in contexts of war, but also of peace (Gregory, 2010; Koopman, 2011; McConnell, et al., 2014; Kobayashi, 2009). Gregory (2010: 181) argues that the discipline of Geography can position itself as 'one of the arts of peace'. Thus, recent research re-situates peace within a geographical framework and unpacks the geographies of peace (Le Billon, 2008; Flint, 2005; Megoran, 2011). Through such endeavour it is able 'to investigate and critique peace as both process and content' (Williams & McConnell, 2011: 4) and to consider peace in broader, complex and more nuanced ways. It has been able to deconstruct normative assumptions about peace. Drawing on ethnographic research, geographers explore peace at different sites and scales to reveal how peace is constructed, materialised, and interpreted (McConnell et al., 2014). In such research, peace is understood as situated knowledge. Within Critical Geography, understandings of peace now seem to shift towards issues of power, politics and agency (McConnell et al., 2014) and therefore seem to parallel, at least to a certain extent, the interest in these issues as they can be found in Peace and Conflict Studies alike.

Indeed, agency has become a buzzword in contemporary research in both Human Geography and Peace and Conflict Studies as it is increasingly evoked as a tool to grasp the ways in which societies at the receiving end of peacebuilding operations comply with, resist, co-opt or challenge the policies promoted by the international community (cf. Kappler, 2014; Richmond & Mitchell, 2011; Björkdahl & Mannergren Selimovic, 2015). At the same time, agency has remained a vague and fuzzy concept, with researchers being unsure how they can recognise, read and interpret it. Including space in the analysis helps to explain why some forms of agency are enabled, while others are disabled (Massey, 1994). Thus, this book will bring together the approaches outlined above to elaborate on spatial practices of agentive subjects, as there is a need to re-theorise in more complex ways the spatial politics of peacebuilding agency in transitions from conflict to peace.

In the field of Peace and Conflict Studies spatial concerns are central, yet they have so far received little consideration. Our contribution shows that war-making and peace-making 'take place' and are spatially driven, engineered and transformed. Furthermore, we show that sometimes the legacy of conflict obscures the visible and tangible manifestations of peacebuilding. The investigation into space-making and place-making adds to this critical debate about the materialisation of peace and the emplacement of peacebuilding agents. By conceptualising peacebuilding agency in relation to space and place we link expressions of agency to spatial practices and thus contribute to the re-theorisation of agency. The ability to turn space into place, and place into space within a broader perspective on transformation of conflict reveals the role that agentive subjects play for change in this analysis. We argue that agency is constituted of, and constituted by, practices of place-making and space-making. Thus, agency is key to understanding any kind of change, including change in a post-conflict environment. One way of reading this change is in a tempo-spatial way, that is, that change can be read in the material and social composition of particular spaces and their transformation over time. The spaces of particular interest in the peacebuilding jigsaw are peace-related spaces in their symbolic and material value to society. At the same time, we suggest that agency is always and by necessity ambivalent in nature. Spatial change can thus be liberating and emancipating on the one hand, or repressive and exclusive on the other hand – or both at the same time, depending on perspective. Spaces are therefore playgrounds of agency, representing platforms on which actors can be empowered or disempowered (cf. Massey, 1994), with both processes often taking place in parallel. By the notion of spatial politics we refer to the ways in which agents in peacebuilding turn symbolic spaces into material places, and vice versa. Peacebuilding agents seek to manipulate strategically and to re-signify the meaning of certain places in which the legacy of war is inscribed by means, as we will see, of deploying certain imaginaries and practices. Place and space thus mould actors. Space may act as a compass of meaning to the exercise of agency, and place is the immediate setting in which agency and practice 'take place' (Therborn, 2006: 512).

Multi-site ethnography

This section introduces the methodological thinking and rethinking of this book. We take as our point of departure the notion of 'reflexive comparison' in the sense of a multi-site ethnography to demonstrate the contested politics of peacebuilding (Marcus, 1995; Hannerz, 2003; Gupta & Ferguson, 1997). The reflexive approach recognises that, while knowledge is context-bound, cases 'speak to each other' and that an analysis of the different circumstances can move beyond the particularities of each case to find commonalities and generate theoretical insights (Gingrich & Fox, 2002). Our choice of multi-sited ethnography is derived from the inter-disciplinary work we undertake to map how space and place structure or question the normative landscape of peace in which ideas about what constitutes peace are transmitted through space and place (Marcus, 1995; Gupta & Ferguson, 1997). Thus the research is designed to move from single site ethnography to multi-site ethnography in order to examine the circulation of meanings, objects and identities in diffuse time-space beyond bounded spatial entities. Our approach to multi-sited ethnography is to read the spatial narratives of the particular spaces and places that are identified as 'diagnostic sites' for our investigation, but in a way that understands the connections and fluidities between those sites.

According to Tedlock (2000: 455), 'ethnography involves an on-going attempt to place specific encounters, events and understandings into a fuller, more meaningful context'. She then concludes: 'as a result, it combines research design, fieldwork and various methods of inquiry to produce historically, politically and personally situated accounts, descriptions, representations of human lives' (Tedlock, 2000: 455). Taking space and place as a starting point for investigation, we aim to explore ethnography as an approach to discover spatial narratives beyond any one individual's experience of space and place. We understand ethnography as a mode of inquiry, open to revisions and modification as we read the multiple and dynamic stories the ethnographic landscape holds. In a way, we apply an ethnographic approach which takes as its entry point the experience of specific individuals whose everyday activities are in some ways connected to, affected by, and constituent of the spaces and places under investigation (DeVault & McCoy, 2002; Kappler, 2013). Such an approach shows us both a place at which to start in the 'everyday' as people experience it and also a way in which to explore the relevant elements of the spaces and places where agency is situated.

When discussing methods of research inquiry, this chapter singles out a number of diagnostic sites of analysis, such as pathways, places of commemoration and of belonging as well as spaces of interaction. The actual combination of sites included in our study enables us to establish linkages between the sites and these linkages make the multi-site study something different from a mere comparative study of various locales (Hannerz, 2003). The selection of places and spaces for closer investigation is based on the following three aspects. First, the site holds a transformative dimension in relation to the transition from war to peace. Second, it possesses a symbolic as well as material presence of war and/or peace. Finally, it can be read through a focus on transitional agency, that is, the types of agency that drive processes of transition. This mode of research reveals how peace and war at one site are reproduced at another site, how meanings circulate, how peace is manifested differently at different sites and how changing sets of peacebuilding agency can be performed in various ways.

Our efforts to map peacebuilding agency, space and place in transitions from conflict to peace are grounded in interview- and field-based research undertaken in Bosnia-Herzegovina, Kosovo, Northern Ireland, South Africa and Cyprus over a period of more than five years (cf. Kappler, 2014; Björkdahl, 2013; Björkdahl & Mannergren Selimovic, 2014, 2016). Our research design combines fieldwork, participant observation and interviews to capture the ways in which peacebuilding agency is not only affected by peace and conflict, but also how it negotiates, resists and challenges these discourses and practices on its own terms. Our observations from fieldwork raise not only questions about scales of peace, but also the question about relational space. How do peacebuilding agents label places and spaces? What does that tell us about social phenomena? How do they appropriate them on their own terms? How do they transform spaces into places and places into spaces? How can we understand agency in terms of space-making and place-making capacity? To what extent does the post-conflict landscape constitute and is it constituted by peacebuilding agency?

We conduct this multi-site ethnography with a keen awareness of being part of the landscape, as the landscape changes across sites. As such, our approach reflects on the researcher as situated in the on-going, never-stand-still of the social and the material (cf. Ellis & Bochner, 2000). Hence, what we discover is always seen, interpreted, heard and experienced by us as researchers and what is discovered is essentially in motion. The selected sites are a point of departure for reading agency through narratives projected onto the sites. This includes the very narratives we bring to the sites as researchers. Certain narratives may be invisible to us, others may be emphasised by certain actors, while others may be disguised to us as outside researchers. We therefore acknowledge our situation as learners ourselves, dependent on the ways in which sites are presented to us on the one hand, but also on our own identities on the other hand. Our aim is not to present a comprehensive list of narratives around the space or place. Instead, we emphasise the very fact that places are not neutral locations, but rather artefacts of meaning which are under constant contestation. It is those contestations which cast light on the power relations at play, yet with an acknowledgement that these are in constant flux and never finished or completed.

Outline of the book

This book hence provides a spatial perspective on the complex architecture of peace. By taking a spatial approach, it advances peace and conflict research. Beginning with chapter one, entitled *Space, Place and Agency*, we develop the original theoretical framework that will guide the subsequent empirical analysis of our selected sites. First, we will provide a thorough re-reading and conceptualisation of the key terms space, place and agency and outline the distinction and tensions between place and space. Second, we explore the role of agency in space and place, linking agency to the capacity to turn place into space (space-making through the recreation of its meanings), and to turn space into place (place-making as the capacity to render ideas into material reality). We then go on to investigate the individual case studies of the book.

In chapter two entitled *Cyprus: Contesting the Island*, we investigate the different manifestations of agency as they can be found on the divided island of Cyprus. The conflict has left a legacy of division that is playing out spatially. Here, agency becomes a question of positionality in the divided landscape of the island. Through an in-depth analysis of places such as the buffer zone and the ghost town Varosha it finds that a number of symbolically laden places have been embedded in political contestation concerning, *inter alia*, the question of whether the island should be reunified.

Kosovo: Emplacing the State and Peace(s) is the title of chapter three in which we explore the anchoring of the state in spatial terms. Place-making in Kosovo has been about giving the state a physical presence. A walk along the Boulevard of Mother Teresa in the capital Pristina reveals how the state is evolving by being inscribed in to the cityscape. This chapter maps place-making and space-making through an analysis of how statebuilding is shaped, resisted and embedded in the post-conflict landscape of the 'newborn' state. Concrete examples from Pristina, Mitrovica and Prizren reflect the extent to which high-level politics are spatially translated into the everyday realities of the inhabitants of those cities.

Moving on from Kosovo to Bosnia-Herzegovina, we explore *Bosnia-Herzegovina: The Ethnic Peace* in chapter four. We investigate how peace is located in place and space, and how socio-spatial relations are remade. We argue that both the war of the 1990s and the subsequent peace process have contributed to the existing spatial order in BiH. To illustrate this, we explore the curbed agency of returnees to Republika Srpska, the place-making efforts to localise peace by a youth centre in Mostar and the space-making processes related to the commemoration of the victims of the siege of Sarajevo.

With a focus on the spatially embedded legacy of the Troubles, chapter five *Northern Ireland: The 'Maze of Peace'* situates peacebuilding agency in the landscape of power in Northern Ireland by revealing the material and immaterial divisions in the cityscape of Belfast as well as the wider structures of dealing with the past in the region. Our analysis demonstrates how the dividing structures of the peace walls and the Maze/Long Kesh are constituted by and constitutive of divisive practices perpetuated by and beyond the Good Friday Agreement. It finds that the limited success of the peace accord in addressing spatial issues indicates an inability to understand the complexities and contestations surrounding transitions, and a failure to acknowledge the material and immaterial legacy of the Troubles as a major spatial factor in the ways in which the (peaceful) future of Northern Ireland is negotiated.

In chapter six, entitled *South Africa: Perpetuating Spatial Apartheid?*, the immaterial and material legacy of the apartheid regime in terms of spatial exclusion, relocation and mobility limitations are exposed, and agents with the ability to resist or go beyond these spatial practices of segregation are analysed. With a particular focus on Cape Town, the chapter foregrounds practices of place-making and space-making in relation to the establishment of structures for the return of previously evicted people as well as the ways in which the country deals with its apartheid legacy and its representation through the prison island of Robben Island.

In our final chapter, the conclusion, we draw out the main findings of our research and emphasise the extent to which agency in transition from war to peace can be read in spatial terms through the processes of space-making and place-making. We note that spatial practices blur the distinction between warscapes and peacescapes, which cannot be seen as separate phenomena, but depend on the observer, narrative and narrator. In consequence, this distinction can change over time. This book demonstrates how peacebuilding, statebuilding and nationbuilding are spatially conditioned and as such cannot be read in abstract, but need to be understood in concrete, grounded terms, with respect to how they affect and are affected by the spatial landscape in which they take place. Furthermore, our empirical analyses show agency as emplaced in time and space and how it evolves through interaction with material and immaterial structures. We also find that the politics of transition and transformation can be read spatially and that spatial practices and mobilities can challenge material and immaterial borders. The cross-case sites reveal how a self-sustaining geography can freeze conflict, whilst at the same time a diverse set of actors keep challenging the spatial setup of war and peace. From our 'spacetime' perspective, we conclude that spaces and places connect the past, present and future in non-linear ways and they offer a platform for intergenerational narratives that cut across time. Finally, we expect these findings to impact upon the future agenda of critical peace research and the practice of peacebuilding, as well as on the theorisation of peacebuilding and agency.

Bibliography

Agnew, J., 2009. Killing for Cause? Geographies of War and Peace, *Annals of the Association of American Geographers* 99(5): 1054–1059.

Björkdahl, A., 2013. Urban Peacebuilding. *Peacebuilding* 1(2): 207–221.

Björkdahl, A. & Mannergren Selimovic, J., 2014. Gendered Justice Gaps in Bosnia-Herzegovina, *Human Rights Review* 15(2), pp. 201–218.

Björkdahl, A. & Mannergren Selimovic, J., 2016. A Tale of Three Bridges: Agency and Agonism in Peace Building. *Third World Quarterly* 37(2), pp. 321–335.

Björkdahl, A., Höglund, K., Millar, G., van der Lijn, J. & Verkoren, W., 2016. Peacebuilding Through the Lens of Friction. In: A. Björkdahl *et al.* eds. *Peacebuilding and Friction: Global and Local Encounters in Post-Conflict Societies*. London and New York: Routledge, pp. 1–16.

Browne, V., 2014. *Feminism, Time, and Nonlinear History*. New York: Palgrave.

Buckley-Zistel, S., 2016. Respecting Complexity: Compound Friction and Unpredictability in Peacebuilding. In: A. Björkdahl *et al.* eds. *Peacebuilding and Friction: Global and Local Encounters in Post-Conflict Societies*. London and New York: Routledge, pp. 17–31.

Crocker, C., Hampson, F. O. & Aall, P., 2001. *Turbulent Peace. The Challenge of Managing International Conflict*. Washington: United Institute of Peace.

Debiel, T. & Klein, A. eds, 2002. *Fragile Peace: State Failure, Violence and Development in Crisis Regions*. London, New York: Zed Books.

DeVault, M. L., & McCoy, L., 2002. Institutional Ethnography: Using Interviews to Investigate Ruling Relations. In: J. E. Gubrium, & J. A. Holstein, eds. *Handbook of Interview Research. Context and Method*, Thousand Oaks: Sage, pp. 751–776.

Dodds, K. & Ingram, A. eds, 2009. *Spaces of Security and Insecurity: Geographies of the War on Terror*. Aldershot: Ashgate.

Ellis, C. S. & Bochner, A., 2000. Autoethnography, Personal Narrative, Reflexivity: Researcher as Subject. In: N. Denzin & Y. Lincoln (eds). *The Handbook of Qualitative Research*. Thousand Oaks: Sage, pp. 733–768.

Flint, C., 2011. Intertwined Spaces of Peace and War: The Perpetual Dynamism of Geopolitical Landscapes. In: S. Kirsh, & C. Flint, eds. *Reconstructing Conflict: Integrating War and Post-War Geographies*. Farnham: Ashgate, pp. 31–48.

Flint, C. ed., 2005. *The Geography of War and Peace: From Death Camps to Diplomats*. Oxford: Oxford University Press.

Galtung, J., 2016. Syria (Minding the Minds II)', Transcend Media Service. Available at https://www.transcend.org/tms/2016/01/syria-minding-the-minds-ii/ Accessed 24 June 2016.

Galtung, J., 2017. Foreword. In: A. Björkdahl, & S. Kappler, *Peacebuilding and Spatial Transformation. Peace, Space and Place*. Abingdon, New York: Routledge.

Gingrich, A. & Fox, R. G., 2002. *Anthropology, by Comparison*. London: Routledge.

Gregory, D., 2010. War and Peace. *Transactions of the Institute of British Geographers* 35(2), pp. 154–186.

Gregory, D., 2011. The Everywhere War. *The Geographical Journal* 177(3), pp. 238–250.

Gupta, A. & Ferguson, J., 1997. Beyond 'Culture': Space, Identity, and the Politics of Difference. In: A. Gupta and J. Ferguson, eds. *Culture, Power, Place: Explorations in Critical Anthropology*. Durham, N.C.: Duke University Press, pp. 33–51.

Hameiri, S. & Jones, L.forthcoming, Beyond Hybridity To The Politics Of Scale: International Intervention And 'Local' Politics. *Development and Change*.

Hancock, L. & Mitchell, C., 2007. *Zones of Peace*. Bloomfiels CT: Kumarian Press.

Hannerz, U., 2003. Being There… and There… and There!: Reflections on Multi-Site Ethnography. *Ethnography* 4(2), pp. 201–216.

Kappler, S., 2013. Coping with Research: Local Tactics of Resistance Against (Mis-) representation in Academia. *Peacebuilding* 1(1), pp. 125–140.

Kappler, S., 2014. *Local Agency and Peacebuilding: EU and International Engagement in Bosnia-Herzegovina, Cyprus and South Africa*. Basingstoke: Palgrave Macmillan.

Kappler, S., 2015. The Dynamic Local: Delocalisation and (Re-)localisation in the Search for Peacebuilding Identity. *Third World Quarterly* 36(5), pp. 875–889.

Kobayashi, A., 2009. Geographies of Peace and Armed Conflict: Introduction. *Annals of the Association of American Geographers* 99(5), pp. 819–826.

Koopman, S., 2011. Let's Take Peace to Pieces. *Political Geography* 30(4), pp. 193–194.

Korf, B, & Raeymaekers, T., 2012. Geographie der Gewalt. *Geographische Rundschau* 64(2), pp. 4–11.

Le Billon, P., 2008. Diamond Wars; Conflict Diamonds and Geographies of Resource Wars. *Annals of the Association of American Geographers* 98(2), pp. 345–372.

Mac Ginty, R., 2006. *No War, No Peace: The Rejuvenation of Stalled Peace Processes, and Peace Accords*. Basingstoke: Palgrave.

Mac Ginty, R., 2011. *International Peacebuilding and Local Resistance*. Basingstoke: Palgrave.

Mac Ginty, R. & Richmond, O., 2013. The Local Turn in Peacebuilding. *Third World Quarterly* 34(5), pp. 763–783.

Marcus, G. E., 1995. Ethnography in/of the World System: The Emergence of Multi-Sited Ethnography. *Annual Review of Anthropology* 24, pp. 95–117.

Massey, D., 1994. *Space, Place and Gender*. Cambridge: Polity Press..

McConnell, F., Megoran, N. & Williams, P. eds, 2014. *Geographies of Peace*. London: I.B.Tauris.

Megoran, N., 2010. Towards a Geography of Peace: Pacific Geopolitics and Evangelical Christian Crusade Apologies. *Transactions of the Institute of British Geographers* 35(3), pp. 382–398.

Megoran, N., 2011. War and Peace? An Agenda for Peace Research and Practice in Geography. *Political Geography* 30(4), pp. 178–189.

Pugh, M., Cooper, N., & Turner, M., 2008. *Critical Perspective on the Political Economy of Peacebuilding*. Basingstoke, New York: Palgrave Macmillan.

Richmond, O., 2005. *The Transformation of Peace*. Basingstoke: Palgrave Macmillan.

Richmond, O., 2014. The Dilemmas of a Hybrid Peace: Negative or Positive?. *Cooperation and Conflict* 50(1), pp. 50–68.

Richmond, O. & Mitchell, A., 2011. Peacebuilding and Critical Forms of Agency. From Resistance to Subsistence. *Alternatives: Global, Local, Political November* 36(4), pp. 326–344.

Richmond, O., Kappler, S. and Björkdahl, A., 2015.
The 'Field' in the Age of Intervention: Power, Legitimacy and Authority vs the 'Local', *Millennium*2015, 44(1), pp. 23–44.

Springer, S. & Le BillonP., 2016. Violence and Space: An Introduction to the Geographies of Violence. *Political Geography* 52(2), pp. 1–3.

Tedlock, B. 2000. Ethnography and Ethnografic Representation, In: N. Denzin & Y. Lincoln, eds. *The Handbook of Qualitative Research*. 1st ed. London: Sage, pp. 455–465.

Therborn, G., 2006. Capital Politics: Why and How Place Matters. In: R. Goodwin and C. Tilly, eds. *The Oxford Handbook of Contextual Political Analysis*. Oxford: Oxford University Press.

Wallensteen, P., 2015. *The Quality of Peace. Peacebuilding, Victory and World Order*. Oxford: Oxford University Press.

Werner, S., 1999. The Precarious Nature of Peace: Resolving the Issues, Enforcing the Settlement, and Renegotiating the Terms. *American Journal of Political Science* 43(3), pp. 912–934.

Williams, P. & McConnell, F., 2011. Critical Geographies of Peace. *Antipode* 43(4), pp. 1–5.

1 Space, Place and Agency

Introduction

This chapter will provide the conceptual framework with which the topics of space and place can be approached in Peace and Conflict Studies. The overall ambition behind this research agenda is to ground the analysis of peace and peacebuilding in their appropriate spatial and temporal context. To do so, we suggest space and place to be vehicles through which peace and agency can be explored. As there has been no sustained inquiry into the relationship of peace with space and place, spatial perspectives have gained scant attention in the study of the contentious politics of peace. Thus, this monograph investigates peace(s) as they are manifested in spatial practices, and in materiality and symbolic representation. This is to argue against a discourse of globalisation, which suggests that the importance and particularity of place is waning in favour of a 'putative expansion of borderless space' (Ley, 2004: 152), and instead to suggest that place and space are key markers in our understanding of peace and conflict as they translate those abstract notions into everyday life practice.

To do so, the chapter will first provide a thorough re-reading and conceptualisation of the key terms space, place and agency. It will then move on to outline the tension between place (as a material phenomenon) and space (as an immaterial, imaginary phenomenon). We will look at the ways in which place and space are mutually conditional and intertwined to explore how they can be understood as geographical, material and structural platforms on which different forms of agency and power unfold. This includes processes of building infrastructures, empowering certain users of space and place and excluding others from their active use. Space will therefore be considered as a possibility in terms of representing a platform of empowerment, while at the same time always being vulnerable to manipulation and co-optation (Massey & Hajnal, 1995; Massey, 2005).

Peace and conflict are manifested and 'take place' in the everyday. A focus on the transformative nature of place and space will thus serve as a point of departure of looking at how different types of space are used to transform the display of power within post-conflict societies. We develop our definition of space and place to take into account their contested nature. Tuan (1979: 421), for instance, points to the differing understandings of 'place' between geographers, architects, poets, moralists and historians. Our approach to space and place emphasizes their interrelationship. Inhabited space is appropriated, given meaning and interpreted and thus it is being transformed into place. In the words of de Certeau (1984: 117), 'space is a practiced place'.

Second, the chapter will look at the role of agency in space and how agency is placed, tying in with the recent body of literature on agency, hybridity, friction and resistance in Peace and Conflict Studies. As agency is always situated, we will situate agency in the tension between place and space. We claim that agency can be found in the capacity to transform place into space (through the (re-)creation of its meanings and possibilities) on the one hand, and the capacity to transform space into place (by rendering ideas into material reality) on the other hand. Such processes of transformation reflect the extent to which power relations, and thus conflicts and peace(s) are located in spatial practice. We will therefore situate spatial agency in an everyday context, where social practices create a sense of belonging as well as a sense of ownership of place. These everyday practices are linked to processes of labelling, symbolising, creating meaning and framing the significance of places and spaces in a given social context. This context in turn constructs divisions, boundaries and bridges within those spaces. Those processes are both material and immaterial in nature, and often reinforced or challenged by artefacts, museums and media representations. In this context, the 'everyday' will not be viewed as the 'primitive' or 'backward', but rather as a practice in which the local, the national and the international meet and negotiate the ways in which places and spaces are framed and used. In a sense, spatiality has the character of situating activities in which we 'make room for' and 'give space to'.

Third, our understanding of spatiality refers specifically to socially produced space, the created forms and relations of a broadly defined human geography. Spatiality is thus the medium and the outcome of situated agency and system of social practices. Soja (2000: 8) reminds us that spatial specificity refers to the particular configurations of social relations, built forms, and human activity in a particular space and its geographic sphere of influence. It arises from the social production of space as a distinctive material and symbolic context or habitat for human life. The notion of spatiality helps us comprehend the moral, political, economic and social contours of space. For instance, it assists in understanding the proliferation of gated enclaves for the wealthier in South Africa (Lemanski, 2006), of the sectarian working class neighbourhoods of East Belfast (Murtagh, 2002), and of the ethnoscape in the divided city of Mostar (Bollens, 2011).

Against this background, the chapter will conclude by arguing that agency can be conceptualised as situated at the intersection between place- and space-making. Therefore, transformative processes in post-conflict societies can be understood as materialising through the active use and transformation of space and place.

Spaces and places for the construction of peace

Almost all processes including war-making and peace-making take place somewhere, in a specific local setting (Koopman, 2011; Megoran, 2011). Capital cities such as Sarajevo or Jerusalem can be read as 'landscapes of power'. As material and emblematic assets, divided cities like Mostar are central and contested places in many identity-based conflicts. An airbase such as the one in Dayton, Ohio, can be a place for peace negotiations giving its name to a peace accord. Conflicts manifest themselves in places, as does peace. Yet, the legacy of the conflict often obscures the visible and tangible materialisations of peace. Contemporary peacebuilding missions profess to bring about 'peace', but what exactly constitutes peace is seldom apparent to the people on the ground. Where peace will 'take place' is hence not always obvious, and not always does such peace materialise in people's everyday (Richmond 2010b; Mac Ginty, 2011; Mac Ginty & Richmond, 2013). Place is thus where peace and conflict affect people in their everyday and it matters to people's experience of conflict dynamics and peacebuilding. Some places are directly affected by violent conflict while other places may be islands of peace in a landscape of violence. Inherent in the distinctiveness of places is their meaning to individuals (Björkdahl & Buckley-Zistel, 2016). The ways in which the latter make sense of and use particular places can therefore be read as the infrastructures of peace and conflict. Hence, while landscapes of conflict are often defined by the exclusive nature of place (the siege of Sarajevo being one example in the attempt to isolate the city from any outside connections), landscapes of peace often aim to transform places to make them more inclusive. The Occupy Buffer Zone Movement in Cyprus, which aimed to overcome the existence of a 'dead zone' strictly dividing the North and the South of the island, is quite telling in this context (cf. Papadakis, 2005). It is exactly this spatial nature of peace and conflict that establishes a connection between the abstract-political aspect of social interaction, and its manifestation in every-day practice. The tactics of manoeuvring that de Certeau (1984) outlines can be read through spatial practice (cf. Mitchell & Kelly, 2011). Peace and conflict, as two sides of the same coin and often taking place in parallel, are thus spatially manoeuvred and translated into the ways in which material places are built, used, and endowed with meaning.

We are curious to find out how space and place structure and question the normative landscape of peace in which ideas about what constitutes peace are transmitted through space and place. One version of peace may be appropriate here, but not there. Spatial structures impact on representations of peace and conflict, while re-politicising agency on an everyday life basis.

Rethinking and situating agency in spatial politics

The agentive subject is always situated in space and in place. A basic under-standing of the meaning of agency has to do with the human capacity to act, a capacity that is not exercised in a vacuum but in a social and material world in which structures shape the opportunities and resources available in a constant interplay of practices and discourses (Giddens, 1984; Gregory, 1981: 16). An initial step in our effort to conceptualise agency is to clarify the blurred border between actor and agent; '...whereas actors are engaged in a consultative mode of participation, agents are better conceived of as transformative of both direct (immediate) and structural (removed) concerns' (Cornwall, 2003: 1327). Thus, a defining component of 'agency is the achievement of change, whereas action presumes no such transformation' (Shepherd, 2011). Central to the concept of agency is the notion of autonomy, the capacity to act independent of material and social constraints. Rethinking agency we want to discuss new forms of autonomy and constraint, as well as the co-constitution of agency and structure, which cannot be understood through conventional dichotomies of the material and social alone.

Thus, our ambition is to transcend the structure–agency debate and account for the blurred boundaries of agency and structures of peace and conflict. To do so, we search for a trajectory between the two poles that foregrounds and situates practice in terms of experience, attitudes and beliefs in the everyday. Then, structure and agency do not occupy two distinct positions but are regarded as mutually constituted through practice (Giddens, 1984; Gregory, 1981). Through practice, agents do not 'create social systems: they reproduce or transform them, remaking what is already made in the continuity of praxis' (Giddens, 1984: 71). When they act conventionally, they maintain a given state of affairs; when they act outside convention, they 'intervene in the world or...refrain from such intervention, with the effect of influencing a ... state of affairs' (Giddens, 1984: 71). Such an understanding may help to question the validity of the binary of actor versus structure as an organising narrative of the human experience and the possibility of knowing whether agency is the consequence of a hidden structure of demonstration of autonomy.

Our concern about turning space into place and place into space within a broader perspective on transformation of conflict calls for a more complex understanding of agency and of the role that agentive subjects play for change. In order to understand what entices space or place to change, we need to understand how differently positioned agents can partake in change (Giddens, 1984; Gregory, 1981). To explain social and material transformation, then, is to understand the interplay between space or place and agents as well as how agents can exercise power to bring about change and drive spatial transformation. At times, however, there may not be a visible, identifiable agent of change, as 'agency may be exercised through fluid, fleeting action in a hidden and obscure space constrained by existing structures and/or existing power relations' (Björkdahl & Mannergren Selimovic, 2015: 171). In such times and spaces, exerting agency in the traditional sense may not stand a chance of bringing about substantial transformation. Critical and situated agency, however, may be able to re-appropriate the everyday spaces and cross to other levels of society from which such agency is traditionally excluded.

Recent re-conceptualisations of agency in the context of peacebuilding have explored the interplay between discourses of power and social practices of resistance (e.g. Richmond, 2010b; Kappler & Richmond, 2011; Kappler, 2013; 2014). While these contributions in critical peacebuilding research have been very valuable in making visible local agents that perform resistance, the search for agency has mostly taken an interest in acts of resistance and, as such, it may reproduce an idea about agency as reactive (cf. Richmond, 2011). Such scholarship has not sufficiently theorised and differentiated between different local agents and thus may run the risk of viewing agency as uniform and unmarked by ethnic, class or gender differences. A preoccupation with the reactive agents narrows the understanding of agency, and obscures the fact that agents, while to a lesser or greater degree socially embedded in relations of power and interdependence, do not lack autonomy, power of initiation, and creativity (Björkdahl & Mannergren Selimovic, 2014). While we recognise that social power and social resistance are always spatial, we find it is important to defy the easy reduction to issues of power and resistance. We recognise that agency is not simply about reaction to power in the form of resistance, but agency can be expressed in various ways and in various enabling or disabling spaces. Rather than stripping agents of identity in terms of class, gender and ethnicity, such dimensions of agency need to be brought to the fore since they drive marginalisation and oppression in post-conflict societies as well as broaden the ways agency can be expressed in unconventional spaces and places. In that sense, we are not only avoiding a dichotomy between power and resistance, but also the binary construction between peace and conflict. By situating peacebuilding agency in spatial practice, we instead point to the fluidities of agency in its ability to move between practices of peace and conflict. Spaces always have the potential to host practices related to peace and conflict, even at the same time, and thus point to the continuous ambiguity of agency in its ability to activate a variety of discourses and practices.

It is the process through which such activities constitute a socio-material world, alter the behaviour of others, change places and spaces as well as modify ideational and material structures that may not necessarily be formulated as intentional acts of resistance. By studying agency from this point of departure, we can reveal relations between agency, space and place as well as unmask power relations played out in such spaces and places. Our investigation finds that agency can be conceptualised as situated at the intersection between place- and space-making. Therefore, transformative processes in post-conflict societies can be understood as materialising through the active use and transformation of space and place. Our interest in the grounds for peace means searching for agency situated in space and place, and mapping the critical agents in the margins that may have transformative effects on conflict. Critical questions must be asked around how agency is situated in space and place, and how exercising agency may transform spaces and places of peace and conflict.

To situate agency in the everyday is one way of linking agency with space and place. The everyday is a space where critical agency can be expressed and where practice 'takes place'. Thus, agentive subjects may transform spaces and places that are imbued with the legacy of conflict in order to promote peace. A grounded peace can be seen as constituted by those inhabiting place and through the spatial practices of these agents. Activities and agencies in the everyday are more likely to be non-instrumental and self-fulfilling than the logics of governing structures of peace (cf. de Certeau, 1984: xi). Situating agency in the everyday assists us in grasping how place is understood differently through individuals' and societies' differing experiences and exploring how meanings of space and place are constructed and articulated by individuals and communities alike.

Place

Peace and peacebuilding are emplaced and constituted in part through location, material form and their imaginings (cf. Appadurai, 1995). In order to detect the significance of place for peace and conflict, it may be useful to distinguish between three kinds of place of relevance (cf. Gieryn, 2000; Creswell, 2004). First, we view place as a 'geographical location' ranging in scale from the body to the globe. Thus, place is the distinction between here and there, that makes people appreciate the near and the far away. Second, place is seen as a 'material' form, created by people's activities. Place has physicality, and processes pertaining to peace and conflict happen through the material forms people build or use. Third, place represents a distinctive, more or less 'bounded' form of space often constructed and defined in the lived experience of people. As such, place is fundamental in expressing a sense of belonging and is seen to provide a locus of identity. Looking at the world as a world of places, we see attachments and connections between people and place. According to Gieryn (2000: 465), places are 'doubly constructed' as they are both built or physically carved out, and interpreted, narrated, named, understood and imagined. Thus, place always encompasses a spatial dimension as well as emplacing and mediating constructions of peace(s) and peacebuilding activities.

Inspired by the work of Lefebvre, Harvey (1990) explores how places are constructed and experienced as material artefacts, how they are represented in discourse, and how they themselves are used as representations. Building on this research, place is here seen to represent a 'fusion' of social and material worlds that are an irreducible part of human experience and without which human experience could not be constituted and made meaningful. Place-based experiences, such as the sense of place and human dwelling in memories of place, are understood to be formative of agents. Yet, the meanings attached to place are often contestable and alterable, and those meanings dictate who belongs, i.e. who is, 'in place' versus who is 'out of place' (Creswell, 1996; 2004). Thus, one's place is clearly related to one's relation to others, according to Creswell (2004: 3). A close reading of place through a power-lens depicts how place reflects and reinforces hierarchy and power relations, hosts power-laden social relations through which agents are constituted and de-centred. Massey (2005) points out how place is a locus of complex intersections and outcomes of power geometries that operate across many spatial scales from the body to the global. Thus, material places are impregnated with power relations, and hierarchies restrain or enable certain forms of agency (Gaventa, 2006). By extending or denying life-chances to people and communities, places such as the ethnic enclaves of segregated urban neighbourhoods in Belfast surrounded by 'peace walls' and suffering from multiple deprivations reflect how fear and violence is place-specific and how the peace dividend is materialised unequally in the city of Belfast.

Place thus moulds actors. It is the immediate setting in which agency and practice 'take place', according to Therborn (2006: 512). In order to get at the compasses of meaning in relation to emplaced agency in times of peace or conflict, we can think of place as: a place to be in, to remain in, to go to, to defend or to liberate, or to commemorate. Agency is thereby constitutive of and constituted by practices of place-making.

In the spatial manifestations of violent conflict, differentiating one place from another and attaching identity to such place is an important feature of territorial conflict. Here identity markers will signal frontiers, at times micro-frontiers, i.e. the borders and boundaries of the place and who belongs and who does not. Where conflict takes place, one might say, is fully impregnated with place. As Enloe (2010) points out, wars are never 'over there' but always in place. Place, however, may also stabilise and give durability to social struc-tural categories, such as peace(s) that re-arrange(s) post-conflict power-rela-tions, hierarchies and embody(ies) and secure(s) otherwise intangible cultural norms, identities, memories supporting the infrastructure of peace. Place can thus sustain both imagined peace(s) and the materialised everyday peace by routinising daily practices in ways that include and bring people and com-munities together, and by embodying the meanings ascribed to them. Through various spatial practices and narratives, agentive subjects become engaged in linking peace with place.

Space

Space can be viewed as the imaginary counterpart to place, referring to the processes of meaning-making and the ideational component of locations. Spaces may or may not coincide with places. At the same time we appreciate that the neat distinction between 'space' and 'place' can be seen as artificial. To cite Massey (2005: 6), 'there are often shared undergirding assumptions: of place as closed, coherent, integrated as authentic, as 'home', a secure retreat; of space as somehow originarily regionalised, as always-already divided up.'

In this book, for analytical purposes, we frame space as the imaginary counter-side of material place, as the ideational extension of physical pre-sence. In that respect, while space is often differentiated from place as non-everyday and abstract, we argue that imaginary spaces tie in closely with the everyday notion of locale, yet accounting for their socially constructed element. Imagination is always linked to place, so the notion of space denotes that which is beyond the material and physical, but the realm which extends to meanings and interpretations of spaces and thus their relevance to their users' everyday lives. This is linked to Tuan's assumption that space is an emotional phenomenon, which needs to be explored through a humanistic lens (Tuan, 1979: 388). As he suggests, we can discover an 'affective bond between people and place or setting' (Tuan, 1974: 4). This socio-political, emotional link, which is filled with meaning will be referred to as 'space' in this study. Although spaces are often considered to be objective, they have attributes which are based on our subjective experiences and therefore reflect underlying structures, needs and grievances (Harvey, 1990). Against this background, space can only be understood with respect to the material (that is, place), but is based on multiple realities in terms of how people make sense of and use them as part of their everyday engagements (Harvey, 1990).

Spaces are therefore always embedded in the socio-political realm, not only as the 'product of interrelations' (Massey, 2005: 9), but also as the initiating platform on which social relations can form and develop. This collective phenomenon is what Tuan (1979: 403) labels 'group experiential space' and illustrates the social nature of space. Given it refers to the meanings created in any given context, 'space' only makes sense in a social environment and can only ever be understood in relation and connection to the socio-political surroundings. In this context, Stevenson (2013: 99ff) has suggested that the social life of cities can, among other things, be accessed through its emotional value as locations are 'imbued with cultural and personal meaning and also have the ability to arouse often very powerful emotions' (Stevenson, 2013: 99). In the light of the power of emotions triggered by particular spaces (with some particularly powerful, such as the Hiroshima monument in Japan), they can be considered influential in the networks of agency deployed in social life. Spaces often trigger emotional responses among their users, and often therefore also political or social mobilisation. Brüggemann and Kasekamp (2008), for instance, describe how the politics of commemoration in Estonia have even led to a 'War of Monuments' around a monument erected to honour Soviet soldiers who had been fighting against Nazi Germany. The emotionality triggered by this monument clearly led to social processes in which the ways in which history would be dealt with spatially were unpacked and discussed.

At the same time, pointing to the potential of spaces to deploy mobilising power, de Certeau (1984) has highlighted the feature of spaces as fields of human creativity and agency. This is in line with Lefebvre's view on space, which he considers to have an active nature in terms of serving as an instrumental and operational tool (Levebvre, 1991: 11). Spaces are hence political, embedded and instrumental to social agency as well as connected to political agendas. Agency unfolds in the processes during the course of which meanings are constructed, challenged and continuously revised. Transformation can therefore be said to have a spatial dimension as agency is situated in the construction of spatial meanings. In this context, Kesby (2005: 2054) argues that transformation requires both material and conceptual spaces in which it can develop. This ties in with Gupta's and Ferguson's argument that calls for 'understanding social change and cultural transformation as situated within interconnected spaces' (Gupta & Ferguson, 1997: 35). The ways in which people relate to spaces (that is, how they feel about spaces, how they make sense of them and how those spaces impact upon social life) can lead to empowerment or marginalisation, inclusion or exclusion. Political action is based on the connection of spaces and is embedded in the spatially laid-out structures of society. In a similar vein, Robinson suggests that 'the imaginative spatialities with which we describe processes of transformation shape our sense of political possibilities and hence our political choices' (2000: 286). Agency is thus an input to and output of practices of space-making. In that respect, spaces are never free of surrounding structures of power and agency, but are imaginary reflections of power relations. The relocation processes of the township inhabitants of South Africa's metropoles, particularly in the context of the 2010 FIFA World Cup, are but one example of the authorities' attempts to demonstrate their power dominance over the more marginalised sections of the population. In this context, Harvey (1990: 226) has argued that the command over space (in our understanding, the command over the imaginary processes of meaning-making associated with place) is a source of social power. Space can therefore act as an inclusionary device in terms of providing a discursive platform of encounter and construction of common meanings, while it can also serve as a platform of exclusion by limiting the discursive realm and construction of meaning to a few selected participants (Kapper, 2014). This ties in with Tuan's 'we-they' syndrome, which denotes the use of both place and space as identifiers of inclusive and exclusive identities (Tuan, 1979: 420). The latter are not necessarily correlated in a linear way with geographical space, but often deviate from it while labelling certain spaces as 'ours' and others as 'theirs' (Tuan, 1979: 420). We can therefore argue that spaces are necessarily linked to agency, with the possibility of embodying violent practices (Springer, 2011: 93), such as social exclusion and hegemonic practices. At the same time, we argue that the type of agency embodied in spaces can be either violent or peaceful, depending on the users active in the space, the audience and social context as such. Spaces of peace therefore turn into spaces of conflict, and spaces traditionally used for peacebuilding are always subject to challenge from inside and outside. The agency to build peace (or refusal to do so) can thus be seen as situated in spatial practice, and as we argue, in the transformation of space into place, and vice versa.

Time

While we have emphasised the centrality of space and place as platforms on which we can analyse peace and conflict, it becomes clear that, considered in isolation of time, they can only provide snapshots and non-dynamic images of a much more complex space-time nexus. Not only are space and place constituent of peace and peacebuilding processes, but so also is time. Time and space intervene in the practice of constructing a durable peace, they condition its construction. Adding a temporal dimension helps us rethink the relationship between space and place. Inspired by Tuan (1977: 6), who has linked space to movement and place to the stops along the way and regarded each stop in the movement as a possibility for space to be transformed into place, we engage with the transformation of spaces and places.

In this context, Latour has argued that the social only becomes visible when it is in the process of making a change and thus clearly relies on the notion of transformation (2007: 108). It is only when the relationship between human and non-human actors (including landscapes) changes that we can observe transformation, brought about through the agency of those actors. The transformation processes that we can read through a spatial analysis can therefore not be read through a snapshot analysis, but instead through an analysis of the changes that the landscape is undergoing and creating over a period of time.

Against this background, a spatial analysis that has as its goal to make visible agency therefore essentially needs to include a time analysis as well. Indeed, the only way of understanding agency is to understand it in a perspective of transformation. What has been changed, and by whose (transformative) agency? This concept in turn includes an interpretation of events as happening in a particular order. This order is not necessarily self-evident or naturally given, but established through practices of argumentation and action. Agency is therefore an inherent part of time, that is, the ways in which actors make sense of a series of events in connection with each other. Hoy (2009: 92) suggests that '[t]here is nothing in the moment of time that tells whether it is past, present, or future. The order comes from temporality.'

At the same time, by taking into account a temporal dimension of agency, we need to avoid falling into the trap of classifying time in a quasi-colonial way. In fact, Stanford Friedman (2006: 428) has warned that, particularly modernist interpretations of time 'typically operate within an unexamined centre/periphery framework that locates the creative agency of modernity in the West.' This results in a dichotomisation of agency during the course of which the West is imagined as full of creative agency, while non-Western societies are accused of backwardness and apathy. Hutchings (2011: 190) therefore points to the tendency of Western cultures to associate 'the non-West as a reminder of its own past'. There is a risk that the researcher will become complicit in a form of 'temporal Orientalism' during the course of which transformation is understood as a temporal progress from non-civilisation to civilisation. This means that the forms of agency that we like are temporally associated with progress (implying the present and the future), whereas less desired forms of agency are ascribed to the past. Instead, in this book, we argue that a temporal understanding of agency always needs to be linked to a more complex, non-linear understanding of time that does not privilege one particular imaginary of time over another, as such Orientalist conceptions of time tend to do. One successful attempt has been made by Browne (2014) who has put forward an argument in favour of poly-temporality, as a non-linear and open understanding of time in a feminist context. With such an approach to temporality, we always need to bear in mind that the imposition of temporal structures of whatever kind can be considered a form of power (Mac Ginty, 2015: 4).

Hence, if we want to explain change and transformation beyond a static notion of space, we need to address the issue of time, not least against the background of Tuan's analysis that '[t]he analysis of spatial experience seems to require the usage of time categories' (Tuan, 1979: 399). In that sense, we need to engage with the fact that time is often not a linear phenomenon – the time-space nexus has often been said to be culture-specific (Tuan, 1979: 390), but is more complex in its creation of links between past, present and future. Narratives and imaginations of time are not neutral, but often selective or instrumental, while different notions of time and space can coexist in any given context. Massey (2005: 71) speaks of competing trajectories in society, which are not necessarily linear, but involve competing conceptions of space in time. And just like space, time can be considered a representation of the surrounding socio-political landscape. To speak with Harvey's words:

> [s]patial and temporal practices are never neutral in social affairs. They always express some kind of class or other social content, and are more often than not the focus of intense social struggle.
>
> (Harvey, 1990: 239).

Indeed, competing notions of time and selective references to the past highlight the embeddedness of spatial narratives in time. This is what Strange and Kempa (2003: 391) refer to as 'palimpsest', namely the 'temporal layering of meanings'.

Monuments are one interesting illustration of which elements of the past are attributed particular significance over other, seemingly less significant elements. At the same time, the choice of which time periods or eras are relevant and which are not, is a highly political one. Such choices reflect the agency of actors to present their perception of 'important time' or 'historical moments' as the one which ends up translating into spatial practice. In the UK, for instance, there are many monuments relating to the 'Great War' as this is deemed a period relevant for both British citizens as well as tourists from abroad (cf. Iles, 2006).

Often, for the sake of coherent narratives, spaces are fitted into stories and time/events are interpreted accordingly to make stories and narratives coherent over time and space. In that sense, places such as monuments not only include a spatial dimension, but also embody a diachronic narrative in time. The stone monument located in front of the Historical Museum in Sarajevo, which calls for the commemoration of victims of previous wars, relates to a way of dealing with the past through a monument as well as providing a critique of the tendency to read 'time' (i.e. the past and its influence on the future) in absolute terms (Simčić, not dated). The monument warns against the violence of the past and thus calls for attention to this with respect to potential future wars. Again, the notion of transformation is inherent in this example as only the time-space connection allows for a transformation of historical narratives. Massey (2005: 71) has therefore pointed to the need to challenge linear conceptions of time, and Starr (2003: 5) suggests that both time and space are dependent on individual or collective perceptions.

Against this background, we need to situate peacebuilding practices not only in space and place, but also in time. This is not least a result of the fact that peacebuilding itself usually takes place in moments of transition, or aims to trigger transitional processes themselves (cf. Suhrke & Berdal, 2012). It is only in moments of transition that agency can be recognised, hence time becomes inextricably linked to a spatial analysis of transformation. For instance, if we are to understand the changing role of the so-called peace walls or interfaces in Belfast, we have to not only account for the physical changes in space (e.g. their presence in arts projects or the removal of selected walls), but also the historical context in which such changes take place. Similarly, the fact that Irish language classes are offered in a community centre in predominantly Loyalist East Belfast can also only be understood in a time dimension, that is in connection with emerging socio-political discourses which encourage such projects (cf. Skainos, 2014).

In this context, we often assume we can clearly localise peace and war in time and space. Where war is present, peace is absent and after war peace will follow. In that sense, it seems difficult to move beyond the binaries of war and peace, since both negative peace (defined as the absence of direct violence) and positive peace (defined as the absence of both direct as well as structural and cultural violence) relate to violence and perhaps must do so (Galtung, 1969). Yet, war and peace are clearly intertwined and if there ever was a clear line between war and peace it has become increasingly blurred. Foucault, for example, argues that war is inside peace while Mac Ginty describes the continuities between war and peace as a situation of 'no war – no peace' (Foucault, 2003; Mac Ginty, 2006). For in the midst of violent conflict there are islands of peace and in times of peace there are outbreaks of violent conflict. By situating peace and war in time and space we are better able to grasp them as fleeting notions and to comprehend how they can co-exist. At the same time, this approach points to the non-linear nature of both space and time in the ways in which they can be read as indicators of transformative agency.

Agency at the intersection between space and place

As the previous sections have shown, both place and space are full of diffuse power relations. But how can we read them? As we argue above, agency manifests itself in transformative practice and therefore becomes visible over space and time. Shome (2003: 40) suggests that space can be viewed as a tech-nology (that is, a means and medium) of power. In that sense, the diachronic notion of transforming material place into imaginary space, and vice versa, is an indicator of transformative practice and thus displays agency through a spatialised lens. In this vein, we argue that we can read agency in the practices of place-making and space-making as we outline here below.

Turning a place into a space (space-making)

The ability of turning a place into a space denotes the process of making a physical place relevant and meaningful to societal and political discourses. For instance, whereas a bridge as such may not seem relevant to people's everyday lives, it can become significant if it enters socio-political discourses in terms of becoming a wider symbol of social life. One example would be the bridge over the Miljacka river in Sarajevo on which Franz Ferdinand was shot in 1914. This bridge has turned into a meaningful space meanwhile, as it has triggered debates around ways of dealing with the past as well as repre-senting a symbolic crossroad in Sarajevo's memorial landscape (cf. Björkdahl & Mannergren Selimovic, 2016; Kappler, 2016). Similarly, the peace walls in Belfast are not merely physical barriers of movements, but at the same time represent a symbolic boundary between the two communities in the city. Examples are numerous, and perhaps most visible in the visual arts. In Cape Town, for instance, a group of artists have put together an exhibition enti-tled 'Talking about Cape Town' (What's On in Cape Town, 2014), which uses the physical city space to narrate spatial stories of the associated social and cultural life. Through such practices, places are equipped with a social meaning, they become part of the social imaginary. The more spatially relevant a place can be made, the more powerful it will be in the transfor-mation of people's everyday lives. The Occupy Buffer Zone Movement in Cyprus is a powerful example of how social activists used the buffer zone as a physical place to reverse its social significance and use it as a space of encounter and dialogue. The place itself only represented the venue, while the wider social and symbolic discourses around it were transformed in favour of an alternative discourse that neither local communities nor international actors were prepared for.

Turning a space into a place (place-making)

Along similar lines, we can read agency from the process during the course of which actors are able to give physical presence to an ideational space. This is based on the realisation that places do not emerge 'like that', but are the result of an on-going process of creative agency. Place does not stay the same, it is continually emerging, that is, place involves a transformation of the physical and the imagined spaces. By inhabiting space, agents appropriate it, interpret it and give it meaning and transform it to place. Thus place is always becoming.

Place can be seen as space filled with people, things, practices and representations (Gieryn, 2000: 465). A sense of place is the attribution of meaning to a built-form or natural spot (Rotenberg & McDonogh, 1993). Places are made as people ascribe qualities to the material and social at that site: ours or theirs; safe or dangerous; public or private; unfamiliar or known; accessible or not.

One prominent example would be the reconstruction of the famous bridge in Mostar, which the World Bank and the EU praise as one of its main achievements in Bosnia-Herzegovina (BiH) (Björkdahl & Mannergren Selimovic, 2016; Forde, 2016). The fact that the international community was able to transform an idea (of reconciliation) into a physical space (the bridge itself) is a marker of agency – although of course it is not the only narrative projected onto the rebuilt bridge. Again, a corresponding example in Belfast would be the marking of territory through flags, graffiti and symbols, all of which are physical illustrations of messages related to identity and difference. The latter have found physical expression in territorial markers, translating ideational processes into material artefacts. In a peacebuilding context, the Youth Cultural Centre Abrašević in Mostar, the youth centre in Srebrenica, Alter Art in Travnik or the Shatro Club in Sarajevo are examples where the idea of creating a social venue, a place of encounter, was at the origin of the creation of the physical space. It was only due to the organisers' power to mobilise local helpers that the abstract ideas of encounter were finally able to translate into material practice. It is the very connection between space and place that points to the agency to translate spatial ideas into material place, which is of particular importance in (post-) conflict scenarios.

Agency through place- and space-making

In that sense, we argue that the ability to transform space into place and vice versa are clear markers of agency, particularly against the background that space does not necessarily equal place. Instead, the agency deployed 'in-between' determines what kind of place is produced from imaginary spatial ideas, or, alternatively, what kinds of imaginary spaces emerge from a physical construction of a place (whether it be a bridge or monument). The bridge in Mostar reflects the agency of the World Bank to reconstruct the bridge on the one hand, yet on the other hand, this agency can be seen as restricted given that the constructed place has limited impacts upon its discursive and symbolic significance. In that sense, the bridge has not really become a symbol of reconciliation locally, but is rather contested and not used to bring people from each of the two communities together. It is simultaneously a contested monument, a place onto which different historical narratives are projected, a competing memory site of a glorious past, a horrific recent past, as well as a site of everyday practices, and a tourist trap.

In this context, basing his work on Judith Butler's ideas of performativity, in relation to the state of Bosnia-Herzegovina (BiH), Jeffrey points to the performative nature of space (Jeffrey, 2013). He suggests that, contingent on available resources, spaces are performed in their manifestation of power and control (Jeffrey, 2013). At the same time, agency and power are not exclusively enacted through top-down measures, but can be seen as playing out in an everyday environment. Places constructed and imposed from the top are constantly challenged in their everyday setting, whether this be through adaptation, ignorance or even demolition of particular spaces (cf. Kappler, 2016). Such performative practices are then projected onto places and produce a multiplicity of meanings around those. Low (2000), for instance, has pointed to the social production (the sum of forces shaping a space's actual physical creation) and social construction (how people use, interpret and produce meanings in space) of space.

It is only through the incorporation of the social enactment of place (i.e. its transformation into space) that we can understand why certain places become shared spaces, while others do not. This also explains why some peace parks (as often cited in African contexts) have been considered successful in overcoming physical barriers (Van Amerom & Büscher, 2005), whereas plans for a peace park in Cyprus have sometimes been referred to as an artificial interruption of natural city life (Papadakis, 2000, 2006). The example reflects the necessity to connect spatial policies and plans to the everyday needs arising in the surrounding communities, as those will determine the ways in which places will be used and which symbolic meanings will be associated with them. Will they be considered places of peace or conflict? Sometimes this is a question of the physical design of a place (is it convenient for people to use, do they pass by there regularly?), while at times it can be a question of how the space is labelled. The Cyprus example is telling here given that the label 'peace' or 'bi-communalism' tends to evoke suspicion locally. Hence if a place is labelled a bi-communal meeting point, it may already lose its symbolic power on either community.

Of course local needs may not always be 'comfortable' or in line with peacebuilding ambitions. As the flag protests in Belfast showed, sometimes local needs can be the reassertion of conflictive identity structures, which may be hard to transcend and transform. In Belfast, the protesters felt they needed to have a physical place to ensure that their identities led to a transformation of symbolic space into physical place, i.e. a position of the flag on the City Council building. At the same time, this example reflects the fluidity of processes between the construction of place and space. Spaces can be signifiers of peace or of conflict and the associated expressions of agency, and even both in parallel, dependent on the respective perspective on them. These processes of meaning-giving are in continuous development and point to the ability of people subtly to transform the use of places as well as the meanings of spaces to change the overall discourse around peace and conflict.

Conclusion

In this chapter we have shown that peace and processes of transition from conflict to peace can be read spatially. The connection between 'place' and 'space' and their mutual transformation allow us to view peace as situated in spatial practice. We have argued that the ability to turn place into space, and vice versa, reflects peacebuilding agency. Therefore, if actors are able to endow a physical location with a particular set of meanings, or if a set of ideas can be translated into material places, they can reconfigure the infrastructures of peace as they play out in lived space. We suggest that this allows us to overcome the binary between peace and conflict, given that spaces and places always embody both at the same time. It depends on the actors using and filling the respective place with meaning how it is read and used locally, but at the same time also challenged and transformed over time by a variety of actors. To fully understand such practices of space-making and place-making, we therefore need to account for variations and fluidities across space and time by investigating meanings associated with peace and conflict on the one hand, but also their materialisation on the other hand. Understanding peace through spatial observation is therefore an innovative way of researching social configurations. This, however requires and engagement not only with the visibilities of place, but also an understanding of the underlying symbolic and social processes of the construction of spatial meaning, which are often not as easily accessible to the researcher. Places and spaces do change over time and are always becoming, and they always embody a multiplicity of discourses and semi-hidden discourses, which can never be fully grasped due to their fluidity. At the same time, a spatial approach to peace and conflict allows us to read peace walls as more than physical barriers, or bridges as more than infrastructures of movement.

Bibliography

Appadurai, A., 1995. The Production of Locality. In: R. Fardon, ed. *Counterworks: Managing the Diversity of Knowledge.* London: Routledge, pp. 208–229.

Björkdahl, A. & Buckley-Zistel, S., 2016. Spatializing Peace and Conflict: An Introduction in A. Björkdahl and S. Buckley-Zistel eds. *Spatializing Peace and Conflict: Mapping the Production of Places, Sites and Scales of Violence.* Basingstoke, New York: Palgrave Macmillan, pp. 1–24.

Björkdahl, A. & Mannergren Selimovic, J., 2014. Gendered Justic Gaps in Bosnia-Herzegovina. *Human Rights Review* 15(2), pp. 201–218.

Björkdahl, A. & Mannergren Selimovic, J., 2015. Gendered Agency in Transitional Justice. *Security Dialogue* 46(2), pp. 165–182.

Björkdahl, A. & Mannergren Selimovic, J., 2016. A Tale of Three Bridges: Agency and Agonism in Peace Building. *Third World Quarterly* 37(2), pp. 321–335.

Bollens, S., 2011. *City and Soul in Divided Societies.* Abingdon: Routledge.

Browne, V., 2014. *Feminism, Time, and Nonlinear History.* New York: Palgrave Macmillan.

Brüggemann, K. & Kasekamp, A., 2008. The Politics of History and the 'War of Monuments' in Estonia. *Nationalities Paper*, 36(3), pp. 425–448.

Cornwall, A., 2003. Whose Voices? Whose Choices? Reflections on Gender and Participatory Development. *World Development* 31(8), pp. 1325–1342.

Creswell, T., 1996. *In Place/Out of Place: Geography, Ideology, and Transgression.* Minneapolis: University of Minnesota Press.

Creswell, T., 2004. *Place: A Short Introduction*. Malden: Blackwell Publishing Ltd..

de Certeau, M., 1984. *The Practice of Everyday Life*. Berkeley: University of California Press.

Enloe, C., 2010. *Nimo's War, Emma's War: Making Feminist Sense of the Iraq War*. Berkeley: California University Press.

Forde, S., 2016. The Bridge on the Neretva: Stari Most as a Stage of Memory in Post-conflict Mostar, Bosnia-Herzegovina. *Cooperation and Conflict*, 51(4), pp. 467–483.

Foucault, M., 2003. *Society Must be Defended: Lectures at the Collège de France 1975–1976*. New York: Picador.

Galtung, J., 1969. Violence, Peace, and Peace Research. *Journal of Peace Research* 6(3), pp. 167–191.

Gaventa, J., 2006. Finding the Spaces for Change: A Power Analysis. *IDS Bulletin* 37(6), pp. 23–33.

Giddens, A., 1984. *The Constitution of Society*. Berkeley: University of California Press.

Gieryn, T. F., 2000. A Space for Place in Sociology. *Annual Review of Sociology* 26, pp. 463–496.

Gregory, D., 1981. Human Agency and Human Geography. *Transactions of the Institute of British Geographers* 6(1), pp. 1–18.

Gupta, A. & Ferguson, J., 1997. Beyond 'Culture': Space, Identity, and the Politics of Difference. In: A. Gupta & J. Ferguson, eds. *Culture, Power, Place: Explorations in Critical Anthropology*. Durham, N.C.: Duke University Press, pp. 33–51.

Harvey, D., 1990. *The Condition of Postmodernity: An Enquiry into the Origins of Cultural Change*. Cambridge: Blackwell.

Hoy, D. C., 2009. *The Time of Our Lives: A Critical History of Temporality*. Cambridge, MA: MIT Press.

Hutchings, K., 2011. What is Orientation in Thinking? On the Question of Time and Timeliness in Cosmopolitical Thought. *Constellations* 18(2), pp. 190–204.

Iles, J., 2006. Recalling the Ghosts of War: Performing Tourism on the Battlefields of the Western Front. *Text and Performance Quarterly* 26(2), pp. 162–180.

Jeffrey, A., 2013. *The Improvised State: Sovereignty, Performance and Agency in Dayton Bosnia*. Malden: Wiley-Blackwell.

Kappler, S., 2013. Coping with Research: Local Tactics of Resistance Against (Mis) representation in Academia. *Peacebuilding* 1(1), pp. 125–140.

Kappler, S., 2014. *Local Agency and Peacebuilding: EU and International Engagement in Bosnia-Herzegovina, Cyprus and South Africa*. Basingstoke: Palgrave Macmillan.

Kappler, S., 2016. Sarajevo's Ambivalent Memoryscape: Spatial Stories of Peace and Conflict. *Memory Studies* Volume (online first) DOI: 10.1177/1750698016650484, pp. 1–14.

Kappler, S. & Richmond, O., 2011. Peacebuilding and Culture in Bosnia and Herzegovina: Resistance or Emancipation?. *Security Dialogue* 42(3), pp. 261–278.

Kesby, M., 2005. Retheorizing Empowerment-through-participation as a Performance in Space: Beyond Tyranny to Transformation. *Signs: Journal of Women in Culture and Society* 30(4), pp. 2037–2065.

Koopman, S., 2011. Let's Take Peace to Pieces. *Political Geography* 30(4), pp. 193–194.

Latour, B., 2007. *Reassembling the Social*. New York: Oxford University Press.

Lemanski, C., 2006. The Impact of Residential Desegregation on Social Integration: Evidence from a South African Neighbourhood. *Geoforum* 37(3), pp. 417–435.

Levebvre, H., 1991. *The Production of Space*. Oxford: Blackwell.

Ley, D., 2004. Transnational Spaces and Everyday Lives. *Transactions of the Institute of British Geographers* 29(2), pp. 151–164.

Low, S., 2000. *On the Plaza: The Politics of Public Space and Culture*. Austin: University of Texas Press.

Mac Ginty, R., 2006. *No War, No Peace: The Rejuvenation of Stalled Peace Processes and Peace Accords*. Basingstoke: Palgrave Macmillan.

Mac Ginty, R., 2011. *International Peacebuilding and Local Resistance: Hybrid Forms of Peace*. Houndsmill and New York: Palgrave Macmillan.

Mac Ginty, R., 2015. *Political Versus Sociological Time: The Fraught World of Timelines and Deadlines, CRPD Working Paper No. 23*. [Online] Available at: http://soc.kuleuven.be/crpd/files/working-papers/working-paper-macginty.pdf [Accessed 13 November 2015].

Mac Ginty, R. & Richmond, O., 2013. The Local Turn in Peace Building: A Critical Agenda for Peace. *Third World Quarterly* 34(5), pp. 763–783.

Massey, D., 2005. *For Space*. London: Sage.

Massey, D. S. & Hajnal, Z. L., 1995. The Changing Geographic Structure of Black–White Segregation in the United States. *Social Science Quarterly* 76(3), pp. 527–542.

Megoran, N., 2011. War and Peace? An Agenda for Peace Research and Practice in Geography. *Political Geography* 30(4), pp. 178–189.

Mitchell, A. & Kelly, L., 2011. Peaceful Spaces? 'Walking' through the New Liminal Spaces of Peacebuilding and Development in North Belfast. *Alternatives* 36(4), pp. 307–325.

Murtagh, B., 2002. *The Politics of Territory*. Basingstoke: Palgrave.

Papadakis, Y., 2000. The Social Mapping of the Unknown: Managing Uncertainty in a Mixed Borderline Cypriot Village. *Anthropological Journal on European Cultures* 9(2), pp. 93–112.

Papadakis, Y., 2005. *Echoes from the Dead Zone*. London: IB Tauris & Co. Ltd..

Papadakis, Y., 2006. Nicosia after 1960: A River, a Bridge and the Dead Zone. *GMJ: Mediterranean Edition* 1(1), pp. 1–16.

Richmond, Oliver (ed.), 2010a. *Palgrave Advances in Peacebuilding: Critical Developments and Approaches*. Basingstoke: Palgrave Macmillan.

Richmond, O., 2010b. Resistance and the Post-liberal Peace. *Millennium – Journal of International Studies* 38(3), pp. 665–692.

Richmond, O., 2011. Critical Agency, Resistance and a Post-colonial Civil Society, *Cooperation and Conflict*, 46(4), pp. 419–440.

Robinson, J., 2000. Feminism and the Spaces of Transformation. *Transactions of the Institute of British Geographers* 25(3), pp. 285–301.

Rotenberg, R. & McDonogh, G., 1993. *The Cultural Meaning of Urban Space*. Westport: Greenwood Publishing.

Shepherd, L. J., 2011. Sex, Security and Superhero(in)es: From 1325 to 1820 and Beyond. *International Feminist Journal of Politics* 13(4), pp. 504–521.

Shome, R., 2003. Space Matters: The Power and Practice of Space. *Communication Theory* 13(1), pp. 39–56.

Simčić, I., not dated. *Braco Dimitrijević: Under this Stone there is a Monument to the Victims of War and Cold War*. [Online] Available at: http://rci.mirovniinstitut.si/Docs/2010%20ASO%20student%20work%204.pdf [Accessed 11 March 2014].

Skainos, 2014. website. [Online] Available at: http://www.skainos.org/tag/irish-language/ [Accessed 07 March 2014].

Soja, E. W., 2000. *Postmetropolis. Critical Studies of Cities and Regions.* Oxford: Blackwell.

Springer, S., 2011. Violence Sits in Places? Cultural Practice, Neoliberal Rationalism, and Virulent Imaginative Geographies. *Political Geography* 30(2), pp. 90–98.

Stanely Friedman, S., 2006. Periodizing Modernism: Postcolonial Modernities and the Space/Time Borders of Modernist Studies. *Modernism/Modernity* 13(3), pp. 425–443.

Starr, H., 2003. The Power of Place and the Future of Spatial Analysis in the Study of Conflict. *Conflict Management and Peace Science* 20(1), pp. 1–20.

Stevenson, D., 2013. *The City.* Cambridge: Polity Press.

Strange, C. & Kempa, M., 2003. Shades of Dark Tourism: Alcatraz and Robben Island. *Annals of Tourism Research* 30(2), pp. 386–405.

Suhrke, A. & Berdal, M., (eds.), 2012. *The Peace in Between: Post-war Violence and Peacebuilding.* New York: Routledge.

Therborn, G., 2006. Why and How Place Matters. In: R. E. Goodin & C. Tilly, eds. *The Oxford Handbook of Contextual Political Analysis.* Oxford: Oxford University, pp. 509–533.

Tuan, Y.-F., 1974. *Topophilia: A Study of Environmental Perception, Attitudes, and Values.* Englewood Cliffs, N.J.: Prentice-Hall.

Tuan, Y.-F., 1977. *Space and Place: Perspective of Experience.* Minneapolis: University of Minnesota Press.

Tuan, Y.-F., 1979. Space and place: Humanistic Perspective. In: S. Gale & G. Olsson, eds. *Philosophy in Geography.* Dordrecht: D. Reidel Publishing Company, pp. 387–427.

van Amerom, M. & Büscher, B., 2005. Peace Parks in Southern Africa: Bringers of an African Renaissance?. *The Journal of Modern African Studies* 43(2), pp. 159–182.

What's On in Cape Town, 2014. [Online] Available at: http://www.whatsonincapetown. com/post/talking-about-cape-town-group-exhibition-at-the-cape-gallery/ [Accessed 02 March 2014].

2 Cyprus: Contesting the Island

Introduction

This chapter investigates the different manifestations of agency as they can be read through the practices of place-making and space-making on the divided island of Cyprus. It finds that, since the violent conflict in the late 1960s and 1970s, a number of symbolically-charged places have been embedded in political struggles either to reunify the island, or to keep it divided. Such dynamics produce contestation around the physical development of Cyprus, and the ways in which the conflict legacy can be dealt with in spatial terms, as well as about who are the legitimate actors and actions that should confront any such development. Agency therefore becomes a question of positionality in the landscape of the island and at the same time relates to the profound effects that lines of division can have on the everyday life of the inhabitants of a comparatively small place.

Indeed, the conflict has left the legacy of a decades-long conflict, with contestations around the ownership and nature of the Cypriot state playing out spatially. The presence of a buffer zone to divide the island, and the capital city Nicosia, is but one example of the sensitive nature of place in the country. The buffer zone has been in existence since 1964 and, despite the relaxation of the border meanwhile to allow for crossings, continues to be monitored by United Nations Peacekeepers. At the same time, local activists have started to question the need for a buffer zone and tried to reclaim the place – with limited success, as this chapter will show.

While these physical places themselves continue to experience symbolic politics, we can, in parallel, observe contestations around space, that is, the meanings behind those physical places. This relates to discussions around the symbolism of division, but also around the meanings of reconciliation, and where and how this would take place. A diverse cluster of agents (including peace activists, politicians, states, international actors and tourists alike) interact in such spaces and contribute to the emergence of competing discourses around the nature and manifestation of peace on the island. They are often found to contest the constrained structures of divisions that shape the internal dynamics of the island, but also its relation with the European Union

(EU), with the *acquis communautaire*[1] being suspended in the Turkish North Cyprus. This in turn means that the North is unable to access the privileges that the EU offers and therefore faces a national and international dividing line at its southern border (Ker-Lindsay, 2005). Peace in Cyprus is thus inextricably linked to a spatial dynamics, as it always involves arguments around the spatial division of the island, access to formerly mixed localities, the (almost exhausted) question of the return of the displaced, potential reunification and the future of the peace negotiations (Senol Sert, 2010). The time factor must certainly not be neglected in this context: not only has the conflict been frozen since the 1970s with little movement or change happening, but the visions for the future as they are being projected by different actors also remain bleak. The EU, having acted as a source of hope for the peace process has effectively contributed to the further division of the island. Other than that, the leadership on both sides has tended to shy away from compromise, so we are left to wonder which actors will continue to make a difference. The proxy role of the UK, Greece and Turkey has certainly been questionable at best.

Against this background, this chapter highlights agency as a spatial concept by outlining practices of place-making as they can be found in Cyprus. To do so, it starts by illustrating the spatial politics on the island by zooming in on Varosha, a suburb of Famagusta in the North-East of Cyprus, which is currently best described as a 'ghost town' after having been attacked in the 1970s during the Turkish military intervention and which has since not been rebuilt or touched. It is an apt example to reflect the ways in which a site can impede or mobilise agency. It is equally illustrative of the powerful role that place plays in the politics of transition – it can inhibit peace and freeze it in time – just as Varosha has been a frozen city.

To illustrate the practice of place-making, the chapter then goes on to investigate Ledra Palace, one of the crossing points of the Nicosia buffer zone. Within that zone, one can find the Home for Cooperation (H4C), which represents the creation of an important place in which peace activism can take place on 'neutral' grounds. The example of Ledra Palace as a crossing point is telling in a wider context, in that it reflects the dividing line as a 'dead zone' on the one hand, and the often-difficult efforts at reunification on the other hand. The H4C has indeed been facing challenges in overcoming the communal split between the two sides of the island, but has nonetheless managed to represent a space in which an encounter is possible. The chapter then investigates the Nicosia Master Plan Walk, which cuts across the buffer zone as a related example of place-making. It is a municipality-based initiative that foresaw the creation of a common place for people to walk in the city of Nicosia. This walk is to a certain extent the materialisation of the idea of a unified city and enables its user to experience the city as a single whole in its structure (spanning, as it does, both sides of it). The municipalities of Nicosia as important agents behind this walk can therefore be considered to have created a possibility of transcending divisions, albeit certainly only on a limited scale.

The chapter then goes on to outline practices of space-making and pays particular attention to a square on the south side of the island, Eleftheria (which means 'freedom') square. This was the square from which a number of protest movements emerged, amongst others the Occupy Buffer Zone (OBZ) movement, which is given attention as part of space-making processes in its attempt to redefine the meanings of the space of the buffer zone. The OBZ movement is one among others that mobilised activists to take issue with the division of the island, not only internally, but also in its external dimensions, that is, the presence of UN peacekeepers maintaining the division. Our presence in and walks through the buffer zone and the cityscape of Nicosia as well as our distant observation of the ghost town of Varosha help us capture the fleeting agency of peacebuilders, understand the transformation of spaces and places as well as the spatial politics surrounding the contested spaces and places of our investigation. A number of interviews, informal conversations and discussions with people who live and work in Nicosia contribute to deepening our analysis of the everyday politics of a divided city.

Before entering into the discussion about spatial politics and space-making and place-making processes, a brief overview of the island's recent violent history is necessary in order to outline the facets of the historical, political and spatial predicament of Cyprus and to get a better grasp of how the conflict and various peace efforts are manifested in the landscape of the island.

Emplacing the Cyprus problem: transformations and continuities

The volatile recent past of Cyprus has fragmented the society and transformed the island into a frozen conflict revealing an ethno-nationalist geography. Yannis Papadakis *et al.* (2006: 1) summarise the last forty years of Cyprus turbulent past in a poignant way:

> Cyprus has experienced anticolonial struggles, postcolonial instability, the divisive effects of opposed ethnic nationalisms, internal violence both between the two major ethnic groups on the island and within each one, war, invasion, territorial division, and multiple population displacements, all facets of the notorious Cyprus Problem.

The year 1960 marked the end of British colonial rule, which began in the late 19th century when Britain assumed control over Cyprus after three centuries of Ottoman rule. During the British colonial era, both Greek and Turkish nationalism intensified in Cyprus. The Greek Cypriot nationalism was expressed in the idea of *enosis*, a will to unite with Greece. The Turkish Cypriots initially preferred British rule, but as a reaction to the Greek Cypriot notion of *enosis* they struggled for *taksim*, the partition of the island (Bryant, 2010). Both *enosis* and *taksim* reveal extreme nationalisms and can be read as blatant nationalisms (cf. Billig, 1995: 43). This type of nationalism is related to the idea of the nation state and how it manifests itself spatially. The nationalist struggle turned violent as the Greek Cypriots formed EOKA (National Organisation of Cypriot Fighters) in the late 1950s, which in turn led the Turkish Cypriots to form their own armed organisation TMT (Turkish Resistance Organisation) (Papadakis, 2005). An anti-colonial struggle against the British and a violent interethnic conflict between the Greek Cypriots and Turkish Cypriots eventually paved way for an independent state, the Republic of Cyprus in 1960 headed by President Archbishop Makarios (Loizos, 1981).

The outcome of independence did not satisfy the aspirations of either of the ethnic groups and both continued to pursue their respective aims *taksim* and *enosis*. Three years after independence, interethnic violence erupted in Nicosia and spread throughout the island. In contrast to the Greek Cypriots who comprised 80 per cent of the island's population, the Turkish Cypriots represented the smaller part comprising only 18 per cent. During the violent period of 1963–1967 these latter bore most of the human costs in terms of casualties and many of the Turkish Cypriots were displaced in refugee camps (Papadakis, 2005; Hadjipavlou, 2010; Bryant, 2010). The crisis damaged the social fabric of interethnic coexistence and resulted in the Green Line dividing the island and separating the two communities (Loizos, 1981).

The Green Line was drawn through the capital of Nicosia and across the island creating a buffer zone on each side to be guarded by UN peacekeepers. Thus, the buffer zone became an empty void in the middle referred to by Papadakis (2005) as the 'Dead Zone'. The division of the island meant that the Turkish Cypriot nationalism played out in the north and the Greek Cypriot nationalism in the south. This in turn put in place two parallel ethnoscapes (cf. Appadurai, 1990).

The partition and the lines of division deepened in 1974 when the Greek fascist junta, in collaboration with EOKA B launched a *coup d'état* to topple the Makarios government which the Greek junta accused of betraying the struggle for *enosis* (Hadjipavlou, 2010). This event prompted Turkey's military intervention, which resulted in the present division of the island into two ethnically homogenous spaces as Greek Cypriots fled en masse to the south and Turkish Cypriots subsequently moved to the north (Loizos, 1981). The Turkish intervention was celebrated as a peace operation by the majority of the Turkish Cypriots, but interpreted as an act of aggression and violation of human rights and international law by the Greek Cypriots (Hadjipavlou, 2010; Bryant, 2010). This time the Greek Cypriots bore the main human cost of the events in terms of people killed, missing and displaced. As pointed out by Hadjipavlou (2010: 88), the demographic changes that took place during the conflict were followed by an influx of Turkish nationals to the North. This added a new element of contention and complexity in the power-sharing and power struggle on the island as the Turkish Cypriot leader Rauf Denktash granted citizenship to the Turkish nationals (Navaro-Yashin, 2012). Due to the intervention by Turkey, the Turkish Cypriots' claim to space in the north of the island was strengthened. As the Turkish Cypriots marked their presence in the North, they rejected the past presence of the Greek Cypriots in the landscape through erasure of memories and memorials of the Greek Cypriots and reinvention of who belonged (Constantinou et al., 2012). Such unconcealed nationalism tends to assign exclusionary meanings to history and ownership of the past and the cultural heritage (cf. Bryant, 2010). The destruction of heritage sites associated with belonging to 'The Other' was part of the intimate violence of the conflict, and today its traces are still visible in the landscape. As argued by Constantinou *et al.*, (2012: 178) it is 'quite common to see vandalised and ruined Greek-Cypriot cemeteries, churches and houses in the north, and similarly to see destroyed Turkish-Cypriot cemeteries, mosques and villages in the south'. Thus, the management of space, place as well as history and memory has become a vital issue in a country where nostalgia has become a patriotic duty and the visions of the future of the island clash.

The events of 1974 paved way for the unilateral declaration of the Turkish Republic of Northern Cyprus (TRNC) in 1983. Only Turkey recognised the state and the international community referred to it as an illegal state while others saw it as a pseudo-state, a de facto state or a liminal state (cf. Navaro-Yashin, 2012; Bryant, 2014; Constantinou & Papadakis, 2001). The TRNC made the Turkish Cypriots feel secure in that they finally had a state of their own and a place of belonging. However, for the Greek Cypriots the declaration of an independent North meant that the island was socially, politically, ethnically and spatially divided and that their 'right to return' was threatened (Navaro-Yashin, 2012).

The international community has over the years undertaken a number of mediation efforts and peace initiatives in addition to the prolonged UN Peacekeeping Operation UNFICYP (United Nations Peacekeeping Force in Cyprus) to resolve the Cyprus Problem (Richmond, 1998). The most prominent effort was undertaken in 2004 in connection with the potential entry of Cyprus into the EU (Anastasiou, 2007). The UN-negotiated constitutional arrangement known as the Annan Plan provided for a federal, bi-communal, bi-zonal solution, which was put to a referendum on each side of the divided island. A vast majority of the Greek Cypriots (76 per cent) rejected the plan, while it was accepted by a convincing majority of the Turkish Cypriots (66 per cent). A few days after the referendum Cyprus entered the EU, but in fact only the south of the island effectively became part of the EU, while the north side remains outside and the Green Line has become the EU's uncertain border (Ker-Lindsay, 2005).

Today, the Turkish Cypriots argue that the past legitimates divisions while the Greek Cypriots claim that it legitimates reunification. Thus, it turns out that history and memory are more concerned with the future than the past and spatial arrangements tend to be fluid as history is constantly reinvented. It is in this context that we can read the contestation on the island. Tensions tend to be concentrated around the area of the buffer zone, but are also high in the northern city of Famagusta, where the question of reconstruction and return keep both the local and the displaced community in conflict.

Spatial politics in Cyprus – Famagusta and Varosha

We argue that the agency situated between space-making and place-making determines what kind of space or place is produced. Space, we find, is performed in its manifestation of power. It is only through the social enactment of place, i.e. its transformation into space, that we can understand how certain places become shared spaces. These performances are then projected onto place. Such politics of spatial contestation play out on a continuous basis across the island of Cyprus, and can be found as condensed in the buffer zone, a highly contested place. It is therefore particularly interesting to investigate the places outside the buffer zone that mirror such dynamics and carry the politics of division out of the dead zone into the lived experience of communities on either side. To illustrate the contestations around the divided island, we now focus on the city of Famagusta, and more specifically, its former suburb, Varosha.

In fact, when it comes to the question of how agency can be read through spatial practices in Cyprus in more general terms, the case of Varosha is particularly interesting. Varosha is a suburb in the south of Famagusta ('Gazimagusa' in Turkish), a coastal town that is now situated in the Turkish Cypriot part, in the north-east of the island. Famagusta, which in its Greek origin means 'buried in the sand' (Global Heritage Fund, 2010: 17), has a rich history. It hosts Byzantine heritage and a walled city. At the same time, the town also has a long military history as it used to be a military base under the Venetians and the Ottomans then continued to use it as such (Önal *et al.*, 1999: 335). Therefore, it is a city of much interest to heritage actors and organisations, whilst acting as a reminder of the connections between East and West (Jaramillo, 2015: 201). What is more, Famagusta used to be two municipalities as it was inhabited by both Greek and Turkish Cypriots (Önal et al., 1999: 339).

Famagusta, and more specifically Varosha, experienced a new wave of interest in the late 1960s and early 1970s when a number of tourist hotels were erected (Sterling, 2014: 1). Whilst the town quickly made itself a name for its sandy beach, this image was destroyed as early as 1974 after a Greek coup and Turkish invasion. The latter was, as Önal *et al.* (1999: 341) point out, 'one of the important turning points for the city of Gazimagusa'. As a result, 39,000 Greek Cypriots left the town and people fled the hotels in panic to escape the violence (Dobraszczyk, 2015: 45). It is from then on that Varosha has been sealed off, held by the Turkish military and with access denied to any human beings. Following from this, Varosha became known for terms such as 'urban annihilation', 'urbicide' (Dobraszczyk, 2015) as well as a 'ghost town'. Sterling cites the journalist Bengtsson who reported in 1977 that 'the asphalt on the roads has cracked in the warm sun and along the sidewalks bushes are growing [...] the breakfast tables are still set, the laundry still hanging and the lamps still burning. *Varosha is a "ghost town"* (my emphasis)' (Bengtsson cited in Sterling, 2014: 2).

Indeed, when visiting Varosha now, what we observe is barbed wire, abandoned hotels with plants starting to grow over them and no signs of life. Sterling (2014: 3) suggests that the term 'ghost town' implies a past dissolved from the present, an image very much visible in Varosha. We find that nothing suggests that the complex of destroyed hotels is linked to the rest of the city of Famagusta, and the past remains almost a frozen myth. Yet this image of destruction has certainly had repercussions for the economy of the entire region and, as such, the image of being a 'ghost town' affected more than just the immediate environment of Varosha (Mullen *et al.*, 2014: 31). The tourism industry was impacted most, and the loss thereof represented a massive economic hit on the city (Önal *et al.*, 1999: 341).

Currently, when visiting Famagusta, we walk along a sandy beach, which is delineated by a barbed wire that stretches out in the water to prevent people from transgressing into the territory of destroyed skyscrapers, rising up in the background of sunbathing tourists. At the same time, the place harbours an imminent insecurity in that no one knows what will happen to Varosha, and to Famagusta as a whole, in the future. Local people have been said to not want to bury their relatives there for fear that Famagusta might be returned to the South eventually (Altay Nevzat, authors' interview, Nicosia, 2014). Therefore, we could argue that the place is a rather grim one, with little planning perspective for its local inhabitants. At the same time, postcards present the ghost town as a tourist attraction (Sterling, 2014: 9), evoking an image of a better past. Famagusta has indeed been activated as a tourist site – partly through the smaller parts of remaining accessible beach, partly through the use of dark tourism as a tool. There is a museum, the Famagusta View Point Museum, which shows a film on the ghost town that is Varosha (Sterling, 2014: 10). We can therefore see that there have been agents activating the space to make use of it for their own purposes – this includes tourism bodies as much as museum staff. Moreover, the surrounding communities can also be considered as part of this process of keeping the space alive. Dobraszczyk (2015: 49) argues that 'Varosha's witnesses – whether the town's former Greek-Cypriot residents or its post-abandonment Turkish overseers – articulate a sense of the town not as a dead place, but rather one that is suspended, waiting to be reanimated.'

Therefore, although the city appears as frozen in the past, it has acquired a central and important position in Cyprus, also in a wider perspective. Varosha has now in fact acquired an important role in the Cyprus conflict and its management. Not least because of its history of mixed population, the town has become a bargaining chip in peace negotiations. Indeed, the Turkish military continues to hold and control Varosha and is therefore able to make demands in return for potentially handing over a certain part of the territory to the Greek Cypriots (Mullen *et al.*, 2014: 26). This was what the Annan Plan had foreseen, namely the return of the former inhabitants to Varosha. However, as the plan was rejected by the Greek Cypriots, the process stalled and Varosha remains a ghost town, with no returns foreseen so far. Hence, despite the town's potential to act as part of a confidence-building measure (Ahmed Sözen, authors' interview, Famagusta, 2014), it continues to stand as an 'inadvertent symbol of division' (Sterling, 2014: 6). It is therefore clear that the 'empty space' in itself can act in two-fold ways, depending on how it is used. If the Turkish military keep controlling the space, there will be fewer alternative forms of agency activated in this space, whereas the use of Varosha as a confidence-building measure could reactivate different types of agency in the town – whether this be local inhabitants, returnees or tourists. In this context, it was suggested that the people in Famagusta would, unlike their leadership, support Varosha being reopened (Ahmed Sözen, authors' interview, Famagusta, 2014).

This would also mean that new controversies and contestations around the use of the thus-far unoccupied space could emerge. Mullen *et al.* (2014: 24), for instance, suggest that there are 'strong feelings about whether buildings should remain standing or be torn down and rebuilt from scratch and whether any initiative will be coordinated or left mainly to the owners'. In that sense, it can be expected that the transition and associated decision-making process would be controversial at best. In addition, there are proposals on the table to turn Varosha into an eco-city (Sterling, 2014: 13). This, however, would mean the unification of Famagusta and Varosha as 'model ecopolis' (Dobraszczyk, 2015: 58) and is expected to lead to political negotiations around the exact use of the space as well. This is certainly further complicated through the expected costs of reconstructing a town that has been frozen for almost half a century, with the estimated reconstruction costs around 100 billion euros (Dobraszczyk, 2015: 57).

We can therefore say that Varosha is captured in the tension between the past and its position of being a frozen ghost town on the one hand, and one of being included in the ways in which a diverse set of actors imagine the future of the city on the other hand. Weisman (2007: 97) captures this as follows:

> Other than the back-and-forth of pigeons, all that moves is the creaky rotor of one last functioning windmill. Hotels – mute and windowless, some with balconies that have fallen, precipitating cascades of damage below – still line the riviera that once aspired to be Cannes or Acapulco. At this point, all parties agree, none is salvageable. Nothing is. To someday once again lure tourists, Varosha will have to be bulldozed and begun anew.

As a result, the agency that was supposed to be eradicated by the military occupation could not be stopped entirely. The place continues to bear relevance and actually plays a key part in the peace negotiations, being evoked by national elites and international organisations alike. On top of that, the ongoing presence of tourists – beach holiday tourists as much as dark tourists – maintains a buzz around the strange atmosphere of the ghost city. And it may be that through the very 'absence' of Varosha as a post-conflict public space, it is gaining particular traction. The space itself, even in the absence of physical activities, thus bears diverse forms of agency and is used and activated by a number of agents to negotiate the post-conflict identity of Famagusta, and the Turkish North of the island of Cyprus as a whole in a space that reaches deep into the local community.

The example of Varosha can therefore be considered a particularly visual example of the ongoing insecurity of the political future of Cyprus. While there is hesitation to regenerate the 'ghost city' due to its token status in the peace negotiations, it remains a canvas on which competing visions of the future are painted – by political actors, proxy powers, political elites, the local communities and tourists alike.

Place-making

Our critical reading of the concepts of space and place recognises that spaces/places are not neatly bounded entities, but instead are fluid and socially constituted through flows and relations with other spaces and places and given new meanings as the past is reinvented. This means we are adept at uncovering relations and variations between different spaces/places, without essentialising them as given entities. Place is thus where peace and conflict affect people in their everyday and it matters to people's experience of conflict dynamics and peacebuilding, as well as where past, present and future come together. Some places are directly affected by violent conflict, while other places (such as the mixed village of Pyla, in the south of Cyprus) may be islands of peace and co-existence in a landscape of violence, divisions and ethno-nationalist geographical claims. Place-making in Cyprus thus relates to the processes through which ideas of coming together as well as separation are given a material spatial presence, as our examples below will show.

Resurrecting the dead zone

In the case of Cyprus, the divided island, it is particularly interesting to take a closer look at the buffer zone as it runs through Nicosia. Here the division runs through the city centre and freedom of movement is restricted as there is still a requirement to formally check out on one side and then check in to the other side by using one's passport. The zone between the checkpoints is often referred to as the 'dead zone', 'no man's land' or 'UN land'. Given the fact that apart from UN personnel, there is no 'normal' population and housing in this zone, it is sometimes seen as 'a space you cannot really grasp' (Confidential source 1, authors' interview, Nicosia, 2014). One of our interviewees even suggested it was more a line than a zone as it is not accessible to people (Altay Nevzat, authors' interview, Nicosia, 2014).

There have been attempts to overcome the divisive character of the buffer zone, as the 2003 project during the course of which a bi-communal team was tasked to redefine it as a 'gluing area' in terms of reuniting the city (Confidential source 2, authors' interview, Nicosia, 2014). Mainly initiated by former mayor of Nicosia and now Turkish Cypriot leader Akıncı, there was a plan to create a Green Belt for the city, which was set to act as a comprehensive belt for the city as a whole. This was, however, only partially implemented (Mustafa Akıncı, authors' interview, Nicosia, 2014). On a general level, there is limited mobility across the buffer zone and the communities continue to be separated along the lines of the zone. Crossings remain rare and the area retains its militarised character with the presence of peacekeepers and control stations (Hadjipavlou, 2007).

Yet, although the buffer zone has long served as a militarised 'dead' place, it has also been serving as a space in which separation and segregation have been resisted by refusing the materialisation of these ideas and instead have emplaced alternative ideas about peace and connection. In that sense, the buffer zone as a place is based on two competing imaginaries: the notion of division to keep the ceasefire, as promoted by the UN, on the one hand, and the imaginary of the buffer zone acting as a place of coming together beyond the community divisions on the other hand. The following sections will reflect in more detail how the place of the buffer zone has been influenced by competing spatial ideas, and how this in turn has shaped the small peace movement that has found a home in this zone.

Housing peace: Ledra Palace and the Home for Cooperation

Situated in the buffer zone in Nicosia, Ledra Palace Hotel was for decades the designated place for bi-communal activities, and peace activists could, after obtaining special permission from the Turkish military, use its facilities for academic conferences and activists' meetings (Demetriou, 2012). It was a place for high politics and the party to celebrate the independence of Cyprus was held in the Ledra Palace on 15 August 1960, attended by, among others, Archbishop Makarios, Dr Fazil Kutzuk, Rauf Denktash and Glafkos Clerides (Epaminondas et al., 2011). Peace talks and negotiations took place here as international diplomats and Cypriot politicians gathered, either to promote peace and reconciliation, or to show their national pride (Maria Hadjipavolou, authors' interview, Nicosia, 2012). Since 1974, the hotel has been under UN control and UNFICYP has since used it as military barracks. In the 1990s and 2000, the UN Day was celebrated in the buffer zone, an otherwise restricted space, allowing free access of citizens from both sides to the Ledra Palace Hotel, where Greek and Turkish Cypriots met relatives, neighbours and friends for a few hours. This was the only time Cypriots could get a glimpse of the buffer zone. In an effort to provide a similar site, the Turkish Cypriots built the Saray Hotel just off Atatürk Square. It never became a place for peace talks and it is mostly recognised for the spectacular view from its rooftop and the casino in the basement (Mustafa Akıncı, authors' interview, Nicosia, 2012).

Political as well as spatial mobility constraints were placed upon Cypriot peace activists. Communication and contacts between Greek and Turkish

Cypriots took place although it was difficult and risky between 1964 and 1974, and from 1974 onwards contact became extremely difficult. For people working towards restoring relations there were few places to meet on the island, and in the early years after the division meetings were mostly organised abroad. In Cyprus the only possibility to meet was at the British Bases in Dhekelia, in the village of Pyla (near Larnaca in the south of the island) and at the Ledra Palace Hotel, located inside the buffer zone. In 1997, the Turkish Cypriot regime imposed an embargo on Turkish Cypriots to take part in bi-communal meetings as such activities were perceived as disguised efforts by the Greek Cypriots to unify the island and permissions to enter the buffer zone where most of the bi-communal work took place were withheld (Maria Hadjipavolou, authors' interview, Nicosia, 2012). This embargo temporarily made the bi-communal movement homeless, as the Ledra Palace Hotel was the only 'bridge' between the North and South of Cyprus.

Ledra Palace can be described as a site for both peace and conflict and for peacebuilding as well as for resistance to peace. Drawing on anthropological, place-based research, Demetriou (2012: 58) characterises Ledra Palace Hotel as a space of the flawed 'peace' of Cyprus. Its 'now crumbling structure embodies the failures of "liberal peace" … on multiple levels: local complicity, global design, gendered marginalisations, politico-economic (dis)advantage, ethnic exclusion'. A critical reading of the Ledra Palace depicts a spatialised narrative of the conflict and its legacy as it now hosts UN peacekeepers while at the same time also captures situated efforts at peace, including bi-communal workshops and high-level peace talks. Thus, conflict and peace are inscribed into place and a double-reading of both reveals places of peace in landscapes of conflict, as they are created by the complex group of actors and the symbolisation of the diversity of actors and discourses are engrained in the place of the hotel.

It can be argued that the bi-communal movement has moved out of Ledra Palace Hotel and into the Home for Cooperation,[2] officially opened in May 2011, by the two leaders of the Republic of Cyprus and the Turkish Republic of Northern Cyprus as the first ever shared space for Cypriots, independent of whether they define themselves as Greek or Turkish Cypriots. The building, now housing the Home for Cooperation (H4C), is well placed in the buffer zone making it a suitable space for shared activities. The transformation of an idea into reality expressed in the restoration of the H4C building is in itself a concrete example of cross-community cooperation in Nicosia and beyond. The H4C is constructed as a place for inter-communal dialogue and cooperation, historical inquiry, to advance an understanding of the past, present and future and to pursue peacebuilding. As such, it houses a multi-functional research and educational centre, which aims for shared discovery of the different narratives of the past that produce the two different and politicised versions of history taught on the island. To quote but one example: the H4C displayed an exhibition entitled 'Topographies of Memory: From the Ermou Market place to Buffer Zone', where visitors were invited to add their own recollections of the city to the map, by means of what is academically referred to as cognitive mapping (Bakshi, 2012). The H4C is also the home of a centre for young people, educators, historians and researchers and a space for exhibitions and archives, a library and a workspace for NGOs (Epaminondas et al., 2011). It hosts the organisation Peace Players Cyprus, which has found that it is easiest for children to meet not on either side of the checkpoints, but between them. It is thus using the buffer zone as a meeting space for their (mainly sports-based) activities (Marina Vasilaras, authors' interview, Nicosia, 2012). Similarly, the NGO Youth Power Cyprus have decided to locate their offices and many of their activities in the buffer zone as it represents an accessible venue and is easy for people to reach (Sezis Thompson and Katerina Antoniou, authors' interview, Nicosia, 2012). It is therefore no surprise that the buffer zone has come to serve as a central platform for bi-communal work, given its accessibility to both Greek and Turkish Cypriots. Indeed, an increasing number of NGOs are locating themselves in the buffer zone, in order to be able to work with both the north and the south of the island. We can therefore argue that, although the space has traditionally served as a place of separation, it is now rebranded as a location for encounters and meetings. At the same time, we need to acknowledge that this bi-communal work in the buffer zone has mainly been restricted to NGOs, and wider local communities are not particularly active in this space (cf. Kappler, 2014).

Located in the buffer zone, an area marked by the scars of confrontation, the Home for Cooperation indeed seems out of place in its surroundings. Everything around it testifies to the normality of conflict and division, whereas the H4C stands for cooperation and unity. The space around it is backward looking, and the ambition of the H4C is to revisit the past to develop visions for the future. Though it is situated in the buffer zone where both local communities and the international community mark their presence, the house creates a physical site where the two communities can work together and also in collaboration with the international community (Epaminondas *et al.*, 2011). Its location means that it breaks with the widely held perception of the buffer zone as a space of separation and transforms the buffer zone into a place for cooperation. However, a place such as the H4C may become a bounded place in the sense that the ideas circulated there and the practices of dialogue become tied to the place and fail to reach the wider community outside the house and outside the buffer zone.

The Nicosia Master Plan walk

Extending just outside the buffer zone, yet still within the city of Nicosia, the Nicosia Master Plan (NMP) is about place-making where the visionary idea of a reunified Nicosia was transformed into a concrete walking plan. Notwithstanding their deeply felt differences and the material division of the city, Nicosia's two communities have together developed a plan to restore and revitalise it as a city for all, both Greek Cypriots and Turkish Cypriots, integrating the two parts, under the auspices of the United Nations Development Programme (UNDP). If implemented fully, the NMP could bring a new future for Nicosia.

The NMP reflects the vision of the two (former) mayors of Nicosia, Lellos Demetriades, representing the Greek Cypriots in the southern part of the divided city, and Mustafa Akıncı, currently leader of the Turkish Cypriot community and former mayor of Nicosia for the northern part of the city. While both leaders looked for a solution to the political situation, they realised that they also needed to deal with the immediate everyday problems of the city, reversing the decay and centrifugal growth of the city and ensuring that collaboration on the sewage system would continue (Lellos Demetriades, authors' interview, Nicosia, 2012; Mustafa Akıncı, authors' interview, Nicosia, 2012).

The NMP enables one to criss-cross from the south of Nicosia, via the opened checkpoints at Ledra street and walk through the UN patrolled buffer zone into the Turkish Cypriot northern part of the city, where Ledra Street changes its name to Lokomaci street (Bakshi, 2015). The political decision to open the checkpoints in 2003, the willingness of the urban dwellers to cross the border exploiting the mobility offered by the opening of the checkpoints and the collaborative work done by Greek and Turkish Cypriot urban planners to plan beyond the divided city and, by means of material symbols along the pathway, now guide the walker through the southern and the northern part of the city and bring the city together into a whole for those who choose to follow the path (Athina Papadopoulou, authors' interview, Nicosia, 2014). The NMP walk takes you through the walled city of Nicosia highlighting two major residential rehabilitation projects for the Chrysaliniotissa and Arabahmet areas. Almost one hundred local NMP projects contributed to the revitalisation of Nicosia as a whole, including the restoration of churches and mosques on both sides of the green line. These projects are numbered and detailed in a guidebook provided jointly by the bi-communal team that works with the NMP in order to help the visitors walking along the marked walkway and to provide a means of recognition once in the place.

After we walked the NMP walk we interpreted it as a place-making process in the sense that it represents the materialisation of the idea of connecting the two parts of the old city together through the spatial practice of walking. It also creates a presence or materiality as well as movement that mirrors the infrastructure of the divided city. It almost makes the checkpoints irrelevant through its deliberate decision to make the process of crossing an integral part of the walk, and reduces the relevance of both the visible and the invisible barriers to movement. Certainly it has to be said that the walk is not used by the majority of the local citizens and is therefore restricted in visibility and not part of everyday practices. Nevertheless, it creates a key avenue to a process, which transforms the physicality of the city and, thereby, the ways in which it is perceived by its users and 'walkers' – even if they are 'only' tourists.

Space-making

The ability to turn a place into a space denotes the process of space-making through which a physical place is inscribed with new meanings making it relevant and meaningful to political discourses. This ability to transform a place into a space, and vice versa, thereby supporting transitions towards peace, is a marker of peacebuilding agency. This process of space-making described below is about connecting a particular place that may or may not be contested in the post-conflict landscape with an imaginary space in which notions of peace are produced.

Freedom postponed: Eleftheria Square

While the process of place-making becomes obvious with the use of the buffer zone and the NMP walk, the example of space-making can best be illustrated by the example of Eleftheria Square (Freedom Square) located in Nicosia. Eleftheria Square is a square, or rather a bridge, connecting the walled city with the more modern shopping malls of the city outside the old Venetian walls. Although Eleftheria Square is located in the south of Nicosia, the Greek Cypriot part, Demetriou (2006: 67) explains how it was not only named 'freedom square' in Greek, but also came to be named as such in Turkish, as a result of the Turkish Cypriots' desire to loosen their dependence on Turkey.

Therefore, in a tradition transcending seemingly neat ethnic boundaries between the Greek and Turkish Cypriot community, Eleftheria Square has a history of protest and serves as a place of activism and campaigns (Demetriou, 2006: 69). It is the place where the 'bufferer movement' (as they call themselves) first started, that is, the movement that, linked to the global Occupy movement, occupied the buffer zone for several weeks in 2011 to point to the need for Cypriots to reclaim the 'dead zone' (Occupy Buffer Zone activist, authors' interview, Nicosia, 2014). It has been suggested that this square is of particular importance, not least because Nicosia has few squares that can be used for public gatherings (Confidential source 3, authors interview, Nicosia, 2014). In that sense, Eleftheria Square acquires a particular importance as a social venue and a mobilisation platform for Cypriots in the articulation of political protest and opinion. In this context, it is interesting to note that Eleftheria Square is located right next to the Town Hall and is visible from the latter, which, again, makes its political and symbolic value rather evident.

At the same time, the square represents an important link between the old and new part of the city and it was therefore identified in 2005 as being in need of refurbishment and re-designing. To the annoyance of many Cypriots, the new design is still far from finished, so the space is a building site and an obstacle rather than a means of connection. As emphasised by a central authority (Confidential source 4, authors' interview, Nicosia, 2014), this is due to the complexity of the works, but there are nonetheless relatively many public voices condemning the increasingly prolonged construction time, as being a deliberate political strategy to keep the city apart. This is not necessarily the case, but can still be interpreted as a way of keeping the different parts of the city divided and as creating obstacles for the political mobilisation of (Greek) Cypriots. Is freedom thus symbolically postponed at 'Freedom Square'?

What is interesting about Eleftheria Square is the fact that it has multiple meanings (Demetriou, 2006: 67), that is, political, social and economic. For instance, while the square is meant to act as a connection between the walled city and its surroundings, the meaning of 'connection' cannot be taken for granted, but must be read also in the light of exclusion as well. Demetriou, for instance, suggests a look at 'how a structure of reunification came to signify the entrenchment of division' (Demetriou, 2006: 55). The square therefore acts both as a bridge between the two parts of southern Nicosia and as a wall in terms of restricting the free flow of movement between the two parts of the city. This is linked to a number of problems, including the seemingly endless construction works that further inhibit the square's function as a bridge within the community of southern Cyprus. In addition, Charalambous and Hadjichristos (2009: 3) suggest that wealthy people have increasingly moved out of the old town, leaving behind an 'urban ghetto' of poorer and elderly people as well as immigrants inside the walls. The inner part of the city thus presents itself mainly as a zone of the disadvantaged, while the more prosperous parts of the population tend to move outside the walled city. Eleftheria Square, which is supposed to connect these two parts, is currently keeping them apart due to the seemingly never-ending construction works.

Against this background, we suggest that Eleftheria Square embodies multiple meanings. While it symbolises unification and connection on the one hand, it is also read as a marker of separation between different groups of inhabitants, almost acting like a socially divisive tool. The politics of space-making thus constantly produce competing meanings, necessitating an analytical lens centred on transformation and process, rather than static outcomes. While the square had been a place of public protest since the 1950s, it is increasingly seen as a space on which hegemonic political interests are played out to prevent protest and to inflame division. It is in this context that some people will suspect the authorities of deliberately postponing the construction works and maintaining a certain degree of chaos in the area around the square. In that sense, symbols of reconciliation can become sites of division in their ability to trigger conflict about meanings, or symbols of division can unite people in their convergent interpretation of those markers. It is the political agency of actors that contributes to the planning of the further development of Eleftheria Square, while at the same time, social actors use their agency to point to the lack of progress at the site and thus highlight the wider symbolical implications of the building site 'Freedom Square'.

Figure 2.1 Eleftheria Square building site with Town Hall in the background, photo taken by authors, 2014.

The Occupy Buffer Zone Movement

One interesting movement in the context of the protests that have started in and around Eleftheria Square is the above-mentioned Occupy Buffer Zone (OBZ) Movement that was launched in 2011 to protest against the division of the island as well as the fact that the United Nations controls the buffer zone. Campaigners, mostly young Cypriots from both sides of the divide, first met on a weekly basis and then started camping in the zone more permanently (Petros Shammas, authors' interview, Nicosia, 2014). Some of their vocalised key goals included the reclaiming of the buffer zone, resistance against the presence of peacekeepers in that area and the eventual reunification of Cyprus as a whole. The movement was linked to a number of protest actions, including a volleyball game across the divide and anti-military walks, but then received an eviction letter from UNDP (Petros Shammas, authors' interview, Nicosia, 2014), the rationale of which is contested. Overall, there was a high degree of scepticism (to put it mildly) on the part of the international community when it came to their perspectives on the movement. The movement eventually disbanded, not least due to the opposition to it expressed by a number of international actors.

Similarly, even at the local level, there is no agreement on whether the movement was able to address broader social questions or whether it was instead a fringe movement and fairly disconnected from local society (Altay Nevzat, authors' interview, Nicosia, 2014). What became obvious, however, is the fact that a number of actors (including institutions such as UNDP or the European Commission) began to feel uncomfortable about the unexpected use of the space, as the case of the 'bufferers' has highlighted. In that sense, the notion as to whether the buffer zone is a zone of disruption or instead a seam that can be used to reconnect the two parts of the city (and the entire island) is contested. The spatial meanings and interpretations of the physical place are therefore divergent and reflect the agency of the advocates of both sides to frame the buffer zone as a zone of peace or of conflict. While international actors and community representatives have voiced criticism of the movement, the activists themselves have instead transformed the meaning of the buffer zone, which has come to denote connectedness and unification. Their aim to reclaim the buffer zone from the UN peacekeepers, and to create out of it a space of unification, was temporally limited. Nevertheless, it has left an important legacy, in that it reflected the extent to which the meanings of the buffer zone are contested and contestable, and it must not be claimed exclusively by the actors directly situated within it. The movement instead highlighted the potential of opening the meanings of the space to a wider audience and demonstrated the agency of an initially small group of activists to make an impact upon the symbolic development of the space. Their notion of what the buffer zone should mean, and its wider symbolic relevance for Cyprus as a whole, are certainly different from the way in which political authorities on either side, as well as the UN peacekeepers, view and police the area. In that vein, the protest movement was able to show that the meanings over the buffer zone (and thus, any other space) must not be viewed as monopolised by politically powerful actors, but can be continuously redefined and renegotiated. The success of the bufferer movement in reclaiming the zone may have been limited in terms of its effect on formal politics, but it certainly managed to challenge the common understanding of what the place stands for and means in its wider social context. The space-making aspect of the movement is thus powerful in understanding the symbolic functions and meanings of places in the context of the peace process on the island.

Conclusion

What this chapter has shown is the extent to which the dividing lines in Cyprus have partially been used to reinforce the social division of the island, but at the same time also used as nodal points around which resistance to the segregation and to the UN presence on the island has been voiced. Competitions around the authority to create and label places are widespread and shed light on the political precariousness the island still endures.

As the chapter has shown, a number of different movements are active in both space-making and place-making processes. There is a complexity of actors active in the contested places and spaces in Nicosia, with political and social activists being particularly active in the use of both the buffer zone and Eleftheria Square. At the same time, we can see attempts by political authorities, local, national and international, to retain control over those spaces and with that, to maintain the status quo, as seems to be the case with the dead city of Varosha. Agency thus lies in the maintenance of the status quo and the transformation thereof alike. The transition from conflict to peace, or from the past to the present, is therefore shaped by a contested interplay of actors who try to materialise their visions for the future in physical places (place-making) on the one hand, and to equip existing places with a particular social function and meaning (space-making) on the other hand. The town of Famagusta gives an interesting insight into how the dynamics of space-making and place-making are generated in parallel, and how these processes can give us important insights into the ways in which agency plays out.

In the context of place-making and space-making, the buffer zone can give us cues in both processes. The zone that separates the island between the Greek and Turkish Cypriots is continuously physically reshaped and restructured to account for the diverse place-making opportunities (a base for the peacekeepers and a peace centre). At the same time, there are processes of play that reshape the symbolic nature of the place, with the Occupy Buffer Zone Movement perhaps being the most prominent (albeit only partially successful) example. But also in other parts of Nicosia can we see spatial politics at work – the Nicosia Master Plan walk as a case of creating physical mobility beyond and across the buffer zone, and Eleftheria Square as a place of contestations, are but two examples that cast light on the diversity of actors engaged in place-making and space-making practices.

It therefore almost seems that if peace is to take place in Cyprus, it importantly needs to be tackled in spatial terms in order to connect to the everyday reality of people's everyday life in the city. The latter is constricted by the buffer zone and the physical division of the island, and unless this issue is addressed, it will remain a lingering problem continuing to haunt and pre-occupy those who want to return to their former properties, to bury their loved ones, or simply to walk around freely on the island that they call home.

Notes

1 The *acquis communautaire* refers to the accumulated legislation, legal acts, and court decisions which constitute the body of European Union Law.
2 Previously known as the 'Mangoian House' or the 'Building with the T-shirt shop'.

Bibliography

Anastasiou, H., 2007. Nationalism as a Deterrent to Peace and Interethnic Democracy: The Failure of Nationalist Leadership from the Hague Talks to the Cyprus Referendum. *International Studies Perspectives* 8, pp. 190–205.

Appadurai, A., 1990. Disjuncture and Difference in the Global Cultural Economy. *Theory Culture Society* 7(2), pp. 295–310.

Bakshi, A., 2012. A Shell of Memory: The Cyprus Conflict and Nicosia's Walled City. *Memory Studies* 5(4), pp. 479–496.

Bakshi, A. 2015. Nicosia Master Plan. Planning Across the Divide. In: A. Björkdahl & L. Strömbom eds. *Divided Cities: Governing Diversity*. Lund: Nordic Academic Press. pp. 197–215.

Billig, M., 1995. *Banal Nationalism*. London: SAGE.

Bryant, R., 2010. *The Past in Pieces: Belonging in the New Cyprus*. Philiadelphia and Oxford: University of Pennsylvania Press.

Bryant, R., 2014. Living with Liminality: De Facto States on the Threshold of the Global. *Brown Journal of World Affairs* 20(2), pp. 125–143.

Charalambous, N. & Hadjichristos, C., 2009. *A Square or a Bridge? The Eleftheria Square Case*. [Online] Available at: http://www.sss7.org/Proceedings/06%20Urban% 20Territoriality%20and%20Private%20and%20Public%20Space/013_Charalam bous_Hadjichristos.pdf [Accessed 16 October 2016].

Constantinou, C. & Papadakis, Y., 2001. The Cypriot State(s) in situ: Cross-ethnic Contact and the Discourse of Recognition. *Global Society* 15(2), pp. 125–148.

Constantinou, C. M., Demetriou, O. & Hatay, M., 2012. Conflicts and Uses of Cultural Heritage in Cyprus. *Journal of Balkan and Near Eastern Studies* 14(2), pp. 177–198.

Demetriou, O., 2006. Freedom Square: The Unspoken Reunification of a Divided City. *HAGAR: Studies in Culture, Polity & Identities* 7(1), pp. 55–77.

Demetriou, O., 2012. The Militarization of Opulence: Engendering a Conflict Heritage Site. *International Feminist Journal of Politics* 14(1), pp. 56–77.

Dobraszczyk, P., 2015. Traversing the Fantasies of Urban Destruction: Ruin Gazing in Varosha. *City*, 19(1), pp. 44–60.

Epaminondas, M. *et al.*, 2011. *The Home for Cooperation (H4C)*. Nicosia: K&L Lithofit Ltd..

Global Heritage Fund, 2010. *Saving our Vanishing Heritage: Safeguarding Endangered Cultural Heritage Sites in the Developing World*. [Online] Available at: http://globa lheritagefund.org/images/uploads/docs/GHFSavingOurVanishingHeritagev1.0sin glepageview.pdf [Accessed 17 October 2016].

Hadjipavlou, M., 2007. The Cyprus Conflict: Root Causes and Implications for Peacebuilding. *Journal of Peace Research* 44(3), pp. 349–365.

Hadjipavlou, M., 2010. *Women and Change in Cyprus: Feminism and Gender in Conflict*. London, New York: I.B. Tauris.

Jaramillo, C., 2015. Memory and Transitional Justice: Toward a New Platform for Cultural Heritage in Post-war Cyprus. *Santander Art and Culture Law Review* 2(1), pp. 199–220.

Kappler, S., 2014. *Local Agency and Peacebuilding: EU and International Engagement in Bosnia-Herzegovina, Cyprus and South Africa*. Basingstoke: Palgrave Macmillan.

Ker-Lindsay, J., 2005. *EU Accession and UN Peacemaking in Cyprus*. Basingstoke: Palgrave Macmillan.

Loizos, P., 1981. *The Heart Grown Bitter*. Cambridge: Cambridge University Press.

Mullen, F., Alexander, A. & Basim, M., 2014. *The Cyprus Peace Dividend Revisited: A Productivity and Sectoral Approach, PRIO Report*. [Online] Available at: https:// www.prio.org/Publications/Publication/?x=7411 [Accessed 6 June 2016].

Navaro-Yashin, Y., 2012. *The Make-Believe Space: Affective Geography in a Postwar Polity*. Durham and London: Duke University Press.

Önal, Ş., Dağli, U. & Doratli, N., 1999. The Urban Problems of Gazimagusa (Famagusta) and Proposals for the Future. *Cities* 16(5), pp. 333–351.
Papadakis, Y., 2005. *Echoes from the Dead Zone.* London: IB Tauris.
Papadakis, Y., Peristianis, N. & Welz, G. eds., 2006. Introduction: Modernity, History, and Conflict in Divided Cyprus: An Overview. In: *Divided Cyprus: Modernity, History and an Island in Conflict.* Bloomington and Indianapolis: Indiana University Press, pp. 1–29.
Richmond, O. P., 1998. *Mediating in Cyprus. The Cypriot Communities and the United Nations.* Abingdon, New York: Frank Cass Publisher.
Senol Sert, D., 2010. Cyprus: Peace, Return and Property. *Journal of Refugee Studies* 23(2), pp. 238–259.
Sterling, C., 2014. Spectral Anatomies: Heritage, Hauntology and the 'Ghosts' of Varosha. *Present Past*, 6(1), pp. 1–15.
Weisman, A., 2007. *The World Without Us.* New York: St. Martin's Press.

Interviews

Ahmed Sözen, authors' interview, Famagusta, 10 July 2014.
Altay Nevzat, authors' interview, Nicosia, 8 July 2014.
Athina Papadopoulou, Head of Nicosia Master Plan (NPM) Municipality of Nicosia, authors' interview, Nicosia, 11 July 2014.
Confidential source 1, authors' interview, Nicosia, 8 July 2014.
Confidential source 2, authors' interview, Nicosia, 9 July 2014.
Confidential source 3, authors' interview, Nicosia 10 July 2014.
Confidential source 4, authors' interview, Nicosia 11 July 2014.
Lellos Demetriades, authors' interview, Nicosia, 26 August 2012.
Maria Hadjipavolou, authors' interview, Nicosia, 25 August, 2012.
Marina Vasilaras, Peace Players Cyprus, authors' interview, Nicosia, 17 September 2012.
Mustafa Akıncı, authors' interview, Nicosia, 22 May 2012.
Mustafa Akıncı, authors' interview, Nicosia, 9 July 2014.
NMP exhibition Ledra Palace, authors' interview, Nicosia 18 May 2012.
Occupy Buffer Zone activist, authors' interview, Nicosia, 11 July 2014.
Petros Shammas, authors' interview, Nicosia, 11 July 2014.
Sezis Thompson and Katerina Antoniou, Youth Power Cyprus, authors' interview, Nicosia, 18 September 2012.

3 Kosovo: Emplacing the State and Peace(s)

Introduction

The post-war situation in Kosovo[1] is often read through the prism of ethnicity, and thus understood as a conflict between Albanians and Serbs, between 'us' and 'them', and clashing territorial claims combined with contrasting visions for the future of the Kosovo territorial space (Björkdahl & Gusic, 2013). In that sense, the practices of place-making and space-making clearly bear a relation to the conflict on the one hand, and to the associated statebuilding exercise of the newly born Kosovar state on the other hand. Contestations around place and space therefore have to be seen in the context of claims to statehood as much as the contested legitimacy of ethnic representation.

As this chapter will show, it is the notion of contested statehood that strongly shapes place-making and space-making practices in Kosovo. Hoxha *et al.*, for instance, have suggested that national identity and political pressure act as sources for urban planners' perception of their work (2014: 85). Indeed, when we consider the famous Mother Teresa Boulevard in Pristina, we can show the extent to which public space is used both as a site of the visualisation of statehood as well as a catalyst for the affirmation and materialisation of identity discourses in the city. Yet, while Pristina can be considered more or less ethnically homogenous, we can see that practices of space-making unfold in a different way in the divided city of Mitrovica. It is the bridge between the northern and the southern part of the city that shows us how this particular place has acted as a basis for the development of meaning-making processes and heavily-laden symbolism around the nature of the Kosovar state. Such struggles are particularly evident as the city of Mitrovica is right on the frontline between the Albanian and Serbian part of Kosovo. Mitrovica has been the epicentre of the ethno-territorial conflict with geo-political consequences. Together with the adjacent Serbian municipalities in Northern Kosovo, Mitrovica is perceived as the last obstacle to stability, to Kosovo's territorial integrity and the peaceful resolution of the conflict. In northern Mitrovica, in other Serb populated spaces of Kosovo, and in Serbia proper the rhetoric since 1999 has been 'Кёсёвё je Србија!' (Kosovo is Serbia!). Such discourse helps us to construct an imaginary Serb space perpetuating the pre-1999 spatial and political order in which Kosovo was part of Serbia and ruled by Belgrade (Gow, 2009; Krasniqi, 2012, Gusic forthcoming 2017). In Mitrovica we investigate how this idea has been materialised in a division of the city between Serbia and Kosovo and considerable autonomy for the Kosovo Serbs. At the same time, the Albanian-dominated south of the city, by means of monuments and flags, firmly emphasizes its Kosovo Albanian identity and its belonging to the Kosovo Albanian space of the newly created state. A bridge across the river Ibar has become the hotspot of ethnic tensions in Mitrovica and we study this bridge from a space-making perspective.

From this on-going issue of urban confrontation and space-making, we then move on to the practices of place-making inherent in the creation of sites of cultural heritage. While this place-making process seems far removed from the everyday politics of ethnic identification and state formation, it stands out as a political choice to counter those narratives and to move towards a notion of shared space – which certainly brings contestations of its own.

As researchers doing fieldwork in Kosovo, we acknowledge our own positionality and identity as well our dependence on the ways in which these particular sites are presented to us by the various people whom we encounter and who have generously given us their time. Thus, what we present below is not a neutral, objective analysis of the Mother Teresa Boulevard in Pristina, of the bridge in Mitrovica, or of the castle in Prizren nor is it a comprehensive list of narratives around the boulevard, the bridge, or the castle or their meanings, which are under constant contestation. From a spatial ethnographic standpoint, we attempt to read these diagnostic sites in order to place specific encounters, events and understandings in a more meaningful spatial context.

Transition towards a state

The statebuilding in Kosovo expressed through the manifestations of its founders as well as through the divisions in Mitrovica are clearly part of the greater Yugoslavian conflict and territorial conundrum. Thus, to grasp this we need briefly to focus on the collapse of the Socialist Federal Republic of Yugoslavia in the early 1990s. The literature on the Yugoslav wars of 1991–1999 has produced a dizzying array of competing interpretations and understandings of the processes of war-making, state-breaking and state-making that took place in the space of Yugoslavia (for an overview of the debates see Ramet 2004a, 2004b; Todorova, 2012; Kaplan, 1993). A common explanation has been that Yugoslavia was an 'artificial state' and that 'Yugoslav' was an 'artificial identity', thus bound to collapse. Following the same line of reasoning Yugoslavism was portrayed as a number of different nations coming together in 'brotherhood and unity' to realise a common socialist community imagined by Marshal Tito. This, however, seems to imply that 'natural states' and 'natural identities' also exist (cf. Wilmer, 2002). Consequently, politics prior to and during the wars in the Western Balkans were seen to be about ethnic groups, imagined nations and clashing statebuilding projects.

The violent break-up of Yugoslavia followed ethno-nationalist logic and was based on an attempt to build a new ethno-territorial order of space and to build an ethnocratic political order upon that space and to erase the old non-ethno-territorial ordering of space. The re-making of the Balkans through war and ethnic cleansing were constitutive of the statebuilding processes that produced new states such as Slovenia, Croatia, Serbia, Macedonia, Bosnia-Herzegovina and eventually Montenegro and Kosovo.

A partial ethno-territorial logic shaped the dynamics of the war and the political geography of the ordering of space. It was based on a particular reading of history and contemporary life, which revealed ethnic identity to be 'the primordial axis of life in Yugoslavia' and that 'throughout history the ethnic groups were in a perpetual competition over land' (Toal & Dahlman, 2012: 4). Politics prior to and during the wars in the Western Balkans has often been read as to be about ethnic groups, imagined nations and different peoples. Democratisation in the midst of economic and political crisis enabled nationalist parties to oust the ruling communists and gain power in the election in 1990. The new powerholders were eager to establish their sovereign states (Woodward, 1995). In an ethnonationalist way of thinking, the different ethnic groups' post-Yugoslav identities were marked by ethnic exclusiveness and polarisation and as such they had a natural homeland, an ethno-territorial place of their own (Kostovicova, 2004). At the same time, there is no broad agreement as to whether the framing of the conflict as mainly ethnic-based is justified, and Ramet has suggested that there is a lack of research into the international factors that contributed to the emergence of the conflict (Ramet, 2005).

Claims to space and control of territory are empowering, since they create an opportunity for the symbolic moulding of identity (Kaplan, 1992: 261). Conflict over territory rearranges space and the new political landscapes reflect and emplace national identity and statehood (Kliot & Mansfield, 1997; Campbell, 1998; Newman, 2002). The process of geographical imagination, and forging 'the mystic bond between people and place', i.e. nation and homeland, is particularly intense during statebuilding processes (cf. Smith, 1991: 91–98, cited in Kostovicova, 2004: 270). These processes are reinforced and sustained by creating man-made landscapes of a symbolically charged character aimed at placing the nation's territory in the mind's eye.

After Tito's death, the province of Kosovo experienced acute ethnic tensions that eventually led to the suspension of Kosovo's autonomy in 1989. This resulted in an escalation of the conflict between Kosovo-Albanian secessionists and the Serbian and Yugoslav authorities. Not until the late 1990s did the Yugoslav war of dissolution reach Kosovo. Until then, the unofficial President of the Kosovo-Albanians, Ibrahim Rugova, had led a non-violent struggle for Kosovo independence (Judah, 2008). The limited success of this endeavour paved way for the emergence of the Kosovo Liberation Army (KLA) in the 1990s, and its violent campaign targeting police stations, Serbian officials and civilians, as well as Kosovo-Albanians, regarded as 'collaborators' escalated the conflict (Independent International Commission on Kosovo, 2000). Three years of violent conflict triggered the contested 1999 intervention by NATO. In its aftermath, Kosovo was placed under UN rule through the United Nations Interim Administration Mission in Kosovo (UNMIK) until its future status could be agreed upon (UNSCR, 1999; Björkdahl, 2007).

Interestingly, peacebuilding in Kosovo took on board the ethnic language and ethno-territorial organisation of the state. According to Visoka and Richmond (2016) '[t]he international community has invoked state-building to satisfy the Albanian majority in Kosovo while utilising peace-building as a tool to accommodate Serbs and minorities'. Clearly, both peacebuilding and statebuilding are processes that reflect past and current violence, ethno-nationalist identities, power and contestation, as well as territoriality and materiality and, as such, both processes have over time operated increasingly well within both informal and formal politics. After the end of the war in Kosovo in the late 1990s, ethnic enclavisation emerged as a security strategy of the Kosovo Serb minority as Serbian security forces withdrew (Kostovicova, 2005: 203). Now there are a total of 120,000 Serbs living in Kosovo, a country of 1.6 million. Most of them are scattered in small communities, but 40,000 live in the north of Kosovo. The Kosovo-Serb minority find that their long-term survival as a minority community rests on their ability to govern themselves spatially, politically and socially separated from the Kosovo-Albanian majority community. In contrast, Kosovo-Albanians favour the integration of the north into the independent Republic of Kosovo (Gusic, 2015). In this contested space Belgrade provides moral, political and economic support for the partition and autonomy of the North, through among other things parallel institutions for the Kosovo-Serb minority in the North, such as education, health care, police etc. Fear, insecurity and the threat of violence tainted interethnic relations in the aftermath of the conflict. Thus, the International Civilian Office (ICO) was tasked to supervise the statebuilding process between 2008 and 2012, as Kosovo was to implement the Ahtisaari Plan – the blueprint for peace and democracy, and a precondition for its sovereignty. During the period of international supervision, many Kosovo Serbs began to cooperate with the newly established state institutions, a moderate political elite emerged, and Kosovo Serb politicians became part of the government. New Serb municipalities were formed and increasing socio-economic benefits for Kosovo Serbs living across Kosovo were granted. Six Serb-majority municipalities were created south of the Ibar and they took over most of the governing role from parallel structures financed by Serbia. North of the river Ibar, it was a different situation. Here, parallel institutions controlled by Belgrade remain in place (ICG, 2012, 2013; Gusic, 2015; Visoka & Richmond, 2016). Thus, the North has been beyond the Kosovo government's control while Serbia has continued to fund local security, judicial, health and educational institutions.

So far, Kosovo's independence has been recognised by more than 100 countries, including the United States and most of the European Union's 28 member states. Serbia still does not recognise Kosovo's independence as it is often portrayed, in Serbian historical, cultural myths and narratives, as the cradle of Serb civilisation. Kosovo is regarded as the birthplace of the medieval Serbian kingdom, a large fraction of the oldest Serbian churches and monasteries are scattered all over Kosovo, and the central Serbian historic event is the Battle of Kosovo in 1389 (Judah, 2008). These powerful and influential narratives clash with the Kosovo Albanian statebuilding project and contribute to strengthening the resistance of the Kosovo Serbs in the North against it.

New power-holders in Serbia keen on advancing Serbia's relations with the EU have paved the way for negotiations concerning Kosovo. Serbia has implicitly agreed to accept the Pristina government's authority over the territory in return for the opening of EU accession talks. Currently, both sides are engaged in an EU-facilitated dialogue aiming to 'normalise' relations. In 2013, authorities in Pristina and Belgrade adopted a draft agreement, mainly relating to the position of the Kosovo-Serbs in the North (ICG, 2013). On the contrary, Kosovo Serbs often feel let down both by the central government and Serbia and many boycott the Kosovo institutions. They resist the statebuilding process that the Kosovo Albanians have embarked on. This frustration is paralleled by intensified efforts in the South, and primarily in Pristina, to prove the success of this process (NGO confidential source, authors' interview, Mitrovica, 2016). A glance at Mother Teresa Boulevard can, in this context, give us important insights into the ways in which this plays out concretely, before we go on to analyse the frictional processes of statebuilding, and the resistance against it, in the divided city of Mitrovica.

Spatial politics: manifesting the state

In 2000, Rexhep Luci, an urban planner for Pristina, launched the initiative 'Vision for Pristina, 2000–2005', which aimed to rid the city of illegal construction works (IKS and ESI, 2006a: 3) and was supported by the UN administration. Yet, shortly after taking the first decisions calling for the demolition of illegal buildings, he was shot dead (ibid.). Although a new law on construction was passed in 2004, 'little has been done to enforce the law' (IKS and ESI, 2006a: 3).

This anecdote all too well illustrates the contestations around space and place that Kosovo experiences. Debates around what can be done against illegal construction works in the bigger cities are just one of the areas of spatial contestation the country faces. When it comes to spatial politics and the negotiation of spaces and places, Kosovo is a particularly interesting example. This is not least in relation to the on-going processes of anchoring the state in spatial terms and giving the recently emerged state a physical presence, most prominently in the cityscape of Pristina and in the divided city of Mitrovica. To a certain extent, this is not completely dissimilar from other post-communist states in Eastern Europe in their attempts to reproduce, spatially, a cultural identity (Kolbe, 2007). Yet at the same time, Kosovo can be considered a unique case in that the idea of statehood is continuously reaffirmed through the anchoring of state symbols in urban landscapes. Thus, reading the cityscape of Pristina, zooming in on Mother Teresa Boulevard we become aware how material symbols and artefacts become divisive in societies that have no common vision for the future or for the state in the making.

In Pristina, the capital city, markers such as the gigantic monument 'NEWBORN', with the letters being repainted regularly, or the numerous monuments dedicated to war heroes and politicians, point to this process of spatial statebuilding as much as to the contestations around properties in this recently-built state. It is in this context that the cityscape offers competing and conflictive monuments to mark the state and offers a strong spatial representation of political contestations and, more specifically, the affirmation of statehood in spatial terms. It is therefore worth taking a closer look at the pedestrian area around the so-called Mother Teresa Boulevard, a small area of Pristina that serves as a microcosm of this contested statehood and reflects the variety of markers through which the state reaffirms itself. In fact, when strolling along this boulevard, the visitor almost feels as if in an outdoor museum, given the plethora of monuments, artefacts and political messages on buildings.

The Mother Teresa Boulevard dates back to the 1950s and was formerly called Marshal Tito and Vidovdanska Street. The latter refers to St Vitus' Day to commemorate the historically-laden Battle of Kosovo of 1389 and, with it, the struggle against the Ottoman Empire (Ermolin, 2014: 164). On the other hand, the street name 'Marshal Tito' is common in the former Yugoslavia and can be found throughout the region. Interestingly, as Tito used to pass through Pristina via this boulevard, the facades are very well-maintained, while the backyards behind are rather run down as they are not visible (Confidential source 1, authors' interview, Pristina, 2016). This phenomenon may date back to the times of Yugoslavia, but is still physically visible on and behind the boulevard – a glimpse back into the history of the area. However, it has been suggested that Pristina is marked by 'a story of destruction and wasted opportunities', with the destruction of parts of the historical monuments going back to deliberate policy of the Communist era (IKS and ESI, 2006b: 3).

Despite this, when walking along and exploring the pedestrian area as a whole, it is striking to acknowledge the density of relatively recent politics made visible in a relatively small place. We enter the area through the Rugova Square as a tribute to the former president Ibrahim Rugova. The area houses the Assembly Building and leads straight up to the Skanderbeg Square with a statue dedicated to George Castriot Skanderbeg, who is often considered to have been at the forefront in defending Western Europe against the Ottoman Empire. The square also houses a war memorial commemorating the victims of the 1999 war as well as a series of photographs of the missing. When walking further down, one enters seamlessly the Mother Teresa Boulevard, marked by a statue to the famous nun. This is followed by posters on buildings representing (mainly Albanian) celebrities and, further down, a statue to the KLA fighter Zahir Pajaziti. At the same time, just in the midst of this politically-laden urban landscape, there is not only the national theatre, but also a plethora of restaurants and shops, with the boulevard representing the main shopping area in the city. In that sense, a large number of residents and visitors alike are exposed to the monuments and historical contestations around the question of statehood and the contested meanings of the state and the nation.

Breaking this down further, it is interesting to investigate the naming of the 'Mother Teresa Boulevard'. Mother Teresa is now located where once the 'Kosovo Maiden' stood, a symbol of Serbia's martyrdom in the Kosovo field (Ermolin, 2014: 164). At the same time, her statue is slightly set back so she is less visible than Skanderbeg or Rugova (Hoxha *et al.*, 2014: 86). The statue is still relevant, because although Mother Teresa had mainly worked in India, she has been claimed by different Balkans states (mainly Serbia, Albania and Macedonia). This in turn has resulted in an on-going battle around her origin and belonging (Alpion, 2004). In Kosovo, she signifies Albanianness as much as orientation towards the West (Ermolin, 2014: 164). In a way, she can be considered a central factor in the discursive construction of a predominantly Albanian identity of Kosovo.

Mother Teresa can be ranked among the non-military people commemorated on the Boulevard, just like the former president Ibrahim Rugova who is often seen as a symbol of unification and pacifism (Confidential source 2, authors' interview, Pristina, 2016). The former president is both praised and criticised for his non-violent stance in fighting for the Kosovo Albanian cause. At the same time, he is confronted with a number of more militarised statues, including those commemorating Skanderbeg (on a war horse) or the armed KLA commander Pajaziti, who can be read as a glorification of the KLA (Ermolin, 2014: 165). Similarly, Skanderbeg tends to be regarded 'as the example of braveness and fearlessness in front of any invader or enemy of the Albanian people' (Ermolin, 2014: 163–4). For some, he represents the protection of Christianity against the Ottomans (Confidential source 2, authors' interview, Pristina, 2016) and is thus a powerful reminder of the identity of the state.

In terms of the agency inherent in spatial politics, that is, which agents are behind the design of the urban landscape, an interesting contestation is emerging. There is a general disagreement as regards whether the monuments outlined above represent the diversity of society, or whether they are 'pure inputs from politicians', and thus have nothing to do with the people themselves (Confidential source 1, authors' interview, Pristina, 2016). Hence, is the cityscape a result of the people coming together as a nation, or does it merely represent a vision of the state that is removed from society? On the one hand, it can be argued that, not least since most statues were contracted from Albania, they are a reflection of political parties (NGO confidential source 3, authors' interview, Pristina, 2016). On the other hand, one interviewee suggested that after all, political leaders also represent the people (NGO confidential source 3, authors' interview, Pristina, 2016). We can therefore see that there is a tension between what is considered political – seen as elite business – or political as representative of society as a whole. The agency behind the construction of those monuments thus remains blurred, as we are unable to identify clearly whether they are a construction of the political elites, or represent a wider societal consensus. The question extends even further as it becomes clear that those monuments tend to represent a societal agreement between Kosovo-Albanians (Confidential source 2, authors' interview, Pristina, 2016), yet exclude citizens of other ethnic backgrounds. In that vein, a number of monuments to the fallen or the missing, such as the photographs of the missing on the fence, tend to reinforce a discourse of victimhood (Ermolin, 2014: 167). It has even been suggested that such monuments may help individuals to gain political points (Fitim Mulolli, authors' interview, Pristina, 2016).

This is certainly not, however, to argue that there is a consensus within the Kosovo Albanian community. In fact, there is an increasing acknowledgement that cultural heritage is an identity issue not only between Kosovo-Albanians and the Kosovo-Serbs, but also within Albanian community (Marija Mirceska and Fitim Mulolli, authors' interview, Pristina, 2016). Certain groups would feel supportive of Rugova's more pacifist approach, while others tend to favour the more militarised approach the Pajaziti statue represents. And others again would feel disconnected from both statues.

There are, furthermore, other controversies beyond questions of ethnicity, one example being the Benetton building. It is located next to the Rugova statue and used to be the Hotel Union building. After controversies about whether it should be preserved as a historic building, or knocked down to provide more space in Rugova Square, United Colours of Benetton restored and reopened it in 2013 (Benetton Group, 2013). This example reflects the extent to which spatial planning brings together social, political and also economic considerations. An unexpected external actor (a corporation) thus turned into a spatial agent and took part in practices of place-making. This is the background against which Hoxha et al., (2014: 86) suggest that a 'young Europeanism' is spatially visible, but is certainly linked to wider political, social and economic questions.

If we then revisit the site constituting the area of Mother Teresa Boulevard, we notice the extent to which the site is politicised. It is a site in which the new state is anchored, (re-)defined, contested and materially embedded in a very central place of the city. In this context, Ermolin (2014: 160) suggests that 'the creation of a new pantheon of heroes is one of the initial steps of any nation-building strategy'. At the same time, it becomes clear that we are not dealing with a unified practice of nationbuilding, or even statebuilding, but instead a competition for the authority of meaning by the different actors involved. The competition revolves around the identity of the state, and thus its public visualisation: is the state based on a violent or non-violent past? How does it relate to Albania? What is the role of women in the state? What is the function of the missing and how can the state deal with their fate? Such processes are continuously reshaped by political authorities on the one hand (including the municipality and political parties) and the population on the other hand. It is the tension emerging at the intersection between those sets of actors that makes the practices of place-making so pressing in Pristina. With the Boulevard making these contestations quite apparent, there is indeed a debate among the people about the degree to which the statues on the Boulevard represent a distant and removed political ideology, or whether it is a reflection of the recent past of the people. The Boulevard itself does not resolve these questions, but opens them up for public debate. The population can take them for granted or resist those practices – as one interviewee suggested 'I don't bring my kids there' (Confidential source 3, authors' interview, Pristina, 2016). It is not clear what will happen to the statues in the future, but so far they have survived and are mainly a national set-piece for visitors who stop to take photographs. Yet this does not reduce their impact as a concrete demonstration of political power structures as they dominate municipal and state structures, as well as narratives around the identity of the Kosovo state.

Yet it would be wrong to focus our attention on the monuments of the Boulevard alone. In fact, not only the shops in the street but also the mostly informal street trade remind us that agency does not necessarily have to follow political (read: ideological) purposes, but has an economic function as well. It is the fact that the memoryscape is situated in a shopping area that it makes the political message more powerful as it reaches out to a wider audience of consumers as well. This is a visual metaphor of the state whose legitimacy ultimately relies on its ability to deliver economically – which, in a country of over 30 per cent unemployment, must be said to be only partially fulfilled. In that sense, the area of the boulevard is not only indicative of the urban landscape in Pristina, but of the socio-economic and political contestations that Kosovo faces as a state. The latter is, however, facing resistance, as our next example of Mitrovica aptly illustrates.

Space-making

Statebuilding invariably produces a re-organisation of space and place as it disrupts various place–identity processes. It produces a sense of belonging but it may simultaneously also be experienced as a form of dislocation. As such it can undermine shared constructions of place and the forms of located subjectivity they sustain. In the case of Kosovo, the Kosovo Serbs seem to perceive the statebuilding process as a loss of place and identity.

Space-making takes as its point of departure the material setting and turns it into a landscape of meaning. Such processes bring to the fore the human–environment relations which are often neglected in peacebuilding processes. The Mitrovica Bridge, as we shall see below, is not an inert backdrop to social relations or a background feature that has a negligible impact on the social psychological processes it frames. Real or imagined places serve as frameworks for integration as well as segregation. Based on our research in Kosovo and elsewhere, we suggest that material places do not simply serve as settings for individuals' activities, actions or behaviours, but are instead actively incorporated as part of the self. Thus we aim to move beyond an abstract notion of agency towards an emplaced understanding shaped through interactions with the ideational and material environments. To examine space-making processes reveals how positioning someone who is in a place can connect people to the multiple established meanings and identities of that place. A sense of place also reveals how material environments such as a bridge can come to symbolise the self. The other side of the coin is then that the physical environment, 'the place', can enable or disable various identity relevant projects.

Thus, we provide a spatial reading of the divided city of Mitrovica by focusing on the Main Bridge over the river Ibar that separates the northern, Serb part of the city from the southern Albanian part of the city. The barricade on the Main Bridge made of stone and sand was transformed into a 'peace park' in June 2014 and then reverted into a barricade. This space-making effort calls for deeper analysis which is the task we engage in below. A close analysis of this particular site helps us reveal the tension between place, as a material phenomenon, and space, as an immaterial, imaginary phenomenon. Recognising that place and space are mutually conditional and intertwined we will explore how they can be understood as geographical, material and structural platforms on which different forms of agency and power unfold. This includes processes of building infrastructures, empowering certain practices and agents connected to place while excluding others. Space will be considered as a possibility in terms of representing a platform of empowerment, while at the same time always being vulnerable to manipulation and co-optation (Massey & Hajnal, 1995; Massey, 2005). The ability of turning a place into a space denotes the process of making a physical place relevant and meaningful to societal and political discourses. By emplacing certain spatial practices, narratives, ideas as well as material artefacts, places are equipped with a social meaning and they become part of the social imaginary. The analysis below reveals how a particular place does not stay the same, but is continually emerging, that is, a place is always becoming and the becoming involves a transformation of the physical places and the imagined spaces.

Dividing the bridge and bridging the divide in Mitrovica

Mitrovica is well chosen as a site for both transformation and contestation as it demonstrates how 'high level politics is played out in a small place', and the bridge across the river Ibar in Mitrovica is illustrative of the 'bridge that divides the two communities' (OSCE official, authors' interview, Mitrovica 2016). The legacy of the Kosovo war clearly divides, and the intangible elements such as the memory of violence, atrocities and murder and displacement as well as destruction of religious buildings have created a mutual geography of fear. In such contested space, the Ibar River has become the material demarcation line to divide the two communities. The river divides Mitrovica into the Kosovo-Serbian North-side, covering one-third of the city-space, and the Kosovo-Albanian South-side, covering the remaining two-thirds of the space.

While there are several bridges across the river in Mitrovica, the Main Bridge is at the centre of the contestation over place. A pedestrian bridge a few hundred metres from it in one direction, right in front of the Tri Solitera (Three Blocks) is located in a largely Kosovo-Albanian populated area of the north part of the city. The Eastern Bridge a few hundred metres from the Main Bridge in the other direction connects the multi-ethnic neighbourhood, Bošnjačka Mahala, in the North with large shopping centres such as Emona and ETC in the South (Pinos, 2016). The Eastern Bridge is open for traffic and has been so for most of the time, even when tension was high. In addition, there is a railway bridge one kilometre from the city centre that is always open (EULEX representative, authors' interview, North Mitrovica, 2016). The Main Bridge has thus become more of a symbol than an actual transportation route.

Since 1999 the Main Bridge and its barricades have been the main flashpoint in interethnic tensions and its role in the politics of statebuilding and resistance to statebuilding is central in both communities. As such, the bridge is a place where peace and conflict affect people in their everyday and it matters to people's experience of conflict dynamics and peacebuilding efforts. For locals, the bridge manifests the social practice of division and is part of the everyday landscape as a reminder that 'the other' lives literally across the bridge (Pinos, 2016: 132). The bridge is seen as a place with a material form, produced by people's practices. It is part of the construction of a bounded form of space that defines the lived experience of people. Therefore, place is fundamental in expressing a sense of belonging and is seen to provide a locus of identity. Such places are experienced as material artefacts, represented in discourse, and are themselves used as representations. Place has physicality, and processes pertaining to peace and conflict happen through the material forms people build or use.

For several years, the Kosovo Force (KFOR) reproduced the division of the city and the physical demarcation of segregation at the bridge. With barbed wire and vehicles, KFOR sought to prevent inter-ethnic clashes. In May 2001, a controversial and stillborn KFOR project on the south side of the bridge set out to erect a fortification system with four walls (2.5 m high and 35 m long) in order to keep the two sides of the city apart (Lemay-Hébert, 2012: 36). In 2005, KFOR removed the two-metres-high sandbag barricades, barbed wire and armoured vehicles from the bridge as part of the confidence-building measures being implemented in order to return the two communities to normal life (New Europe, 2005). When Kosovo Police and KFOR troops dismantled barricades Kosovo-Serbs came out to protest and clashed at the bridge and they were quickly rebuilt.

To prevent the Kosovo Albanians from crossing, the Kosovo Serbs in Mitrovica North built a barricade made of stone and sand on the Main Bridge. It is a material manifestation, which came to symbolise the refusal of

Figure 3.1 Main bridge Mitrovica. Photo by authors, 2016.

Kosovo Serbs in northern Kosovo to merge with the rest of the country. Such barricades were not limited to the Main Bridge. Others were also erected near the west and east bridges but positioned a few blocks north of the river and thus not on the bridges. The streets between those barricades and the bridges are shared spaces where Mitrovica's only multi-ethnic neighbourhoods exist. They are also places where ethnic violence most frequently flares up. During the years 1999–2002, the bridge watchers guarded the bridge and monitored crossings. They would sit on rooftops and in cafés near the riverbank governing the space and discouraging people from interethnic contact. The bridge watchers are still operational but in a less visible way and expressing a more hidden agency, organising violent protests by means of payments to young people, intimidating civil society members with bombs, building barricades, monitoring the city through CCTV, and maintaining social cohesion through threats (Clark, 2014). In recent years, the bridge has been watched around-the-clock by the men of the Civil Protection Force who, according to hearsay, receive Serbian-dinar salaries from Belgrade.

As the barricades are removed, new ones are put in place in response to political tensions and insecurities felt by the Kosovo Serbs. A new barricade was erected on the bridge in 2011 in a protest against the presence of Kosovo police and customs on the contested border with Serbia (Balkan Insight, 2014; OSCE official, authors' interview, Mitrovica, 2016).

The Kosovo Serbs who dominate the northern part of the town believe it is their right to inscribe their presence in the city and mark it as Serb territory (Balkan Insight, 2014). For most Kosovo Serbs, keeping the bridge closed for traffic has become central in creating a sense of security – making them go head on with the Kosovo Albanian community that wants the bridge opened and freedom to cross. The Serb narrative projected onto the bridge reflects insecurity and the vulnerability felt by the Kosovo Serbs and the fears of Kosovo Albanian attacks from the south. The bridge materialises the fears of the Kosovo Serbian community. Still today, the Main Bridge is always guarded by Italian Carabinieri accompanied by a Serbian member of the Kosovo Police, and occasionally KFOR troops make an appearance, while a number of European Union Rule of Law Mission in Kosovo (EULEX) and UN marked cars can be seen at times (OSCE official, authors' interview, Mitrovica, 2016).

The barricades on the bridge clearly define the particular meanings attached to place. These meanings are contestable and alterable as we see in the trans-formation of the place, yet those meanings dictate who belongs, i.e. who is 'in place' and who is 'out of place'. The guarding of the bridge by KFOR, EULEX, the Italian Carabinieri, the Bridge Watchers and the Civil Protection Force is a meaning-making practice that situates agency in a particular place.

The barricade made of stone and sand that symbolised the refusal of Kosovo Serbs in northern Kosovo to integrate with the Kosovo state was removed in 2014 after three years and replaced with a large patch of soil in preparation for what would become a 'peace park'. For a while, vehicle traffic moved freely across the bridge, but it was once again blocked one afternoon when workers showed up to place a series of flower boxes containing small trees across the span. Concrete flower pots were thus placed at the Main Bridge at the spot where the block once stood, and the bridge was opened for pedestrians, but remains closed to traffic. The peace park attracted a lot of attention from diaspora visiting the town and the park opened up visions of the other side, allowed for people to come together and some individuals tended the flowers and the trees and used the benches in the garden (OSCE official, authors' interview, Mitrovica, 2016).

Just outside the peace park, on the Kosovo-Serbian side of the bridge, we noted as we crossed a dark-coloured memorial entitled 'the Monument of Truth', and to us it seemed like a stark reminder of a heavily contested past. The monument dedicated to the fallen Serbian heroes of the Kosovo war gives meaning to the bridgehead. In the eyes of many Kosovo Albanians these heroes of the recent war were the same men who engaged in the government-sponsored campaign of ethnic-cleansing during the war. Thus, by crossing the bridge war heroes from the recent past are turned into contemporary war criminals. This reveals how different meanings are connected to place and time and how these meanings change as we move through the place. The place moulds actors and a barricade constitutes certain spatial practices whereas a peace park can be thought of as constituting other spatial practices, even though the transformation of a barricade into a peace park is given different meanings, depending on which side of the bridge you stand.

Situating agency on the bridge

We can read agency from the process during the course of which actors are able to transform places that are imbued with the legacy of conflict into a space of peace by connecting a particular version of peace to a place. The mayor of the Kosovo Serb part of the city, Goran Rakic, adopted a decision to build a peace park to replace the barricade. The transformation of the barricade into a peace park materialised through replacing the barricade with concrete flower boxes (Rakic, 2014a).

In the eyes of the Kosovo Albanians the peace park was a new barricade, and Kosovo Albanian rioters gathered at the bridge to protest against the reintroduction of a new barricade and clashed with external and internal security forces. Cars were set on fire, teargas grenades detonated to disperse the crowds. Numerous rioters and security personnel were hospitalised, and many were arrested. What was meant to be a peaceful march against the latest move by Kosovo Serb authorities in the northern part of Mitrovica to block traffic across the bridge turned into violent protest (EULEX representative, authors' interview, North Mitrovica, 2016). 'The aim of the Peace Park is an expression of the desire that the point which separated the two nations over the past 15 years becomes a place where they meet,' and that the removal of the park could be seen 'as a threat to peace' Rakic (2014b) said in a statement. South Mitrovica mayor Agim Bahtiri claimed that the peace park, which sparked violent protests by Kosovo Albanians, would be removed 'very soon' and that the bridge would be restored to its original state. It was clear from Rakic's statement that he had not taken the decision independently but it followed from consultations with Belgrade (Rakic, 2014a). The mayor of northern Mitrovica was instructed by Belgrade to remove the barricades in June 2014. This unpopular action was carried out in the middle of the night to avoid protest. Yet, it resulted in immediate confrontations and, with the unofficial support of Belgrade, Rakic erected another barricade narrated as a 'peace park'.

The peace park on the Main Bridge has been an issue on the agenda for the Brussels talks and has been negotiated. The EU Special Representative in Pristina, Samuel Zbogar, has been engaged in the transformation of the bridge and proposed a resolution of the dispute concerning the bridge in Mitrovica to participants at the technical dialogue in Brussels (InSerbia, 2015). The aim of the talks was to reopen the bridge in June 2016. At point of writing this has not yet happened.

Spatial segregation through barricading the bridge can be understood as a mechanism to cope with insecurity and vulnerability of being a minority in a Kosovo Albanian state. Individual interactions are very limited. The present segregation did not emerge from the war, nor from the NATO-intervention but in the aftermath as Kosovo Serbs felt defenceless and vulnerable to retaliation. Standing at the bridge that has been given often contradictory meanings in the narratives of the two communities, it becomes more apparent than ever that places and spaces are transformative and frequently those driving the transformations are guided by different ideas and understandings of peace and it is possible to see peace in plural manifest itself at different times on the bridge. The eventual removal of the Peace Park will not be enough to reverse or accommodate these spatial narratives. Thus it becomes apparent that the bridge is both an ideational space containing competing meanings in the narratives of the Kosovo Serbs and the Kosovo Albanians and as such it is a product of the material manifestation of the ethnic divide in Kosovo, the politicisation of ethnic cleavages, and the difficulties of both Kosovo Serbs and Kosovo Albanians to co-exist in one state.

Place-making

Place-making is the process through which an abstract idea or symbolic meaning is translated into material reality. This means that ideas such as the state become visible in material terms (as the creation of the Mother Teresa Boulevard above shows, for instance). This is certainly of great importance in the context of Kosovo where the physicality of places represents a statement of the right to the state and therefore the importance of ethnicised places. It is therefore particularly interesting to cast light on place-making dynamics that aim to de-ethnicise place to a certain extent and both reinforce and also counter the strength through which the newborn state reinforces itself in place. A focus on the work around cultural heritage that increasingly receives attention not only from national, but also international actors reflects the extent to which a temporal focus away from the recent conflict and on 'places of the past' can be read as a tool of agency in a landscape otherwise heavily shaped by ethnic contestation.

The conservation of cultural heritage as a place-making strategy

The question of the conservation of cultural heritage seems to be an important concern in contemporary Kosovo. This process involves the notion of travelling back into the past, the ultimate goal often being a Kosovo before and beyond conflict. Indeed, given the contested and conflict-ridden urban landscape in cities like Pristina and Mitrovica, preserving the past can be used as a way to celebrate a Kosovo with its shared, rather than divided, heritage.

This tendency has not least been taken up by the government of Kosovo as it now protects 45 'Special Protective Zones' across the country in its attempt to preserve and maintain cultural heritage. Those 'Special Protective Zones' that are part of the Ahtisaari plan of 2007 are legally defined as a

> defined area surrounding a monument, building, group of buildings, ensemble, village, or historic town centre that is safeguarded from any development or activity which could damage its historical, cultural, architectural or archaeological context, natural environment or aesthetic visual setting
> (Law on Special Protective Zones, article 2).

As a result, the government is legally obliged to comply with this law and the responsibilities that come with it and has to come up with the respective mechanisms of implementation. Hence, these zones are often protected through and coupled with municipal development plans that are set up context-specifically. At the same time, as the OSCE has pointed out in their involvement and advisory functions with respect to the 'Special Protective Zones', this approach is also aimed at the harmonious cohabitation of surrounding communities (OSCE, 2014: 16). We can therefore say that the work on cultural heritage is not only relevant to the ambition of 'freezing the past', as the case of Varosha in Cyprus has illustrated above. It is also of relevance to the present and the ways in which communities relate to shared heritage, yet with lesser degrees of ethnically-laden vocabularies and with a potential to refer back to a time during which shared spaces and places were still possible. It is in this context that the creation of heritage sites as places of peace can be situated, not least as they need to protect areas of groups other than the Kosovo Albanian majority. As a result, many of those zones include sites of Serbian Orthodox churches (Marija Mirceska, authors' interview, Pristina, 2016).

This is an agenda increasingly pursued by international agencies operating in Kosovo, with the OSCE taking a lead role in this thematic field. On a legal level, the OSCE is keen to press the institutions of Kosovo to implement fully the legal framework on cultural heritage protection (OSCE, 2014) and it focuses much of its work in the country on this aspect. The OSCE emphasises its approach that includes the sites of all cultural groups of the country (OSCE, 2014: 7) and monitors those sites (Marija Mirceska, authors' interview, Pristina, 2016). It also contributes to the drafting of the heritage and culture law in terms of providing comments (ibid.). Interestingly, the OSCE frames the question of cultural heritage as a human rights issue (OSCE, 2014: 8–9) and thus puts it in direct relation to a political agenda that otherwise may seem only distantly related. However, in its approach, it does state the importance of public engagement with heritage sites (OSCE, 2014: 27) and therefore considerably raises the profile of mechanisms of heritage protection. This is further reinforced by the involvement of the Council of Europe (CoE) and the EU in the programme 'EU/CoE Support to the Promotion of Cultural Diversity (PCDK)'. Similarly to the work that the OSCE does, this programme primarily involves the CoE's and EU's contribution to the draft of the Cultural Heritage Law (Barber & Španzel, 2015). In this context, it can be said that the fact that the government – not all that long ago – started taking an interest in this issue area (Fitim Mulolli, authors' interview, Pristina, 2016) is not least due to the pressure of international organisations, such as the OSCE, the EU or the CoE. The attention of those international actors to the preservation of cultural heritage – not only in terms of the funds that come with it, but also the political pressure on the government of Kosovo to deal with this issue, has certainly had a strong influence on the political attention given to the maintenance of the special protective zones as places worthy of protection.

This is certainly not to claim that cultural heritage is de-politicised as an issue. Indeed, an interviewee emphasised that, while it is less emotional than other contemporary political issues, it is still being used as a political tool (NGO confidential source 1, authors' interview, Pristina, 2016). There have been, reportedly, controversies around the ways in which places of cultural heritage should be maintained within meetings dealing with special protective zones as well as with whether it is more important to restore the tangible, material, or the intangible, symbolic, dimension of heritage as a priority (NGO confidential source 2, authors' interview, Pristina, 2016). In that sense, the decision about which places are 'made' in the context of cultural heritage protection has to be seen in the light of the political context and the forms of agency (of governments, NGOs and other societal actors) that surround this decision-making process. The example of the city Prizren and its castle in the south of Kosovo illustrates the different actors involved as well as the political negotiations at play in the field of cultural heritage protection.

Creating a place for the community in Prizren

In Kosovo, the city of Prizren, the second-largest city of Kosovo, and specifically its castle, are often evoked when it comes to discussions around cultural heritage. The historic centre is the biggest special protection zone in the country as Prizren has a rich history as well as cultural heritage that goes back to the Middle Ages, the Ottomans and the Kingdom of Serbia, to name but a few. Whilst Pristina and Mitrovica are often considered epicentres of conflict, Kosovars, in conversation with us, tended to refer to Prizren as 'the real Kosovo', 'a place you have to visit'. An interviewee made it very clear to us that Prizren is different from Pristina (Confidential source 4, authors' interview, Pristina, 2016). The interviewee emphasised that Pristina could not be considered representative of Kosovo and that even Mitrovica was rather artificial (ibid.). According to this interviewee, people feel more nostalgic about Prizren than about Pristina and, as a result of the greater popularity of the city, people use its public space more than the one in Pristina (ibid.). Such statements tend to be invoked in the light of the historical artefacts that can be found in Prizren to this date, rather than employment or housing opportunities.

Both in the context of Prizren, and also in other heritage related areas of Kosovo cultural heritage has been used as a way of mobilising the surrounding communities. One way to implement this approach have been the 'Local Cultural Heritage Forums' as a platform for the establishment of participatory planning structures and mainly led by the NGO Cultural Heritage Without Borders (CHWB) (Cultural Heritage Without Borders, 2015). The organisation has launched a four-year programme with seven municipalities to engage in the development of 'local cultural heritage plans'. This means that, in each municipality, a group of civil society actors and local stakeholders are involved in the development of this plan and feed it to the government through CHWB. This in turn is aimed to attract international, national and municipal funding whilst at the same time ensuring the inclusion of civil society in the process. The programme places emphasis on including minorities in the process. With this approach, cultural heritage is viewed as a resource for local development, education and even capacity-building (NGO confidential source 2, authors' interview, Pristina, 2016). It becomes clear that there is not only a peace-related agenda underlying these plans and the joint development of place-making strategies in the communities, but also an economic motivation. It is the latter that often gets on board people in the community who would otherwise be less interested in cultural heritage and protection of the relevant sites. Yet it has been observed that some community members have opened Bed & Breakfasts in old buildings, thus benefiting from the site's attractions for tourists (ibid.).

This approach, amongst others, has been used in the preservation of Prizren castle project. CHWB has aimed to engage the surrounding community and stakeholder groups in the planning process in order to make sure that the site and the way it is used would be in line with emerging community needs (NGO confidential source 3, authors' interview, Pristina, 2016). It has to be said that the consultation and negotiation process between the authorities and the community as well as between the government and local institutions was rather conflictive as the authorities had preferred to retain the status quo of the castle whereas NGOs and the communities preferred the site to be transformed into a useable public space (ibid.). Against the background of such heated debates, a final plan was developed that created a place (the castle) that would take into account those competing demands. This plan involves the rebranding and refurbishing of one half of the castle as a museum, whereas the other half could be used as a function or conference room to serve a variety of audiences (ibid.). The place that it was decided to create thus became an open site to serve the general public, including a park (ibid.).

What this example reflects is the interplay between different forms of agency in the process of place-making with respect to Prizren's cultural heritage sites. What type of place is constructed from the castle is subject to the negotiations around it, not least in the light of available funds and international pressure factors as well. The interest of a number of international actors has certainly been conducive to the attention given to this process of place-making and has contributed to the shaping of the agenda. The ideas of space (that is, the perceived need of a space for meetings, economic income and conservation of the city's history) have therefore translated into a place-making project that aims to cater to this complexity of needs.

Conclusion

The case study of Kosovo highlights the relevance of place-making and space-making to both the affirmation and the contestation of statehood. Spatial politics in Kosovo are part and parcel of the state building exercise and tend to make visible societal divisions in the material landscapes of urban areas. Whether it be the Mother Teresa Boulevard in Pristina, the bridge in Mitrovica or the castle in Prizren, those places tell us about existing dividing lines in society as well as how those have been resisted by a variety of agents. In fact, while the underlying infrastructure of the state tends to be translated into the microspheres of spatial politics, there are agents actively engaging in changing this spatial narrative and creating shared places – as the example of the Prizren castle illustrates. In that sense, the process of moving back and forth in time through the construction of heritage sites creates a constant spatial transformation that allows for multiple meanings to enter historic sites. Yet such processes are faced with powerful spatial structures that the Mother Teresa Boulevard, amongst others, demonstrates and through which places create infrastructures of division that are visible to passers-by and users of the place. In that vein, places can embody conflict and peace at the same time, as the example of the Mitrovica Bridge illustrates. While the image of a bridge itself stands for unity and cooperation, this particular bridge has equally performed the function of a dividing line in Mitrovica. Conflict is therefore spatially embedded in the everyday, just as much as the transformation of places and spaces can embed agency working towards peace and shared space.

Note

1   We use 'Kosovo' as it is the more common use in English (and in Serbian) while we acknowledge that Kosova is the preferred use in Albanian.

Bibliography

Alpion, G., 2004. Media, Ethnicity and Patriotism – the Balkans 'Unholy War' for the Appropriation of Mother Teresa. *Journal of Southern Europe and the Balkans* 6(3), pp. 227–243.

Balkan Insight, 2014. 'Park' on Bridge Causes Confusion in Divided Mitrovica. [Online] Available at: http://www.balkaninsight.com/en/article/new-barricade-causes-uncertainty-in-northern-kosovo [Accessed 26 May 2016].

Barber, J. & Španzel, Š., 2015. *Joint Project EU/CoE Support to the Promotion of Cultural Diversity (PCDK) Final Report*. European Union and Council of Europe.

Benetton Group, 2013. The United Colors of Benetton megastore in Pristina opens. The historic Hotel Union, in the heart of the capital, is returned to the city following an important refurbishment and restoration. [Online] Available at: http://www.benettongroup.com/media-press/press-releases-and-statements/the-united-colors-of-benetton-megastore-in-pristina-opens-the-historic-hotel-union-in-the-heart-of-the-capital-is-returned-to-the-city-following-an-important-refurbishment-and-restorat [Accessed 31 May 2016].

Björkdahl, A., 2007. To Practice What They Preach: International Transitional Administrations and the Paradox of Normal Promotion. In: A. Swain, R. Amer & J. Öjendal, eds. *Globalization and Challenges to Building Peace*. London: Antheme Press, pp. 145–164.

Björkdahl, A. & Gusic, I., 2013. The Divided City – A Space for Frictional Peacebuilding. *Peacebuilding* 1(3), pp. 317–333.

Campbell, D., 1998. *National Deconstruction: Violence, Identity and Justice in Bosnia.* Minneapolis, MN: University of Minneapolis Press.

Clark, J. N., 2014. Kosovo's Gordian Knot: The Contested North and the Search for a Solution. *Nationalities Papers* 42(3), pp. 526–547.

Cultural Heritage Without Borders, 2015. *Local Cultural Heritage Plan.* Pristina: Cultural Heritage Without Borders.

Ermolin, D. S., 2014. When Skanderbeg meets Clinton: Cultural Landscape and Commemorative Strategies in Postwar Kosovo. *Croatian Political Science Review* 51 (5), pp. 157–173.

Gow, J., 2009. Kosovo – The Final Frontier? From Transitional Administration to Transitional Statehood. *Journal of Intervetion and Statebuilding* 3(2), pp. 239–257.

Gusic, I., 2015. Contested Democrac(ies) – Disentangling Understandings of Democratic Governance in Mitrovica. In: A. Björkdahl & L. Strömbom, eds. *Divided Cities – Governing Diversity.* Lund: Nordic Academic Press, pp. 215–234.

Gusic, I.,forthcoming. *War, Peace & the City: Urban Conflicts over Peace(s) in Belfast, Mitrovica, and Mostar.* Ph.D. thesis. Lund: Lund University Press.

Hoxha, V., Kimitrovska Andrews, K. & Temeljotov Salaj, A., 2014. Cultural Factors Affecting Urban Planners' Intentions to Regulate Public Space in Prishtina, Kosovo. *Urbani ivviv* 25(2), pp. 76–89.

ICG, 2012. *Setting Kosovo free: Remaining challenges. Report No. 218*, Pristina/Istanbul/Brussels: International Crisis Group.

ICG, 2013. *Serbia and Kosovo: The Path to Normalization. Report No. 223*, Pristina/Belgrade/Brussels: International Crisis Group.

IKS and ESI, 2006a. *Utopian visions: Governance failures in Kosovo's capital.* [Online] Available at: http://www.esiweb.org/pdf/esi_document_id_78.pdf [Accessed 1 June 2016].

IKS and ESI, 2006b. *A Future for Prishtina's Past.* [Online] Available at: http://www.esiweb.org/pdf/esi_future_of_pristina%20booklet.pdf [Accessed 1 June 2016].

Independent International Commission on Kosovo, 2000. *The Kosovo Report: Conflict, International Response, Lessons Learned*, Oxford: Oxford University Report.

InSerbia, 2015. Zbogar Proposes Solution for Peace Park in Mitrovica. [Online] Available at: https://inserbia.info/today/2015/06/zbogar-proposes-solution-for-peace-park-in-mitrovica/ [Accessed 8 June 2016].

Judah, T., 2008. *Kosovo.* Oxford: Oxford University Press.

Kaplan, D. H., 1992. Nationalism at a Micro-scale: Educational Segregation in Montreal. *Politial Geography* 11(3), pp. 259–282.

Kaplan, R., 1993. *Balkan Ghosts: A Journey through History.* New York: St. Martin's Press.

Kliot, N. & Mansfield, Y., 1997. The Political Landscape of Partition: The Case of Cyprus. *Political Geography* 16(6), pp. 495–521.

Kolbe, L., 2007. Central and Eastern European Capital Cities: Interpreting www. pages-history, Symbols and Identity. *Planning Perspectives* 22(1), pp. 79–111.

Kostovicova, D., 2004. Republika Srpska and its Boundaries in Bosnian Serb Geographical Narratives in the Post-Dayton Period. *Space and Polity* 8(3), pp. 267–287.

Kostovicova, D., 2005. *Kosovo: The Politics of Identity and Space.* London and New York: Routledge.

Krasniqi, G., 2012. Overlapping Jurisdictions, Disputed Territory, Unsettled State: The Perplexing Case of Citizenship in Kosovo. *Citizenship Studies* 16(3–4), pp. 353–366.

Law on Special Protective Zones. Law Nr. 03/L-039. [Online] Available at: http://www.assembly-kosova.org/common/docs/ligjet/2008_03-L039_en.pdf [Accessed 04 November 2016].

Lemay-Hébert, N., 2012. Multiethnicité ou ghettoïsation? Statebuilding international et partition du Kosovo à l'aune du projet controversé de mur à Mitrovica. *Études Internationales* 43(1), pp. 27–47.

Massey, D., 2005. *For Space*. London: SAGE.

Massey, D. S. & Hajnal, Z. L., 1995. The Changing Geographic Structure of Black–White Segregation in the United States. *Social Science Quarterly* 76(3), pp. 527–542.

New Europe, 2005. Nato Removes Barricade from Bridge in Mitrovica. [Online] Available at: https://www.neweurope.eu/article/nato-removes-barricades-bridge-mitrovica/ [Accessed 15 June 2016].

Newman, D., 2002. The Geopolitics of Peacemaking in Israel-Palestine. *Political Geography* 21(5), pp. 629–646.

OSCE, 2014. *Challenges in the Protection of Immovable Tangible Cultural Heritage in Kosovo*. OSCE Mission Kosovo.

Pinos, J. C., 2016. Mitrovica: A City (Re)shaped the Division. In: É. Ó. Ciardha & G. Vojvoda, eds. *Politics of Identity in Post-Conflict States: The Bosnian and Irish Experience*. London and New York: Routledge, pp. 128–142.

Rakic, G., 2014a. Interview with AFP. [Online] Available at: http://www.i24news.tv/en/news/international/europe/34660-140618-kosovo-serbs-replace-barricade-with-flower-boxes-in-flashpoint-town [Accessed 26 May 2016].

Rakic, G., 2014b. Interview Balkan Insight. [Online] Available at: http://www.balkaninsight.com/en/article/peace-park-in-divided-mitrovica-causes-dispute [Accessed 26 May 2016].

Ramet, S. P., 2004a. Explaining the Yugoslav Meltdown, 1 'For a charm of pow'rful trouble, Like a hell-broth boil and bubble': Theories about the Roots of the Yugoslav Troubles. *Nationalities Papers* 32(4), pp. 731–763.

Ramet, S. P., 2004b. Explaining the Yugoslav Meltdown, 2 A Theory about the Causes of the Yugoslav Meltdown: The Serbian National Awakening as a 'Revitalization Movement'. *Nationalities Papers* 32(4), pp. 765–779.

Ramet, S. P., 2005. *Thinking about Yugoslavia: Scholarly Debates about the Yugoslav Breakup and the Wars in Bosnia and Kosovo*. Cambridge: Cambridge University Press.

Smith, A. D., 1991. *National Identity*. London: Penguin.

Toal, G. & Dahlman, C., 2012. *Bosnia Remade*. Oxford: Oxford University Press.

Todorova, M., 2012. *Imagining the Balkans*. 2nd ed. Oxford: Oxford University Press.

UNSCR, 1999. *Security Council Resolution 1244 (1999)*. New York: United Nations.

Visoka, G. & Richmond, O., 2016. After Liberal Peace? From Failed State-building to an Emancipatory Peace in Kosovo. *International Studies Perspectives*, DOI: http://dx.doi.org/10.1093/isp/ekw006.

Wilmer, F., 2002. *The Social Construction of Man, the State, and War: Identity, Conflict, and Violence in the Former Yugoslavia*. New York and London: Routledge.

Woodward, S. 1995. *The Balkan Tragedy*. Washington D.C.: Brookings Institutions.

Interviews

NGO confidential source, authors' interview, Mitrovica, 14 April 2016.

Confidential source 1, authors' interview, Pristina, 13 April 2016.

Confidential source 2, authors' interview, Pristina, 13 April 2016.
Confidential source 3, authors' interview, Pristina, 15 April 2016.
Confidential source 4, authors' interview, Pristina, 13 April 2016.
EULEX representative, authors' interview, North Mitrovica, 14 April 2016.
Fitim Mulolli, authors' interview, OSCE, Pristina, 15 April 2016.
Marija Mirceska and Fitim Mulolli, authors' interview, OSCE, Pristina, 15 April 2016.
Marija Mirceska, authors' interview, OSCE, Pristina, 15 April 2016.
NGO confidential source 1, authors' interview, Pristina, 15 April 2016.
NGO confidential source 2, authors' interview, Pristina, 15 April 2016.
NGO confidential source 3, authors' interview, Pristina, 15 April 2016.
OSCE official, authors' interview, Mitrovica, 14 April 2016.

4 Bosnia-Herzegovina: The Ethnic Peace

Introduction

The war-scape of Bosnia-Herzegovina (BiH) provides us with ample opportunities to explore different expressions of peacebuilding agency. It also helps us to rethink the interconnectedness between space and place and their relationship with peace and conflict and, in doing so, to generate new insights to the understanding of where peace and conflict 'take place'. The central contention of this chapter is that the organisation of space and place is significant for the structure and function of peace as well as of war in BiH. Peace is located in place, but it is also about socio-spatial relations that are always being made and remade. Through peacebuilding agents' efforts at space-making and place-making, peace becomes connected to space and place and agents contribute to the transition from war towards peace in BiH – whether the current situation is referred to as post-conflict or in similar terms. The analysis of BiH presented in this chapter thus helps us to understand how peace and conflict are socially and materially situated, which in turn makes it possible to reconceptualise and contextualise transformations of the legacy of conflict and the building of peace.

This transformation of the legacy of conflict and the emergence of peace in Višegrad in Eastern BiH, as well as in Mostar and Sarajevo, reveal how both conflict and peace are performed through everyday practices, and thus can be changed through altered spatial practices. It also reveals the spatial politics, which is what dictates and sets up the spatial order. Thus, this chapter also maps the agency performed by minority returnees attempting to return to the ethnically more or less homogenous Republika Srpska. We zoom in on refugee return to Višegrad, which can be read as a failed effort to counter the transformation, in war and peace, of the demographic and spatial landscape of Eastern BiH. In so doing we unmask the curbed agency of refugees and displaced persons as well as of the international community in the spatial politics at play in the country. The ethnically cleansed places produced through the war and cemented through the peace process have indeed resulted in an 'ethnic peace'. De-ethnicising this peace requires power shifts and entails a coherent strategy of minority return and an actual process of minority returnees reclaiming territory and restoring their place of belonging.

Furthermore, with a focus on space-making, the chapter analyses how agents transform the material wounds of the siege of Sarajevo. Through a process of space-making, peacebuilding agents transform the scars of the mortar shell explosions by giving them new meaning and turning them into the Sarajevo Roses. For those who survived, the siege is forever inscribed into the cityscape of Sarajevo through the small craters left from mortar damage now filled with red resin into a symbolic rose. These Roses now act as constant reminders of the horror and tragedy of the longest siege of a city in the history of modern warfare whilst acting as powerful symbol of conflict prevention. Today, such space-making efforts shape the memoryscape of Sarajevo. Through a spatial perspective we can explore how places are negotiated and how they shape peoples' experiences, memories, feelings and interpretations. The transformation of these material wounds of the war through a process of space-making are thus analysed in this chapter to highlight the peacebuilding agency of ordinary citizens and of the urban dwellers passing the Roses in their everyday lives. These places foreground the politics of belonging (Yuval-Davis, 2006), and the Sarajevo Roses are discursive sites for the construction of narratives in which experiences of the siege are rendered meaningful.

Finally, we investigate the place-making process to localise peace at the Youth Cultural Centre Abrašević, a youth centre located on the former front line of the fighting in the divided city of Mostar – a place linked neither to the Bosniaks nor to the Bosnian Croats that inhabit the city. We show that the centre, in similar ways to many other cultural and youth centres across the country, represents the materialisation of a de-ethnicised logic. In that sense, we reflect the extent to which the place-making practices of the centre defy the overall logic of BiH's post-war spatial organisation and instead suggest a public space organised beyond the ethnic dichotomies that shape Mostar as a city.

Transition from war to ethnic peace

The war in BiH has to be seen in the context of the breakup of the former Yugoslavia in the early 1990s. It was a war that was set in the context of the death of Tito, but also of the associated transition to democracy and market economy. BiH was eventually drawn into the war after Serbia and Croatia had clashed, and after Croatia's unilateral declaration of independence was rejected by both Serbia and by the Socialist Republic of Yugoslavia. Violence in BiH lasted from 1992 to 1995. It included the almost four-year long siege of Sarajevo, a 'war within the war' in the city of Mostar where former allies turned into enemies, and also the ethnic cleansing of various regions of the country such as Eastern BiH and Herzegovina. This devastating war has left its imprints on people, villages, towns and cities around the country (Woodward, 1995).

Despite the UN presence in the country, and a number of efforts, of varying seriousness, to end the war through peace negotiations, it ended only in 1995 with the signing of the Dayton Peace Accord (DPA) (Gow, 1997). Both the EU and the UN were indeed criticised for their failure to end the war at various earlier stages as negotiations, mediation efforts and sanctions remained ineffective and even strengthened Milosević's position, while weakening the Serbian opposition (Glenny, 1996: 211). A spatial perspective draws our attention to the secure spaces UN peacekeepers in UNPROFOR attempted to create during and after the war. These spaces were intended to create a sense of everyday security for the Bosniaks, Bosnian Croats and Bosnian Serbs (Higate & Henry, 2010). For example, the international community, in the shape of the UN peacekeeping presence on the ground, aimed to create 'safe havens' in Srebrenica, Žepa, Goražde, Tuzla, Bihać and Sarajevo.[1] According to Higate and Henry (2010: 44), 'peacekeeping is an exemplary territorialising practice that shapes perceptions of everyday security through its transformation of space, performed through particular security practices'. These security measures temporarily transformed the villages to safe havens in BiH, saving lives and offering a degree of sanctuary from ethnic cleansing and mass killings. Over time, however, their credibility was eroded. The military protection put in place was insufficient to deter attacks and, in the absence of political will to provide resources to protect the enclaves, in combination with the requirement to demilitarise the safe havens, two of the six supposedly safe havens fell to the Serbs. Neither the UN nor NATO were able to prevent the Srebrenica massacre with an estimated 10,000 casualties in Eastern BiH where the majority of the ethnic cleansing took place. The Srebrenica massacre, which Malcolm (2002: 264) describes as the blackest moment of UN involvement in BiH and as a humanitarian disaster, has subsequently been acknowledged as genocide by the International Criminal Tribunal for the former Yugoslavia (ICTY).

The transition towards peace in BiH has generally been associated with the DPA of 1995, which put an end to the war that had scarred the country for almost four years. It was mainly the international community that took charge of the planned transformation of the country and largely drove the process. Richmond and Franks (2009) suggest that, instead of addressing the very roots of the conflict, the DPA was instead used to implement the liberal peace and its associated elements, such as the free market, democracy and the rule of law. In order to supervise the implementation of the peace agreement, the institution of the Office of the High Representative (OHR) was created.[2] The OHR together with other international organisations managed to take over functions of sovereignty which allowed them to govern BiH in a trusteeship-style way (Caplan, 2004: 54). This has been done through the construction of parallel systems of governance through international involvement (Coles, 2007: 267).

This included the fact that the externally negotiated peace agreement formed the new Bosnian constitution as well as envisaging the geographical division of the country both territorially as well as in terms of political representation. The formation of Republika Srpska, a mainly Bosnian Serb-dominated area with its own geographic boundaries, the Federation (mainly Bosniak and Bosnian Croat-dominated) as well as the self-governing Brčko District were an attempt to order BiH geographically after the war (Dahlman & Ó Tuathail, 2005; Jeffrey, 2006; Bieber, 2005) and to respond to the demands of the ethnic leaders of the war. This reordering of territory according to ethnic cleavages made the signing of the DPA possible. On the other hand, it became an obstacle to minority return, to rebuilding ethnically divided cities and to the materialisation of a shared non-ethnic peace. In addition, all political offices and institutions were split up to include representatives from the three majority ethnic groups – a basic precondition for the peace agreement to be signed by all three parties. While this meant the possibility of ending the violence, it also cemented the ethnically segregated structures of war in BiH's social and political life. The consociational political arrangement solidified ethnic affiliation (Finlay, 2011) and created an obstacle to cross-ethnic collaboration in the long run. This in turn is not conducive to the reunification of the country and impedes a sustainable political settlement that would include minority groups other than the three so-called 'constituent peoples'.[3] It promotes an emphasis on identity division and exclusiveness of categories. At the same time, it maintains a geographical and spatial division between different ethnic groups in BiH, not least as their interests are presented in a mutually exclusive way.

We could therefore go as far as to argue that the internationally conceived and mediated peace institutionalised the war gains throughout BiH's spatial, political and social structures. This persistent segregation is still visible even today, with most political parties being affiliated ethnically and geographically situated. The international community have indeed struggled to deal with these obstacles that they helped to create. As Belloni (2007: 5) suggests, overcoming these cemented ethnic cleavages is further complicated by the international community's focus on stability and the status quo and thus the failure to respond to social, economic and political challenges as they emerge out of a deeply-divided political system and segregated geographical space.

Transformation is thus not a coherent, mono-directional process, but contains its own internal contradictions (Belloni, 2007), with largely separated political and social spaces. We can therefore argue that the transition from war to peace in BiH is shaped by a dual process: on the one hand, there is a strongly institutionalised and territorially organised continuing ethnic segregation of the country with more and more ethnically homogenous countryside, neighbourhoods, villages, towns and cities testifying to the perpetuation and permanence of ethnic cleansing through other means. On the other hand, we can now observe the mobilisation of large parts of the population across ethnic groups, to seek social justice, as could be seen with the 2014 protests throughout the country (Murtagh, 2016). These protests took place in various cities and resulted in the removal of politicians from office as well as the creation of citizens' plenums in which political affairs were discussed and communicated to the formal political sphere (Mujkić, 2015). Such attempts aiming at a transformation of deeply engrained ethnic structures are now pointing at possible changes, but only 20 years after the signing of the actual peace agreement. However, spatially speaking, the country remains divided as a whole, though segregation tendencies are visible in urban landscapes as well, with Sarajevo, Mostar and Višegrad representing particular points in case. In this context, controversies about the use of space are still commonplace, not least illustrated by the contestations around minority returns, emplaced ethnic divisions in cities and fragmented memoryscapes. Against this background, we suggest that the spatial structure of BiH is shaped by two tendencies that are unfolding in parallel: on the one hand, a number of agents and actors are keen to reinforce the dividing lines, both material and symbolical, in order to keep the country divided. The 2016 call for a referendum for independence by Milorad Dodik, president of Republika Srpska, to launch another attempt to make his entity independent is but one example. On the other hand, as we will show below, actors such as cultural youth centres or citizens' initiatives are actively resisting these segregative tendencies through their own place-making and space-making initiatives. We could therefore argue that, whilst the overall spatial politics of BiH suggest an increasing division of the country, this is countered by a multiplicity of opposing activities and forms of agency that strive to overcome this tendency.

Spatial politics and the ethnicisation of peace

The post-war landscape constrained the international and local peacebuilding agents attempting to reverse wartime displacement through post-war returns to Eastern Bosnia and to the village of Višegrad. We therefore suggest that this village is a useful example that reflects larger spatial politics in BiH and the difficulties encountered by the reversal of deeply engrained policies of segregation. Efforts to do so challenged the ethnicised peace of the DPA, and the reclamation of territory was sternly resisted by local ethno-nationalist powerholders, and continues to be so. Transforming the post-war landscape and de-ethnicising the peace accord through minority returns is therefore proving to be an enormous challenge to the Bosniak Internally Displaced Persons (IDPs) and to the international community. The atrocities and extent of ethnic cleansing that took place during the war in south-eastern and eastern BiH have been well documented.[4] During the 1992–1995 war, Višegrad was synonymous with mass killings, ethnic cleansing and rape camps. During the first month of the conflict in BiH, Serbian paramilitaries embarked on a policy of ethnic cleansing of Bosniaks from towns like Višegrad and surrounding villages (Björkdahl & Mannergren Selimovic, 2015). Those who survived sought refuge in Bosniak-controlled territory such as Tuzla and Sarajevo as well as abroad. Once Višegrad became a space controlled by the Bosnian Serbs, Bosnian Serb refugees who had fled from the war in other parts of BiH sought refuge here (Women's organisation Most, authors' interview, Višegrad, 2014). These Bosnian Serb IDPs took over abandoned houses in Višegrad, and lived in schools and government buildings, thus taking over places that had once belonged to Bosniaks or that had once been shared and multi-ethnic. Thus, the Bosnian Serbs claimed and reframed the space, and the appropriation of physical places was a way of manifesting agency as well as of inscribing the Serbian ethnic identity on the landscape. As a consequence, and in a parallel process pertaining to the politics of belonging, the Bosniaks lost 'their sense of place' in Eastern BiH. These processes cannot be said to be unique to Višegrad as similar processes of consolidating claims to space and place were made by the other ethnic communities in places where they sought to maintain control over space, place and population.

As a consequence of this transformation of place, Višegrad and Eastern Bosnia were formally granted to Republika Srpska under the DPA. The international community through the DPA can be said to have brought a negative peace to BiH – a peace that has been termed 'ethnic peace' – as the settlement did not resolve the underlying ethno-nationalist conflict and spatial contestation. The peace accord was a compromise that endorsed the creation of a unified and independent state, but also accepted the partition of the state into two discrete ethno-territorial entities, Republika Srpska and the Federation of BiH, separated by an internal 'inter-entity boundary line' as well as the semi-autonomous Brčko District. Thus, the peace materialised through the construction of Republika Srpska and the inter-entity boundary line and, as such, the territory and the border were given some form of agency. The DPA's conception of BiH reflects an ambivalence concerning statehood (Dahlman & Ó Tuathail, 2005). On the one hand, the DPA remains committed to the 'sovereignty, territorial integrity, and political independence of BiH in accordance with international law'. On the other hand, BiH consists of two entities, the Bosniak-Croat Federation, occupying 51 per cent of the territory, and Republika Srpska occupying 49 per cent. Republika Srpska roughly coincides with the ethno-nationalist homeland claimed by the Bosnian Serb leadership before the war, and the DPA can thus be seen as having rewarded war efforts and ethnic cleansing. This construction of BiH, based on three constitutive peoples, two entities and one state, was a result of the inconsistencies inherent in the DPA and, as a consequence, the fate of BiH oscillates between reintegration and partition (Belloni, 2009).

The DPA legalised and legitimised Republika Srpska, the territorial space which was claimed through large-scale ethnic cleansing and genocide (Belloni, 2005). Yet the DPA also sought to reverse the ethnic cleansing via Annex VII pertaining to refugee return. Over time, international agencies hoped that minority returns would return BiH to its multi-ethnic character. However, the practical reality at the end of 1995 was that the houses of IDPs had been either destroyed or occupied. During and immediately after the war, legislation was passed preventing access to property owned and lived in before the war. In places like Višegrad, local authorities were openly hostile to returns and continued to enforce wartime laws that 'legalised' the reassignment of former Bosniak property to displaced Bosnian Serbs in an effort to secure their newly constructed ethnoscape. Ethnonationalists were thus long successful in blocking minority return, while the international community imposed a legal framework to facilitate returns and allow returnees to (re)take place. Local associations of displaced persons, often acting without the support of international agencies, made initial visits, provided information to potential donors and assessed the security situation on behalf of potential returnees. The Bosniak nationalist party, Stranka demokratske akcije (SDA), provided construction material for refugees returning to destroyed pre-war homes in an effort to capitalise politically from the refugee return (Belloni, 2005: 441).

During the spring of 1996, thousands of displaced persons attempted to return to or visit their pre-war homes in eastern BiH, in order to celebrate a Muslim holiday close to family graves (Björkdahl & Mannergren Selimovic, 2015). In anticipation, local Bosnian Serb nationalists mobilised and threatened violence against any 'Muslim terrorist' returning to Republika Srpska (Dahlman & Ó Tuathail, 2005). So, in addition to legal barriers, IDPs did not feel safe returning to areas controlled by another ethnic group as the fear and hate left by the legacy of war crimes was inscribed into spaces of minority return (Fischel de Andrade & Delaney, 2001).

Thus, in the first five years after the DPA, only 6 per cent out of the 42 per cent who were displaced from South-Eastern BiH returned to what had become Republika Srpska after the war and, labelled as BiH's 'black hole' known to be a hiding-place for several indicted war criminals and the stronghold of nationalist radicals (Fischel de Andrade & Delaney, 2001). Many displaced persons felt that not enough arrests had been made for them to return. In Višegrad, returning Bosniaks encountered former neighbours who had attacked them during the war, some of whom continued to threaten violence upon the returnees (Duinzings, 2007; Kolind, 2007). Furthermore, they often found that their house had been illegally occupied by Bosnian Serb IDPs who claimed the houses as theirs, and local police were reluctant to enforce their evictions (Confidential source, authors' interview, Srebrenica, 2014).

Post-war efforts to implement the Annex VII, according to Dahlman and Ó Tuathail (2005: 644) developed into 'a struggle over place between entrenched local ethnonationalists, multiple international agencies and displaced persons'. Having people return, house by house, and town by town was an ambitious 'spatial (re)engineering and place (re)building' effort with the aim of restoring places to their pre-war multi-ethnic character (Dahlman & Ó Tuathail, 2005: 651). In contrast, local authorities used refugees and IDPs to consolidate their control over a territory and majority returns fulfilled this ambition. By controlling the allocation of housing the local elite ethnically engineered the return process. As in many places in Republika Srpska, allocating land plots to Bosnian Serb IDPs, mainly war veterans, widows and those evicted from illegally occupied property, represented another strategy to consolidate spatial claims to territory. Thus, IDPs and 'refugees were instrumentalised to consolidate war time gains' (Zaum, 2010: 301). Such spatial practices were used to create facts on the ground that eventually both Bosniak potential returnees and the international community had to accept.[5]

The return process has therefore been a long and protracted power struggle throughout BiH's localities. The dynamics of minority return to Republika

Srpska in general and to Višegrad in particular provide insights into the relation between agency, space and place as well as into power relations that are played out in certain places, not dissimilar from those in other parts of a country that has been unable to shed its post-war structures of ethnic segregation. The demographic character and the cultural landscape of Višegrad in particular were radically changed by the war and the town remains the most difficult space for returnees. Peacebuilding agency in this context is constrained by powerful spatial practices and consolidated claims to space as the entity structure of the country acts as an ethnoscape that can barely be challenged. The example of Višegrad thus reflects the strong power of highly controlled spaces to intervene in people's daily lives and prevent societies from returning to 'normality'. It is indeed difficult to see how in such spaces, less visible or politically resourced manifestations of peacebuilding agency can counter the ethnic organisation and domination of space. It also demonstrates the agentic force of the ethnoscape and how it shapes agency that supports, constructs, reacts, resists, or challenges ethnicised spaces and places. It is this context in that, not only in Višegrad, but also beyond, actors have to manoeuvre, either accepting this spatial logic and finding their own place within, or alternatively challenging it on their own terms. The examples of place-making and space-making that we provide below will illustrate the ways in which actors have been challenging such a constraining structure through an attempt to reverse the ethnicised spatial logic.

Space-making

In line with Doreen Massey (2005), we conceive of space as always under construction and, as such, being connected to an anti-essentialist notion of politics. Such an approach to space acknowledges that the ordering of post-war space, like any other order is political (Mouffe, 2005: 18). Space-making is a process that takes as its point of departure the physical, material place and through meaning-making processes transforms it into an abstract, ideational, social space. Through a process of space-making peacebuilding agents give a particular meaning to a physical place, which turns it into a social space that resonates with political discourses. Spaces, according to Massey (2005: 9) are a 'product of interrelations', and relational, connected to place through social discourses and practices. Such practices are the product not only of relations between people acting around particular places but also of the relations between the urban dwellers and the place and there is an 'affective bond between people and place' (Tuan, 1974: 4). Marking territory has been at the core of the politics of memory and competing symbolism in Sarajevo (Kappler, 2016) and this will be explored through the perspective of space-making below.

The memoryscape of Sarajevo

We turn our attention now to Sarajevo, a city that historically has defied demands for consistency and national boundedness. It is a city that has changed its colours and there are public reminders of Ottoman rule, of the Central European Habsburg Empire and of the spread of Islam, Serbian Orthodoxy, Roman Catholicism and Sephardic Jewry (Markowitz, 2010). There are manifestations of two 20th-century Yugoslav projects and now the statebuilding project of BiH. Sarajevo embodies the competing, coexisting and intertwined results of a convoluted past and it was one of the most cosmopolitan cities in Yugoslavia. As such it used to be a showcase of ethnic, religious and cultural diversity. This image of the city was shattered in the war of dissolution in Yugoslavia. Between 1992 and 1995, Sarajevo was held in a thousand-day siege (Maček, 2009). It was 'the epicentre of the Bosnian "memoricide"' according to Halilović (2013: 103). Since the war the city has been divided into Sarajevo proper, where Bosniaks greatly outnumber Bosnian Croats and Bosnian Serbs, and the Bosnian Serbian-majority suburb of East Sarajevo known as Istočno Sarajevo, the de jure capital of the autonomous Republika Srpska (Jansen, 2013). Today Sarajevo is in transformation between mirth and melancholy, heterogeneity and hybridity, products of ethnic separatism and interethnic blends that constitute Sarajevo as 'a cosmopolitan society and its enemies' (Beck, 2002 cited in Markowitz, 2010). BiH's cultural heritage represents exactly this: the civic identity of the city and the material marks that people of different ethnicities and religions could live together sharing common cultural heritage as part of their collective cultural memory (Halilović, 2013; Donia, 2006). The cityscape reflects the fragmented memories of a fragmented country (Moll, 2013) and the contemporary spatial stories of the conflict depict Sarajevo's ambivalent memoryscape (Kappler, 2016). In this war-torn city we explore the spatial narratives of the cityscape and zoom in on the materiality and symbolism of the so-called Sarajevo Roses as an attempt to instil a different logic into the otherwise ethnicised memoryscape. In this context, we note that places such as those where the Sarajevo Roses are displayed carry meaning through the inscription and reconfiguration of identities in relation to place. As the geographer Edward Soja puts it, '[p]lace emerges as a particular form of space, one that is created through acts of naming as well as the distinctive activities and imaginings associated with particular social spaces' (cited in Hubbarb *et al.*, 2004: 5). In the section below we investigate the construction of space through the altered experience and narrative of place, and the reconfiguration of identity in how it shapes spatial practice in an ethnicised environment.

The Sarajevo Roses: a meaning-making process

War greatly impacts upon the narratives and interpretations of places, and thus the construction of space. Bevan (2006) writes that war destroys memories, but in some regards also creates another layer of memory. The symbolic and political power of any given place can be seen in its ability to mould thoughts, evoke memories and emotions, reinforce and create discourses and practices, and to relay to the world the experiences of a place. Wise's (2011: 12) notion of 'landscape remembrance' can be applied to the post-conflict cityscape of Sarajevo in the spatial expression of memories all over the cityscape. While the spatial narratives of Sarajevo often refer to the Sarajevo Roses, which sound like something beautiful, the story of the Sarajevo Roses refers to the emplaced legacy of the Bosnian war of the 1990s and the siege of Sarajevo, the longest siege of a city in modern history. During the siege, Bosnian Serb forces shelled the city of Sarajevo from the surrounding hills. The number of shells that landed in Sarajevo during the 1,335 days the city was under siege amounts to an average of around 300 hits in Sarajevo every day (Maček, 2009). The Roses can therefore be considered as a memorial and testimony of the everyday experiences of the Sarajevans during the war.

The Roses were made in 1995 and are often considered a 'peoples' monument' as they represent a memorial made by the Sarajevans themselves.[6] The Roses were placed in some of the places where a mortar shell explosion made a material scar in the pavement and they were later painted with red resin as a memorial to those who were killed at that particular place during the siege. There are Sarajevo Roses in front of churches and of bakeries, and on pedestrian streets, and they serve as a reminder of the constant horror in which the people of Sarajevo lived for almost four years. Yet, their origins are a mystery and the Sarajevans' memories blur as regards when the first Rose appeared and the extent to which this matters.[7]

The Sarajevo Roses, the highlighted areas in which mortar shells exploded, are not just material places, but they also symbolise the serious scars in the hearts of those affected and on the cityscape. They are inspired by the image of an open wound and they signal brutal death. To compare the crater left by an exploded mortar with the beauty of a rose may thus seem morbid, but the unique fragmentation pattern of a mortar round hitting concrete can be interpreted as having a floral look. Still, while roses are a symbol of love and beauty, the Sarajevo Roses represent a collective memory of the physical scars of war. Someone who lived through the siege in Sarajevo (Confidential source, authors' interview, Sarajevo, 2013) suggested that 'during the siege we were divided into those who grew these Roses with their lives and those who survived and watered the Roses with their tears. And that was the only difference.' From interviews and 'being in place' we are able to capture how agentive subjects produce narratives and counter-narratives that help make sense of the events that took place during the siege. These narratives are not only discursively constructed but materialised in the place such as the streets of Sarajevo.

Today, however, the Roses present a moral dilemma. Some Sarajevans feel sad looking at them when they walk by, because they recall past traumas. The Roses are close reminders of terrible deaths in the midst of where the Sarajevans' everyday lives still go on. Yet many Sarajevans feel uncomfortable and do not want to think about their traumas. Activist Jasmin Halilović (authors' interview, Sarajevo, 2013) argues, however, that 'we must keep them as we have to remember what happened, because what will happen if we

Figure 4.1 Sarajevo Rose next to the Catholic Cathedral, Sarajevo. Authors' photograph, 2013.

forget?'. By walking from Rose to Rose we were able to trace a scar running
deep across the local memoryscape. We found that walking the streets of
Sarajevo became a way of tracing as well as collecting the spatial narratives of
the siege and, as walkers, we compose a 'manifold story that has neither
author nor spectator' (de Certeau cited in Björkdahl & Mannergren
Selimovic, 2015: 5).

While the maintenance of the Roses has often been said to be an initiative
of the municipality, the latter left them to decay until they triggered debates in
the media (Halilović, 2011). Although many Sarajevo Roses have disappeared

in the years since the conflict ended, there are still many left and many others are being restored in an effort to ensure that this monument of the siege of Sarajevo is not forgotten. It was through the initiative of a number of non-governmental organisations, universities and social movements that the Roses were revived, repainted and given more importance in the public sphere. Since 2010, volunteers from the Youth Initiative for Human Rights Bosnia and Herzegovina have been repainting the Sarajevo Roses around the city. In the morning on the anniversary of the siege, they painted the resin in red. Many of the Roses that used to exist all over the city after the war disappeared during post-war reconstruction (Korchnak, 2014). 'Sarajevans failed to realise their value' (Halilović, authors' interview, 2013). In this context, individual activists designed, together with members of the Association 'Save the Sarajevo Roses', an art project under the name '7 Spots – 7 Sarajevo Roses'. The idea was to connect the Roses with true stories of people and thus point to the importance that these Roses have for the citizens of Sarajevo. The growing concern about the maintenance of the Roses resulted in a petition to the Sarajevo City Council (Halilović, not dated), and as a consequence the Sarajevo Canton signed a contract with a Bosnian company in 2012 to reconstruct the Roses, and a total of 200 Sarajevo Roses were reconstructed to preserve them as a symbol of shelling and thousands of casualties (Jukić, 2012). Thus, the Sarajevo Roses still remain etched in asphalt as a testament of what the city and its inhabitants had to endure. The spatial memory of war appeals to many Sarajevans, independent of their ethnic background, in a context in which many monuments have served as an artefact of memory for one nationality only (Zupan, 2006: 336).

The Sarajevo Roses are increasingly becoming part of the cultural discourse of post-war Sarajevo, which in many ways connects the local everyday experiences of war and post-war to the global metanarratives of peacebuilding, reconciliation and remembrance. The movie 'Sarajevo Roses – A Cinematic Essay' is directed and produced by Roger Richards, an award winning film-maker who was in Sarajevo at the height of the conflict and has witnessed and filmed its restoration on numerous returns. This movie, shown at the Sarajevo Film Festival 2016, tells the story of Sarajevo through five ordinary citizens who lived in an extraordinary time, survived unimaginable horror and have struggled to rebuild their city and their lives. It has now been twenty years and a generation has reached adulthood since the siege of Sarajevo ended. It is long enough for many of the city's war scars to heal, but the experiences shared by the survivors and the lessons they brought have compelled many Sarajevans to make a record of those times and of their journeys to find peace for those who follow. Through these narratives the movie attempts to bridge the gap between the war and its aftermath, and depicts how its impact has been felt even by generations that were as yet unborn (Sarajevo Roses – A Cinematic Essay, 2016).

The Sarajevo Roses can be read as an effort at space-making during the course of which the ways in which the war and the siege of the city can be spatially remembered are negotiated through various political and social groups and initiatives. They are a recollection of the suffering of the Sarajevans. The Roses avoid any personalisation of any particular site, yet they represent an unavoidable part of the history of this city, a monument to the dead, engraved in the cityscape of Sarajevo. The fact that they are placed in the asphalt in the streets makes them easy to ignore while walking over them. Yet, once noticed, the shiny crimson-coloured concrete splashes disrupt the grey monotony of the sidewalks and abruptly remind passers-by of the city's history of deadly mortal shelling. They do not hinder your path, nor obstruct your pace or disturb your peace of mind. They can be read as a reflection of the past, without obstructing a move towards the future and they are there to enable those who lost their loved ones to remember them in the present.

Place-making

The aforementioned place-making refers to the practice of physically locating social relations and social practice in a material place. Places express a sense of belonging for those appropriating them. As we shall illustrate below, 'being in place' involves a range of cognitive (mental) and physical (corporeal) performances that are constantly evolving as people encounter place. Our fieldwork in Mostar assists us in capturing local voices and agencies that enable us to portray the divided city and transformations of places to counter the material and immaterial division in the city. It shows us how a divided city can develop shared places through the materialisation of ideas of togetherness and resistance to an ethnic gaze on the urban space.

Mostar and the divided peace

Mostar has been one of the places where the imprints of war have turned into deep scars on the social landscape of a once multi-ethnic city. It became the site of some of the most serious violence and destruction in the region, to the extent that the devastation of Mostar has been characterised as an urbicide (Kresimir cited in Yarwood, 1999). Historic monuments, cultural property and religious buildings were deliberately targeted during the war to destroy the memory of the city.

Before the war, Mostar was characterised by mixed residential areas, apart from the Old Town Mostar where mainly Bosniaks resided, and about one-third of marriages were ethnically mixed (Bollens, 2007: 186). During the 1992–1995 war Mostar was the site of a three-way war, initially between Bosnian Serb militias supported by the Yugoslav National Army (JNA) on the one hand, and Bosniak and Bosnian Croat defenders on the other. In the late 1992, once the frontlines with the Bosnian Serbs and the JNA were established outside the city of Mostar, the war entered a second phase during which the Bosniak and Bosnian Croat allies became enemies (Yarwood, 1999; Halilović, 2013). Like most of the region of Herzegovina, Mostar was ethnically cleansed of the 'other' resulting in massive movements of people; displacement within and from the city combined with a huge influx of refugees from the surrounding villages. The demographic balance of Mostar shifted drastically during the course of the war. The total city population dropped sharply despite a large influx of displaced persons from surrounding areas into both sides of the city, altering the composition of the city's population. In the direct aftermath of the war, the communal division was strict and few dared to cross the border which ran throughout the city. However, the end of the war did not mean an end to the ethnic cleansing, which continued in a quieter version for years after the DPA had brought (at least formal) peace to BiH and members of other ethnic groups either left voluntarily or were forcibly expelled. Resettling refugees and internally displaced persons as frontier populations was another strategy in using urban space to foster confrontation (Björkdahl, 2012). The territorial division of the city continued and was cemented in the post-war era. The public, collective sphere that had existed prior to the war became fragmented, subordinated and manipulated, and the collective interests of the city collapsed and dissolved. The divide in the city was the result of a politics of confrontation and negotiation in the war and the post-war period. This 'ethnisation' of urban space production resulted in an ethno-nationally fractured cityspace. In this context, the Youth Cultural Centre Abrašević, which builds on a long tradition of Yugoslavianism, challenges the ethnic divides in the city. The Youth Cultural Centre Abrašević attempts to emplace a non-ethnic peace based on pan-Yugoslav nostalgia by creating a place where youth from different communities can meet and feel at ease, thus challenging the obvious dividing line(s) of Mostar.

The Youth Cultural Centre Abrašević

Youth centres in BiH can be found in many different towns across the country and have a long history, and many of them go back to the socialist era. Despite the diversity of centres, many of them have acted as microcosms of an almost pan-Yugoslav nostalgia (Katie Hampton, authors' interview, Mostar, 2010). In the case of the quite well-known Youth Cultural Centre Abrašević in Mostar, this includes an engagement with older generations of the town as well as celebrations of pan-Yugoslav holidays. Interestingly, the centres we have visited in Sarajevo, Srebrenica, Travnik and Mostar refrain from the ethnic language prevalent in the political sphere and instead celebrate diversity and creativity. They can be said to be the material presence of the idea of young people living together irrespective of their ethnic identities. That means that, very often, the centres take as their point of departure neither the peace nor reconciliation agenda, but instead an ambition to respond to the needs of young people in the respective town or city, and to offer them a space in which they feel at ease.

The Youth Cultural Centre Abrašević in Mostar is an example which fulfils an important function in the divided city in its ability to represent a space for those at the cross-roads of identity formation. It is located at the former front line of the fighting, which is a place that is not linked to either of the two sides of the city. This is rather important in a city which is shaped by its geographical division based on ethnic belonging and in which there are hardly any spaces that would be equally accessible to both sides of the community. The street in which the youth centre is located has two names, accounting for both sides to the conflict. The decision to keep the centre, which dates back to long before the war in the 1990s, on the front line can therefore be read as a clear spatial statement of resistance against the ethnic division of the city. Actively challenging the ethnification of space, the Youth Cultural Centre Abrašević has transformed a part of the former battle frontline on the Austro-Hungarian Boulevard into an alternative place (Björkdahl & Gusic, 2013). The organisers, many of whom work on a voluntary basis, contribute to the success of the centre, which, in the absence of sufficient public funding, would otherwise be unable to function.

Yet the goal of the Youth Cultural Centre Abrašević is not necessarily to represent or reach out into society as a whole, given the risk of reproducing social divisions, but, according to one of the centre coordinators, 'to create a micro-society' (Youth Cultural Centre Abrašević, authors' interview, 2013), that is, a space in which social divisions can be challenged. In that respect, this is not an attempt to follow the internationally-led and mainstreamed approach to fuse narratives of the different ethnic communities, but a more pragmatic approach during the course of which those young people who feel comfortable interacting with people of the other ethnicity use a joint location, which can serve as a cinema, a theatre, a place to spend time or as a sports venue. The centre can therefore be considered a materialisation of the idea of multi-culturalism and the physical reproduction of this idea, yet without falling into the trap of reproducing the heavily ethnicised discourse that local politicians and international peacebuilders have long tended to pursue. This also means that the way in which the youth centre brings about change and transformation in Mostar does not rely on the same inter-ethnic logic that at times international peacebuilders or local politicians pursue, but instead on the side effects of bringing together young people independent of their ethnic or religious belonging.

Youth centres across the country

This approach is somewhat similar to the work of other youth centres in the country. Rather than acting as a political venue, the president of the youth council in Srebrenica has emphasised that, while she would not want to be a politician, the youth centre has given her a different way of bringing about change (Milena Nikolić, authors' interview, Srebrenica, 2010). Their work involves activities such as music rehearsals, concerts, artwork or similar projects, just like what the centre Alter Art in Travnik, for instance, promotes. 'Alter Art' has brought young people together since 1995, as musicians in the first place. And although the centre does not necessarily see itself as a space of resistance, it nevertheless serves as a creative place for young people in which 'expression without restrictions' is possible (Darkco Saračević, authors' interview, Travnik, 2011). It can be said that these centres serve as 'alternative' venues, praised by some for their non-conventional approaches for peace, and criticised by others for attracting mainly a particular kind of people, that is, those who are already open to non-ethnicised languages. At the same time, this allows them to give material presence to their alternative approach and, instead of getting bogged down by quotaled ethnic representation, they can make use of their spaces to respond to the needs of youth independent of the often ethnicised peacebuilding logic. This also means that funding is scarce for the centres which therefore retain a certain degree of independence from international and national political actors.

The youth centre examples illustrate the extent to which certain places (that is, places of former conflict such as the front line in Mostar where the local youth centre is located, or the centre in Srebrenica which is accessible to both sides) have been used by local activists to materialise their idea of potential cross-ethnic cooperation. Their agency lies in their effort to transform the idea of a 'common space' into material presence, even in most adverse circumstances and resisting the fact that they are often referred to as 'alternative' by their host societies. It is the agency of the organisers to create a place in which the dynamics of otherwise ethnically homogenised spaces are reversed. Indeed, the youth centres are often seen as spaces of 'a few alternative people' and are thus often viewed critically in the surrounding communities. What they reflect, however, is the extent to which persistent activism, as seen on the part of the organisers of the centres, can lead to a material presence of a shared place in a city, where interethnic cooperation is otherwise believed to be impossible. At the same time, those people visiting the centres, helping with their construction and engaging with them in regular terms make these spaces 'lived spaces' (cf. Lefebvre, 1991: 396). In that sense, the agency of the youth centres can be seen as located with the organisers on the one hand. They have the courage to overcome social divisions as present in their surroundings and often work in a heavily constrained and under-funded environment. In fact, many of the centres are run by volunteers who flexibly take over any job that may be required of them. On the other hand, the young people using and attending the centres also have to be considered as bearers of agency. In a context in which identity is defined by one's ethnicity it is often hard visibly to resist this framing and instead to attend a youth centre. The fact that the use of the physical place always means a certain degree of visibility, also means that every user's positionality in society is affected by this. The agency to create an alternative place for young people is therefore the materialisation of the desire to avoid the ethnic logic of both conflict and the peacebuilding process and has had a lasting effect on places such as Mostar.

Figure 4.2 Youth Cultural Centre Abrašević, Mostar, photograph taken by authors, 2011.

Conclusion

In BiH, war is now an event of the past, but its scars, visions and legacies remain. BiH exists in the long shadow of war. As demonstrated in this chapter, identity-based wars secure and engrain ethnicity and ethnic identities by inscribing them into the landscape and cityscape, and when identities become merged with territory, spaces and places become ethnicised. We also show that post-conflict memory landscapes embed and convey meaning, and are thus indissolubly linked to the legacy of the conflict, to struggles over interpretations about the violent past and to the sites where remembering takes place. In such a context it becomes urgent to explore where peace comes about, that is, where the overpowering logic of ethnic segregation is overcome or challenged by a variety of actors. To do so, we have explored emplaced agency, transitions from war to peace, expressions of transformative power as well as space-making and place-making by investigating the contestations surrounding minority returns, youth community's place-making efforts, and space-making processes, all of which contribute to our understanding of the dynamics of constructing a sustainable and grounded peace. We have pointed to the mutual constitution of social and material spaces of peace. By situating agency, we are able to demonstrate that people make places by investing them with meaning. In the precarious post-conflict everyday, these meanings are often deeply contested.

The narratives of minority return, the fragmented memoryscape of Sarajevo and a youth centre challenging the materialisation of ethnic cleavages in a divided city come together to reveal the relationship between agency, space and place and expose how power relations play out in certain places and spaces. Agentive subjects and efforts at space-making and place-making are constrained by powerful spatial practices, contestation and consolidated claims to space as different ethnoscapes have been produced through the war and the peace in the war-torn territory of BiH. Nonetheless, the youth centre in Mostar, like other youth centres, produces a non-conventional place for peace to avoid the overwhelming presence of ethnicity in the city and all over post-war BiH. In doing so, youth has been able to establish its version of cross-ethnic cooperation. Sarajevo is a spatial compendium of multiple narratives that coexist as different people, through their place-making and space-making practice, come to perceive and inhabit the city of Sarajevo differently while trying to nourish the spirit of Sarajevo. Yet, the meanings of the Sarajevo Roses are diverse, with some passers-by ignoring them and other people stopping to contemplate and reflect on them. The political contestations around whether the Roses should be left to decay, to allow for the siege and killings to be forgotten, are thus challenged by a need to keep the memory of the past alive, and even as a warning against any potential future violent attacks. We therefore argue that the nature and quality of peace can be seen as spatially contested in the practices of giving competing meanings to places in processes of space-making. The Roses keep being alternately activated and silenced by a variety of agents in this context, ranging from non-governmental organisations to universities, all equipping them with a particular narrative and meaning. As researchers, walking the streets of Sarajevo, conducting interviews and collecting narratives, we are conscious of the fact that many discourses may be invisible to us, other discourses may be emphasised in particular by certain agents, while other narratives may be disguised to us as outside researchers.

Yet the examples that we find in the post-conflict landscape of BiH reflect how highly-controlled spaces intervene in peoples' daily lives and prevent societies from healing their social and material wounds. It also demonstrates the agentic force of the ethnoscape and how it shapes agency that supports, constructs, reacts, resists or challenges ethnicised spaces and places, whilst competing forms of agency constantly challenge this strong spatial logic at play.

Notes

1 On April 16, 1993 the UN acting under Chapter VII, passed UNSCR 819 setting up a safe area in Srebrenica. UNSCR 824 extended the concept to the towns of Žepa, Tuzla, Sarajevo, Goražde, and Bihać.

2 Together with a large number of international organisations present in BiH – including OSCE, the ICTY, UNHCR, the UNDP, the European Convention on Human Rights (ECHR) and others, the OHR steers and guides the post-conflict peace process. The latter has recently been primarily guided by the EU in the context of its enlargement process.

3 In 2006, the Sejdić-Finci case took the Bosnian state to the European Court of Human Rights, for its failure to allow those who are not part of the three major ethnic groups to stand for election for the presidency and parliament (cf. Claridge, not dated). Although Sejdić and Finci, a Bosnian Jew and Roma, won, changes to the constitution have not been implemented, and people who do not declare themselves as part of the 'constituent peoples' of Bosnia-Herzegovina are denied public representation in those institutions.

4 Over half of Bosnia-Herzegovina's population of 4.4 million people were driven from their homes during the war. More than three-quarters of Bosnia's housing stock was damaged or destroyed by war, often as a deliberate tactic of ethnic cleansing. Approximately 250,000 were dead, over a million had fled the country as refugees and about a million were internally displaced.

5 Over one million returns, of which 467,297 are minority returns, and a PLIP implementation rate of 93.3 percent. However, in some cases, high restitution rates correspond with high rates of sale or exchange, instead of return. The Housing Verification and Monitoring Unit of OHR's Reconstruction and Return Task Force found that while about three-quarters of pre-war occupants return to their reconstructed houses, only a part of the family actually returns in a third of those cases (Haider, 2010).

6 Many thanks to Lejla Sumon-Krupalija for pointing this out.

7 Some would trace the origins of the Sarajevo Roses to Neza Kurto, a Professor of Architecture at the University of Sarajevo, who conceived of the memorials following the Markale Massacre.

Bibliography

Belloni, R., 2005. Peacebuilding at the Local Level: Refugee Return to Prijedor. *International Peacekeeping*, 12(3), pp. 434–447.

Belloni, R., 2007. *State Building and International Intervetion in Bosnia*. London, New York: Routledge.

Belloni, R., 2009. Bosnia: Dayton is Dead! Long Live Dayton. *Nationalism and Ethnic Politics* 15(3–4), pp. 355–375.

Bevan, R., 2006. *The Destruction of Memory: Architecture at War*. London: Reaktion Books.

Bieber, F., 2005. Local Institutional Engineering: A Tale of Two Cities Mostar and Brčko. *International Peacekeeping* 12(3), pp. 420–433.

Björkdahl, A., 2012. The EU Administration of the Divided Bosnian city of Mostar: Implications for EUs Evolving Peacebuilding Approach. *Australian-New Zealand Journal of European Studies* 4(1), pp. 2–17.

Björkdahl, A. & Gusic, I., 2013. The Divided City – A Space for Frictional Peacebuilding. *Peacebuilding* 1(3), pp. 317–333.

Björkdahl, A. & Mannergren Selimovic, J., 2015. Gendered Agency in Transitional Justice. *Security Dialogue* 46(2), pp. 165–182.

Bollens, S. A., 2007. *Cities, Nationalism, and Democratization*. Abingdon, New York: Routledge.

Caplan, R., 2004. International Authority and State Building: The Case of Bosnia and Herzegovina. *Global Governance* 10(1), pp. 53–65.

Claridge, L., not dated. *Discrimination and Political Participation in Bosnia and Herzegovina: Sejdic and Finci v. Bosnia and Herzegovina.* [Online] Available at: http://m inorityrights.org/wp-content/uploads/old-site-downloads/download-787-Briefing-Pap er-Discrimination-and-political-participation-in-Bosnia-and-Herzegovina.pdf [Accessed 11 July 2016].

Coles, K., 2007. Ambivalent Builders: Europeanization, the Production of Difference, and Internationals in Bosnia-Herzegovina. In: X. Bougarel, E. Helms & G. Duijzings, eds. *The New Bosnian Mosaic: Identities, Memories and Moral Claims.* Burlington: Ashgate, pp. 255–272.

Dahlman, C. & Ó Tuathail, G., 2005. Broken Bosnia: The Localized Geopolitics of Displacement and Return in Two Bosnian Places. *Annals of the Association of American Geographers* 95(3), pp. 644–662.

Donia, R. J., 2006. *Sarajevo: A Biography.* Ann Arbor: University of Michigan Press.

Duinzings, G., 2007. Commemorating Srebrenica: Histories of Violence and the Politics of Memory in Eastern Bosnia. In: X. Bougarel, E. Helms & G. Duijzings, eds. *The New Bosnian Mosaic: Identities, Memories and Moral Claims.* Aldershot, Burlington: Ashgate, pp. 141–166.

Finlay, A., 2011. *Governing Ethnic Conflict: Consociation, Identity and the Price of Peace.* New York: Routledge.

Fischel de Andrade, J. H. & Delaney, N. B., 2001. Minority Return to South-eastern Bosnia and Herzegovina: A Review of the 2000 Return Season. *Journal of Refugee Studies* 14(3), pp. 315–330.

Glenny, M., 1996. *The Fall of Yugoslavia: The Third Balkan War.* Harmondsworth: Penguin.

Gow, J., 1997. *Triumph of the Lack of Will.* New York: Colombia University Press.

Haider, H., 2010. The Politicisation of Humanitarian Assistance: Refugee and IDP Policy in Bosnia and Herzegovina. [Online] Available at: https://sites.tufts.edu/jha/a rchives/700. [Accessed 29 September 2016].

Halilović, H., 2013. *Places of Pain: Forced Displacement, Popular Memory and Trans-Local Identities in Bosnian War-Torn Communities.* New York, Oxford: Berghahn Books.

Halilović, J., 2011. *Nestaju Sarajevske ruže.* [Online] Available at: http://zrnomudrosti. blogspot.co.uk/2011/11/nestaju-sarajevske-ruze-imaju-li-graani.html [Accessed 11 November 2013].

Halilović, J., not dated. *Sarajevo Roses.* [Online] Available at: http://udruzenjeurban. ba/english/sarajevo-roses/ [Accessed 5 September 2016].

Higate, P. & Henry, M., 2010. Space, Performance and Everyday Security in the Peacekeeping Context. *International Peacekeeping* 17(1), pp. 32–48.

Hubbarb, P., Kitchin, R., & Valentine, G. eds, 2004. *Key Thinkers on Space and Place.* London: SAGE.

Jansen, S., 2013. People and Things in the Ethnography of Borders: Materializing the Division of Sarajevo. *Social Anthropology/Anthropologie Sociale* 21(1), pp. 23–37.

Jeffrey, A., 2006. Building State Capacity in Post-conflict Bosnia and Herzegovina: The Case of Brčko District. *Political Geography* 25(2), pp. 203–227.

Jukić, E., 2012. Reconstruction of 'Sarajevo Roses' Started. [Online] Available at: http:// www.balkaninsight.com/en/article/reconstruction-of-wartime-shelling-street-scars-sta rted [Accessed 15 August 2016].

Kappler, S., 2016. Sarajevo's Ambivalent Memoryscape: Spatial Stories of Peace and Conflict. *Memory Studies*, Volume (online first) DOI: 10.1177/1750698016650484, pp. 1–14.

Kolind, T., 2007. In Search of Decent People: Resistance to the Ethnicization of Everyday Life among the Muslims of Stolac. In: X. Bougarel, E. Helms & G. Duijzings, eds. *The New Bosnian Mosaic: Identities, Memories and Moral Claims.* Aldershot, Burlington: Ashgate, pp. 123–140.

Korchnak, P., 2014. *Roses of Sarajevo: Wounds of Remembrance in the Streets of Bosnia.* Compass Cultura.

Lefebvre, H., 1991. *The Production of Space.* Oxford: Blackwell.

Maček, I., 2009. *Sarajevo Under Siege: Anthropology in Wartime.* Philadelphia: University of Pennsylvania Press.

Malcolm, N., 2002. *Bosnia: A Short History.* London: Pan Books.

Markowitz, F., 2010. *Sarajevo: The Bosnian Kaleidoscope.* Urbana, Chicago, and Springfield: University of Illinois Press.

Massey, D., 2005. *For Space.* London: SAGE.

Moll, N., 2013. Fragmented Memories in a Fragmented Country: Memory Competition and Political Identity-building in Today's Bosnia and Herzegovina. *Nationalities Papers* 41(6), pp. 910–935.

Mouffe, C., 2005. *On the Political.* New York: Routledge.

Mujkić, A., 2015. In Search of a Democratic Counter-power in Bosnia-Herzegovina. *Southeast European and Black Sea Studies* 15(4), pp. 623–638.

Murtagh, C., 2016. Civil Mobilization in Divided Societies and the Perils of Political Engagement: Bosnia and Herzegovina's Protest and Plenum Movement. *Nationalism and Ethnic Politics* 22(2), pp. 149–171.

Richmond, O. P. & Franks, J., 2009. Between Partition and Pluralism: The Bosnian Jigsaw and an 'Ambivalent Peace'. *Southeast European and Black Sea Studies* 9(1), pp. 17–38.

Sarajevo Roses – A Cinematic Essay, 2016. *Sarajevo Roses – A Cinematic Essay.* [Online] Available at: https://fromtheheartproductions.networkforgood.com/projects/11872-documentaries-sarajevo-roses-a-cinematic-essay?entity_id=fromtheheartproductions [Accessed 27 September 2016].

Tuan, Y.-F., 1974. *Topophilia: A Study of Environmental Perception, Attitudes, and Values.* Englewood Cliffs, N.J.: Prentice-Hall.

Wise, N. A., 2011. Post-war Tourism and the Imaginative Geographies of Bosnia and Herzegovina and Croatia. *European Journal of Tourism Research* 4(1), pp. 5–24.

Woodward, S., 1995. *Balkan Tragedy: Chaos and Dissolution After the Cold War.* Washington D.C.: The Brookings Institute.

Yarwood, J., 1999. *Rebuilding Mostar: Reconstruction in a War Zone.* Liverpool: Liverpool University Press.

Yuval-Davis, N., 2006. Belonging and the Politics of Belonging. *Patterns of Prejudice* 40(3), pp. 197–214.

Zaum, D., 2010. Post-conflict Statebuilding and Forced Migration. In: A. Betts & G. Loescher, eds. *Refugees in International Relations.* Oxford: Oxford University Press, pp. 285–304.

Zupan, N., 2006. Facing the Past and Transitional Justice in Countries of Former Yugoslavia. In: M. Fischer, ed. *Peacebuilding and Civil Society in Bosnia-Herzegovina: Ten Years After Dayton.* Munster: Lit Verlag, pp. 327–342.

Interviews

Women's organization Most, authors' interview, Višegard, 23 September 2014.
Katie Hampton, Youth Cultural Centre Abrašević, authors' interview, Mostar, 18 March 2010.
Milena Nikolić, authors' interview, Srebrenica, 2 April 2010.
Darko Saračević, authors' interview, Travnik, 2 March 2011.
Jasmin Halilović, authors' interview, Sarajevo, 3 September 2013.
Youth Cultural Centre Abrašević, authors' interview, Mostar, 5 September 2013.
Confidential source, authors' interview, Srebrenica, 2 July 2014.
Confidential source, authors' interview, Sarajevo, 3 September 2013.

5   Northern Ireland: The 'Maze of Peace'

Introduction

As peace and war are spatial phenomena they are embedded in space and place. Our investigation into the maze of peace in Northern Ireland explores how peacebuilding agency can be expressed in the transformation of spaces and places that are associated with the legacy of the conflict. Both the conflict, colloquially known in Northern Ireland as the 'Troubles', and the peace, reached through the Good Friday Agreement[1] (GFA) in 1998, demonstrate that peace and war are emplaced. This chapter analyses how the Troubles, as well as the GFA, have left material marks on the spatial topography of Belfast. As a place characterised by profoundly emplaced patterns of sectarian separation, operating on multiple scales, Northern Ireland's capacity to embrace peacebuilding is contradicted by the spatial narratives and spatial segregation of the Loyalist and Republican communities.[2]

The divides between Republicans who historically have favoured unification with the Irish Republic and Loyalists who assert that Northern Ireland should remain a part of the United Kingdom are persistent. The divisions are evident through different understandings of the conflict and its causes, but also of where and for whom the peace dividend has materialised.

In Belfast the first peace wall was constructed in 1969 during the darkest days of Northern Ireland's thirty-year conflict as a military response to sectarian violence and disorder. The peace walls separating the two dominant communities remain today despite the GFA that was expected to make such spatial arrangements unnecessary. In the post-peace accord era the communal separation is engineered partly by the idea that 'good fences make good neighbours', partly by lack of practices that transgress conceptions of segregated space (Byrne, 2011; Shirlow & Murtagh, 2004). The heritage development has been controversial in the post-Trouble era. The Maze/Long Kesh (MLK)[3] prison is part of the material legacy of the Troubles and occupies a prominent place in the history of the Troubles as it was often seen as a microcosm of the conflict. The peace accord provided for an early release programme for prisoners connected to the Troubles and the MLK prison was closed in 2000 (Graham & McDowell, 2007; Flynn, 2011; Michael *et al.*, 2016). The future of the prison is contested and it remains in limbo. Below, this chapter explores efforts made to transform the peace walls and the prison as part of the peace process in Northern Ireland.

By following the spatial turn in Peace and Conflict Studies it is possible to rethink the relationship between war and peace on the one hand, and place and space on the other. In adopting such an approach to peacebuilding that connects with space and place, we are able to read agency in the post-conflict landscape. This chapter situates space-making and place-making in the transition of the Northern Ireland conflict, reflecting on peacebuilding agency as a means to understand how the conflict and the peace have been spatialised. It reads the landscapes of power and politics in Belfast and Northern Ireland through a spatial lens revealing the persistence of material and immaterial divisions in the cityscape (cf. Gaffikin & Morrissey, 2011; Brand, 2011; Brand & Fregonese, 2013).

Our approach of 'being in place' allows us to examine closely the presence of the peace walls in the cityscape and critically listen to the voices in the MLK debate. By being in place we read the everyday as a practice in which the two communities in Belfast meet and negotiate the ways in which places and spaces are narrated, used and transformed. This enables us to conduct an in-depth analysis, which demonstrates the spatial politics of the interfaces and reveals how these dividing structures of the peace walls are constituted by and constitutive of divisive practices perpetuated in the everyday. Furthermore, we also find that a broad register of agents spur processes of space-making to transform these divisive places into shared spaces, while at the same time being constrained by these material and immaterial urban structures linked to the peace walls. Through a close reading of the debate about the MLK and listening to various voices, we are able to trace the place-making process and to emplace the abstract notion of peace at the MLK prison. Furthermore, the reading of the peace walls and the MLK as sites in transformation assists us in mapping peacebuilding agency as well as identifying the fluidity of agency and spatial practices.

Segregating the peace

The history of the conflict in Northern Ireland, as in most conflict-affected societies, is complex and dates back centuries. Northern Ireland has been embroiled in conflict and division since its inception in 1921. The island was divided as a response to the 'Irish problem' and the resentment towards the partition was manifested in waves of violence, peaking in the 1960s when the Troubles started. Often viewed as a conflict centring on religion, the conflict is multifaceted and includes competing political, colonialist, religious and national ideologies spatialised in the city of Belfast, in Northern Ireland, between the United Kingdom and the Republic of Ireland, and between Loyalists and Republicans (Nagle, 2009; Goldie & Ruddy, 2010; McDowell &

Shirlow, 2011). During the Troubles, it is estimated that approximately 3,600 people were killed, and a further 30,000 plus injured (Dixon, 2008; Finlay, 2011). Much of the violence took place in Belfast (Nagle, 2009; Gaffikin & Morrissey, 2011).

In 1994 a ceasefire was reached and in 1998 the GFA was signed. Following the signing, a referendum on the agreement was held in Northern Ireland and it was ratified in the Republic of Ireland, meaning that the peace agreement had the necessary 'buy-in' from the population. It was a political alignment of polar opposites that would have been unimaginable in the darkest days of the Troubles (Belloni & Deane, 2005). The peace process attempted to address a series of sensitive and contentious issues relating to the legacy of the conflict, such as prisoner release, decommissioning, power-sharing and the peace walls (Finlay, 2011; Byrne, 2011; Shirlow, 2006; McGarry & O'Leary, 2006; Mac Ginty, 1999).

Disagreements over contentious issues like the annual Loyalist Orange Order marches, policing and the decommissioning of paramilitary weapons have occurred on a regular basis. Furthermore, dissident groups opposing the peace accord have attempted to derail the peace process. Dissident paramilitaries reverted to violence and the bomb attack by the Real Irish Republican Army in 1998, which killed 29 people in Omagh was one of the deadliest (Horgan & Morrison, 2011). However, instead of derailing the peace process, the attacks spurred demands for peace and the efforts to implement the GFA intensified (McEvoy, 2009; Belloni & Deane, 2005). Yet, the peace in Northern Ireland is still precarious and continues to be challenged by protest marches, debates around which flag should be placed on Belfast City Hall (and how long) and controversies about the future of the peace walls continue (Confidential source, authors' interview, Stormont, 2014). And what is more, with the 2016 referendum through which a majority of the United Kingdom's population (as opposed to the majority in Northern Ireland) expressed their wish to leave the EU, the situation has not become any easier, given the GFA was not least based on an EU framework (Meager, 2016).

The example of Northern Ireland shows that transitions towards peace in divided societies are notoriously difficult to grasp. In this chapter we provide one understanding of transitional processes in post-conflict societies through a spatial reading of the active use and transformation of space and place. Northern Ireland reveals the continuities between periods of conflict and times of peace, as the conflict spills over in times of peace through persistent claims to space and control of territory.

Spatial politics – the peace walls in Belfast

Spatial politics reveal the contestation surrounding space and place in the city of Belfast where both communities live closely together yet divided by the physical infrastructure of the peace walls that cut across the urban landscape.

Erecting peace walls

The first temporary barrier at Cupar Way was installed by the British Army after large-scale rioting between Loyalists and Republicans in August 1969, which led to the burning of homes on Bombay Street and in several other Republican areas in West Belfast (Hocking, 2015). As sectarian violence persisted, more barriers were constructed to separate the two communities.

Most of the security barriers and forms of defensive architecture have been erected at interfaces. An interface is sometimes a visible site in the urban settings of Belfast. They are often associated with parades-related disputes, rituals and locality-specific violence and as such they are often seen as contested spaces (Nolan, 2014; Belfast Interface Project, 2011). Most days mundane activities take place along the peace walls, including people dog-walking, jogging, biking or just passing by on their way somewhere else. Some days low-intensity stone-throwing, so called 'recreational rioting', disturbs the precarious peace (Hocking, 2015). Though many walls now have gates that are open for part of the day, many local residents still avoid passing through the area of the other community (John O'Donnel, authors' interview, Belfast, 2013).

Violence and spatial competition continue to be concentrated on various interface areas such as the Shankill and the Falls neighbourhoods. Thus, the largest peace wall in Belfast runs along Cupar Way where the two neighbourhoods border each other (see Fig. 5.1 below). These Loyalist and Republican working class areas continue to suffer from the conflict in terms of continued presence and activities of paramilitaries and from the consequences of the conflict in terms of multiple deprivations such as high unemployment rates, poor health indicators and low educational qualifications (Komorova & O'Dowd, 2016). Each of the neighbourhoods is visibly marked with sectarian symbols such as murals, flags and colour-coded pavements, which reflect the alignment between territory and identity. Here identity is spatialised as a means of 'placing' the community in territory (Campbell, 1998). This creates 'man-made landscapes of a symbolically charged character' (Kostovicova, 2004: 270). Thus, the material residue of the Troubles is still part of people's everyday life and the turbulent past disturbs the efforts to emplace peace in a post-conflict landscape littered with the fabric of the conflict (Brand, 2011; Graham & McDowell, 2007; Murtagh, 2002).

The peace walls are very much part of the material and visual cityscape of Belfast. Sometimes decorated with political art the peace walls are part of the muralscape, which has come to reflect the Troubles as well as efforts to emplace peace in the post-conflict landscape.[4] The mural painting is tied to the sectarian politics of Northern Ireland and most of these murals reflect community identity or commemorate historic events such as the Battle of Boyne hailed by the Loyalists. Within Loyalism, murals are traditionally aggressive in their nature such as the Ulster Volunteer Force (UVF) mural on Sandy

Row portraying Loyalist paramilitaries. Other murals celebrate Republican martyrs like Bobby Sands, who died in a hunger strike at the MLK (Hill & White, 2012).

Almost twenty years after the GFA Belfast is still weighed down by the various forms of defensive structures often referred to as peace walls. According to recent assessments, almost 100 walls, fences and gates divide communities across the city, and approximately one third was constructed after the signing of the GFA. Byrne (2011: 15) concludes that 'these barriers have institutionalised the separation between the two communities, reinforced different cultural identities and continue to illustrate the deep enduring antagonisms that exist between communities'. The peace walls can be read as a product of fear, threat and actual use of physical forms of violence (Jarman, 2005). They are constitutive of and constituted by segregated communities. As such, they foster inner community cohesion, solidarity and socio-cultural obligations towards local community institutions, which in turn consolidate and maintain local systems of authority (Abdelmonem & McWhinney, 2015).

Despite their physical presence within the city, there is an ambiguity about the peace walls. Already in 1971 in the secret Stormont report by the Northern Irish government the construction of walls, gates and fences to separate the two communities was criticised. The 'peace lines', the report stated, were creating an 'atmosphere of abnormality' in the city. Yet, the report did 'not expect any insurmountable difficulty' in bringing down the barricades once the violence had subsumed (Byrne, 2011). Still today, there is no coherent government policy, strategy or framework in place to address the walls, as this has been a policy area largely absent from the politics of the peace processes (John O'Donnel, authors' interview, Belfast, 2013). So far, the defensive architecture has proved far easier to erect than to tear down (Byrne, 2011).

Dismantling peace walls

Dismantling the peace walls is not an uncontested endeavour and the residents living in the area of interfaces are reluctant to see them brought down (Nolan, 2014; John O'Donnel, authors' interview, Belfast, 2013). This reveals how complicated the issue of the peace walls has become and how the walls both constitute and are constituted by the practices of the residents of the interface areas. A vast majority (86 per cent) of the inhabitants from the two main communities in Belfast would not enter an area dominated by the other group or travel through such an area at night even by car (79 per cent) (Byrne *et al.*, 2012). This signals a firm spatial order of segregation and that the peace walls – a key pillar in such a spatial order – are difficult to dismantle. A survey undertaken in 2012 showed that 69 per cent of respondents who lived closest to the peace walls felt the walls were still necessary because of the threat of violence and 76 per cent indicated their belief that the walls made people feel safer (Byrne *et al.*, 2012). According to the survey, 58 per cent of respondents who lived closest to the walls were very/fairly worried about the

Figure 5.1 Cupar Way Peace Wall, Photo by authors 2014

police's ability to preserve peace and maintain order if the peace walls were ever removed. When asked about the future, 58 per cent of respondents said that they *would like to see* the peace walls come down now or sometime in the future. However, only 38 per cent could actually envisage a time when no peace walls would be visible in Northern Ireland, indicating that the public may be unable either to visualise what a city without walls might actually look like or to have faith in a process that could facilitate such a change. According to an updated survey in 2015, opinion had changed so that in 2015 only 35 per cent would like to see the walls come down in the future (Byrne *et al.*, 2015). Ironically, this comes at a time when the Northern Ireland Executive has published the 2023 target date for the removal of all the peace walls (Housing Executive, authors' interview, Belfast, 2014). This suggests that the political circumstances surrounding the peace walls, notably the climate of intercommunity relations and sense of safety, has deteriorated over the last three years and that the peace process in relation to interfaces has, in part, gone into reverse.

Attempts at both a political and a community level to try to address issues of community identity, integration and sectarianism have recently taken on increased importance. The peace walls became the policy responsibility of local politicians in Northern Ireland first in 2010 under the devolution of Policing and Justice Powers to the Northern Ireland Assembly (Housing

Executive, authors' interview, Belfast, 2014). In 2013, the Northern Ireland Executive published *Together: Building a United Community – A Policy Strategy,* which set out the power-sharing government's approach to building a shared society in Northern Ireland. In it, the government made a commitment to reduce and remove all peace walls by 2023 (The Executive Office 2013). As a consequence, a number of government strategies and funding schemes support the goals of expanding shared space and improved relations between previously conflicted communities, in the hope of removing the peace walls.

The opening of the Alexandra Park and the demolishing of the Crumlin Road peace wall are illustrative cases of how the dismantling of peace walls may play out. Throughout the Troubles, the park was a flashpoint for sectarian conflict, a fiercely contested space where clashes between Loyalists and Republicans regularly broke out. Despite this legacy, a peace gate was officially opened in September 2015 (Young & Bell, 2013). Attended by politicians, residents and children from one Protestant and one Catholic school, the ceremony was loaded with symbolism. In 2016, the Crumlin Road peace wall, an eight-foot brick structure situated at what is considered one of the most contentious interfaces was demolished to make way for railings and decorative panels. A community-led decision which came about after years of relationship-building and talks within and between communities in north Belfast paved the way for the removal of the interface barrier (*Belfast Telegraph*, 2016). The demolition of the Crumlin Road peace wall is linked to the peacebuilding effort lower down on Flax Street, part of the Crumlin Road peace wall. The dismantling of peace walls and the new murals depicting the peace process, shared future, re-imagined communities can be read as 'the first evidence of the area's renewal and regeneration' and contribute to transform the post-conflict landscape (McCromick & Jarman, 2005: 64).

A number of constraints exist that prevent the dismantling of the remaining peace walls. As pointed out in a comprehensive study (Goldie & Ruddy, 2013), the greatest impediment to the transformation of the interface area is the 'chill factor' that comes from fear, distrust and reluctance to use space that is identified as 'belonging to the other side'. Youth-led thrill-seeking behaviour, low-intensity violence, stone-throwing and parades-related disputes reinforce segregation, as do the symbolism of marking territory, hostile sectarian displays of graffiti, flags and emblems as well as sectarian practices. The potential of losing territory, which is to say relinquishing territory originally inhabited exclusively by a particular community also works to constrain efforts to dismantle the peace walls (Murtagh, 2002; Murtagh & Keaveney, 2006).

In a very different way the highly developed Troubles heritage tourist industry works to maintain the peace walls as the industry capitalises on the presence of the walls, casting the walls as key attractions in a landscape 'where memory of the recent conflict is never far away' (Belfast City Council and Northern Ireland Tourist Board, 2011: 13, cited in Hocking, 2012). Wiedenhoft Murphy's research (2010: 543–544, 555) reveals that 'the [peace] lines have become one of the "sites" that local and citywide tour guides include in their itineraries to visibly express that the peace process is still being negotiated'. Part of the tourists' attraction to post-conflict societies is the adventure in consuming conflict (Wiedenhoft Murphy, 2010). Monuments and other forms of commemoration 'function as landmarks, alerting visitors to an important event that has occurred there, thus enabling them to experience the spirit of the place' (Marshall, 2004: 102, cited in Wiedenhoft Murphy, 2010: 539). To satisfy the tourist search for authenticity and 'otherness' 'local communities may be in danger of being marginalised or mere objects of the voyeuristic tourist gaze if they are not empowered to tell their own version of the past' (Wiedenhoft Murphy, 2010: 539). The tourist audience is a key component in shaping the meaning of many public spaces in Belfast, and their presence does not necessarily build peace, but may reproduce processes of the past conflict, particularly territoriality and as such tourism has wider social and political implications. The tourists are not just passively taking in the narratives of the Troubles presented to them. They can also be important political subjects with an ability to move across borders, access localities that are outside the historical narratives and disrupt official as well as unofficial narratives of the Troubles and, in that capacity, express a type of peacebuilding agency.

Business people and entrepreneurs in tourism argue that tourism is an important factor in the economic development of Northern Ireland, and that such tourism requires that the legacy of the conflict such as the murals and the peace walls remain, to satisfy the desire of tourists to experience the Troubles. In a sense there has been a commodification of the Troubles through tourism and tour operators invest in this lucrative business of dark tourism (Leonard, 2011). Black cab drivers and ex-paramilitary prisoner groups on both sides of the sectarian divide forge partnerships to cash in on the tourist demand to visit these former zones of conflict.

Thus, efforts to transform the peace walls are obviously not an uncontested endeavour and many people from the interface communities strongly resist such efforts. Like politicians, urban designers and bureaucrats, the interface communities are intimately involved in the shaping of meaning for public spaces. Although Belfast is in many ways an archetypical violently divided city it possesses a rich history of non-sectarian social movements and agencies mobilising to forge political actions that suspend ethnic encapsulation and dismantle peace walls (Nagle, 2013).

At first encounter, we found that Belfast has an atmosphere of mundane normality. It is not until we walk into the working class Loyalist and Republican areas we see the city for what it is: a divided, conflict-affected society. What struck us is the everyday segregation of the city where three-quarters of the city space is segregated. When we walk along one of the many remaining peace walls we also note that the materialisations of division takes different forms: from tall wire fences that run along the backs of terraced houses to actual brick walls that divide one neighbourhood from another. The most visible interfaces are high brick walls topped by reinforced steel panels and made taller still by heavy wire fencing. Despite or perhaps because of the murals on some of the walls, we feel the oppressive nature of the imposing material structures, and realise how these structures restrict the mobility and define the movement of people living on either side of them. Yet many of the interfaces do not represent physical barriers. Instead there is an invisible dividing line that we fail to see, but local people are aware of, because, historically, they were, and to a degree, still are, threatening and unsafe places. By being in place, we find that the peace walls have become normal, and part of the built environment, and efforts to establish peace have taken place without taking down the walls. In post-conflict Belfast the peace walls seem to be the most troublesome reminders of a divided society.

Space-making

As peace and conflict are manifested in different ways, space-making becomes a process that enables us to cross-cut between a variety of those manifestations. The peace walls re-inscribe the Troubles and become spatial boundaries that become psychologically coded barriers. In our reading, peace walls are not simply a physical place, but are linked to the ideas of the Troubles and of the GFA. Thus they oscillate between contradictory significations of continuation of conflict and peace processes. The space-making that departs from peace walls takes into account moments and memories of both extra-ordinary and ordinary everyday life and the stories that reveal it in terms of violence, rioting, segregation, murals and art connected with the walls. The peace walls are both perceived in terms of their concrete and material aspects as well as their ideational meaning, i.e. the representation of imagined boundaries. They are also places experienced by the communities living in the interface areas, but also by those living in other areas of the city or visiting Belfast. The spatial patterns and everyday practices of local people and communities may uphold or challenge the territorial and sectarian claims manifested in the peace walls. Transforming such places is an immense challenge to peacebuilding actors.

The process of turning contested places such as the peace walls into shared spaces denotes the process of making a physical place relevant and meaningful to societal and political discourses of peace (cf. Lefebvre, 1991). This in turn demonstrates the ambivalent potential of space-making in that physical places can be activated as spaces of divisions or, as spaces of connection. As physical barriers to movement the peace walls represent the bounding of place as well as the boundaries of the communities (Byrne *et al.*, 2012). Through peacebuilding strategies, the peace walls can be transformed through new everyday practices that alter the use of the barriers and provide them with new social meanings. Developing shared spaces signals conflict transformation, reduced levels of segregation and division, greater freedom of movement, promotes equality and an improved quality of everyday life for local people. Regenerating interfaces is therefore crucial to peacebuilding. Transforming the peace walls is a key post-conflict issue, given the high levels of violence and residential segregation experienced in many neighbourhoods of Belfast. How then can the most important marker of social division in Belfast – the peace walls – be transformed into a shared space? With respect to the peacebuilding efforts to transform the peace walls, we explore the community art-project Draw Down The Walls in more detail, in order to identify transformation as well as creative peacebuilding agencies.

Draw Down The Walls

One particular space-making project that aims to deconstruct the peace walls through re-imagining the city without them, is the focus of our analysis. This project can be seen as representational for similar ambitions to transform the peace walls and it can be contextualised in the cultural practice of painting murals and recent attempts to paint peace as a way to counter sectarian imagery.

One project to re-imagine Belfast without peace walls was the Draw Down The Walls project. It was a North Belfast-based cross-interface community relations' initiative of 2012 that held a vision of 'creating the conditions to imagine a city without barriers' (Clarke, 2012). Developed by the North Belfast Interface Network, the project expanded to focus more broadly on cross-interface community relations in North Belfast and came to include the areas of Ardoyne, Lower Shankill and New Lodge/Newington through the partnership of the Golden Thread Gallery, North Belfast Interface Network and Lower Shankill Community Association. Working with some of the most divided and contested places of the city, the project developed an approach of utilising art as an engagement tool to explore mutual understanding and promote dialogue between local communities separated by contested interface barriers. The project invited and provoked discussion about barriers, visible or invisible. 'We developed the Draw Down The Walls project to map our relationships and thinking on the physical barriers, the interfaces and segregation walls which scar North Belfast' (Clarke, 2012). According to Clarke, the walls are merely a manifestation of the divisions which lurk beneath the surface of the city almost two decades into the peace process (Breandán Clarke, authors' interview, Belfast, 2013). Identity, cultural expressions, social exclusion, social mobility, access to education and employment, an inequality of opportunity and ultimately poverty, were the real issues and the peace walls can be read merely as representations of these multiple deprived societies.

When it comes to the Draw Down The Walls project, the actors driving the transformation were part of the local communities. The ambition was to engage with young people and adults who rarely took part in the conversations and processes of peacebuilding. It was initially developed in order to build and foster improved community relations in the area, and engage with those hard to reach groups which have previously not been attracted to, or involved in traditional dialogue techniques. Part of the project focused on youth, and they made visits to interface barriers around the city, took part in discussions around key issues and some were appointed ambassadors for peace and underwent training in good relations. By involving the youth, the aim was to allow for them to express their political agency in a way that was creative and transformative rather than as resistance, which is the way much of what has been termed recreational rioting has been described (Breandán Clarke, authors' interview, Belfast, 2013).

Re-imagining Belfast

Within the Draw Down The Walls project and as part of the worldwide truce for the Cultural Olympiad, a large-scale international initiative was undertaken. It aimed to temporarily transform the place between the Flax Street gates through a large art project, and the artist Oscar Muñoz was carefully selected to work on this project. For the project – the Ambulatorio installation – to be convened and open to the public, the two gates at Flax Street needed to be opened to allow for equal access from both communities (Curator Golden Thread Gallery, authors' interview, Belfast, 2013). A consultation process was undertaken which included leafleting the wider community and inviting all to participate in a public meeting (Young & Bell, 2013). The questions that emerged focused on the practicalities of the gates opening and the security that would be in place. For easier access, a third gate was opened from another neighbouring area as well. Thus, the three gates were open between the 9th July and the 4th August 2012 to provide open access for visitors to the exhibit. Over the course of the event nearly 2,000 people passed between the Flax Street gates and experienced the artwork (Curator Golden Thread Gallery, authors' interview, Belfast 2013). The entire event was staged, without trouble, during a traditionally contentious time in the Northern Ireland marching season. This novel spatial practice, to make use of a place that most of the time is off limits, provided insights into, and an experience of, what that neighbourhood would be like in the event that the peace wall were to be taken down.

Several attempts to re-imagine Belfast without the peace walls have been undertaken. One is the Urban Innovations, which was commissioned by the Northern Ireland Housing Executive's BRIC programme. It was set up for the Housing Executive to work together with community representatives to re-imagine the interface area without the peace walls. One particular difficulty for local residents emerged around visualising such material change as dismantling the peace walls and what the cityscape would look like in their absence. To help the process of re-imagining visual models of what a particular change at an interface may look like were developed (Housing Executive, authors' interview, Belfast, 2014). These re-imagined models were incorporated into the consultation process to help visualise change and discuss different ideas.

Many artists and community cultural workers have pushed for less offensive and intimidating murals that are not territorial and connected to Troubles (*Belfast Telegraph*, 2010). In response, political parties and community organisations have put up schemes to remove nationalist murals. One initiative is the Art of Regeneration project funded by the Northern Ireland Department of Culture, Arts and Leisure and the Arts Council of Northern Ireland. The project provides funding for local authorities to initiate arts projects in areas in need of social and economic regeneration, such as the arts projects in two Loyalist areas to replace paramilitary murals and graffiti. A similar initiative is the Re-imagining Communities programme, which is the most extensive programme to address the visible manifestations of sectarianism and racism. This programme provides funding for transforming the murals on the peace wall in Lower Falls. The peace wall on Conway Street now holds a message of inclusiveness and depicts 'the sky' based on a poem by Tom Kerr. It is the only Republican mural funded by the re-imagining community project (Hill & White, 2012). Today, we see that some new murals are co-constructed by artists from the two communities (Hill & White, 2012).

Place-making

Thinking with Massey highlights the necessity of understanding the relationship between abstract notions of space and concrete notions of place. Place is always being made, never finished, never closed. Contestations and conflicts over place create new spatial arrangements, a new way of ordering space which give rise to new symbolic and political landscapes reflecting and emplacing a given vision of national identity and imagination of the community (Kliot & Mansfield, 1997; Campbell, 1998). To consolidate peace, to embed the abstract idea of peace, and to realise the peace dividend, the spatial order of conflict needs to be transformed. Agents of peacebuilding are the drivers behind such process – the place-making process. Furthermore, peace, peacebuilding and peacebuilding agents are emplaced and constituted in part through place and space. In the context of Belfast the idea of peace seems still abstract and intangible, while the material legacy of the Troubles is tangible and visible. The transformation process of emplacing peace is analysed through the efforts to transform the MLK into a peace and conflict resolution centre.

The Maze/Long Kesh Prison – a legacy of the Troubles

As a historic site, the MLK prison on the outskirts of Belfast has a short history. It was used to hold both Loyalist and Republican paramilitaries during the Troubles.[5] Today, it is a politically contested site and an eerie, grey place in limbo, and one can peek through the deteriorating maximum-security fence into the debris of disconnected barbed wire and dismantled searchlights.

Located in the city of Lisburn, about ten miles from Belfast, the MLK comprises more than 300 buildings on a 360-acre site. The site was vacated by the RAF shortly after World War II, and renamed the 'Long Kesh Detention Centre'. The introduction of internment in 1971 increased detentions of men from the nationalist communities without trial (Graham & McDowell, 2007). It has been rather conservatively estimated that more than 10,000 men were imprisoned at the site during the Troubles (Purbrick, 2004). The prisoners' status and release as well as the future of the MLK were important issues during the peace talks and as an agreement was reached the GFA could provide for an early release programme for prisoners connected to the Troubles. As a consequence, the MLK prison was closed in 2000 and a couple of years later the government decided to transfer the estate to the public as a symbolic gesture (Flynn, 2011; Michael *et al.*, 2016). The Maze Regeneration Unit was created in 2002 as a subsidiary of the Office of First Minister and Deputy First Minister to respond to the perceived need that something had to be done with the MLK (Michael *et al.*, 2016).

The MLK prison holds a prominent place in the history of the Troubles. It shaped the identity of the prisoners within it and the construction of narratives of the past within their associated communities. Particular events took place here, at important moments in time, shaping both the conflict dynamics and the peace process. The Republican protests, i.e. the 'blanket protest' and the 'dirty protest' took place here when the Special Category status was removed. The removal of their status as political rather than criminal prisoners provoked the Republican prisoners to undertake a hunger strike in 1981. Ten IRA and INLA hunger-strikers died and the martyrdom of these volunteers reified the role of the prison within the Republican narrative of the Troubles (McAtackney, 2014). In Northern Ireland, the prison is now seen as a place fundamentally linked with the Republican movement.

In contrast to the Republicans, the Loyalist prisoners did not tend to question the right of the state to dispense justice, and imprison the paramilitaries on both sides. This placed the Loyalist prisoners on the same side as the policemen, soldiers and civilian authorities fighting against the Republicans. It was also to the MLK the then Secretary of State, Mo Mowlam, came in order to persuade the Loyalist leaders to maintain the ceasefires and support the peace process (Graham & McDowell, 2007; McAtackney, 2014). Although the MLK prison is most prominently associated with a Republican past, the Loyalist narrative and identity are also inextricably linked to this place, but perhaps in more subtle and ambiguous ways.

The MLK can be read as a 'hypertrophy of historical awareness' (Leerssen, 2001: 217) where zero-sum classifications of public space – 'ours' or 'theirs' predominate (Nagle, 2009: 329). As a key heritage site the transformation of the MLK is contested and it is likely to exclude those not subscribing to its new meaning. In this case, the issue of place-making is closely connected with the remembering of a violent and divided past. The past is valued and understood differently by different peoples, groups or communities and how the past is understood validates their sense of place (Smith, 2006: 80). The transformation of the MLK by giving it new meaning will thus have to take into account that 'a heritage place may represent or stand in for a sense of identity and belonging for particular individuals or groups' (Smith, 2006: 77) and such connection between identity and place may constrain the process of transformation and hamper the transition towards peace.

Opinion had been split between those who wished to see the prison and all it represented, destroyed, obliterated and forgotten, and those who argue that the site must be fully retained as a 'Museum of the Troubles' or, as referred to in the media debates, 'a monument to and invocation of the Ghosts of the Troubles' (*Belfast Telegraph*, 2013a). Clearly, the dark legacy of the MLK continues to haunt the present and in the debates the prison has been portrayed both as a 'sacred site of martyrdom' (Graham & McDowell, 2007), and a 'shrine to terrorism' (*Belfast Telegraph*, 2013b). Whilst the place remains in limbo, our excavation of the competing narratives reveals anxiety about the past, present and future as Loyalists worry about the strong Republican identification with the place and fear that preserving the prison will turn it into a pilgrimage site of Republican martyrdom (cf. McAtackney, 2014). Republicans, on the other hand, fear that destroying the remains of the site will mean that the memory of all that Republican prisoners fought and died for will be lost.

Making place for peace at the Maze/Long Kesh

The advent of peace spurred a heated debate surrounding how to deal with a difficult heritage and the meanings of such material places in the present and future of Northern Ireland. This is particularly true for the MLK, which has acquired an emblematic status in terms of dealing with Northern Ireland's contested past. As a cultural heritage site, the prison may not represent the 'right memory'. It can become a memorial with the ability to encapsulate and perpetuate ethno-national identities and claims (Schramm, 2011). The MLK is a particular material remnant of the Troubles and it has been read as a 'reminder of a painful past and disputed presence' (McDowell, 2009: 216) and it can readily slide into contested and contradictory narratives about history, specific events, victimhood and victory. Furthermore, the MLK is constituted as a place that is occupied by the troubled past and this particular past limits the kind of ideas and meanings that can be emplaced there in the future. A temporal reading of the MLK reveals how the past, present and future are linked, and how different agents constitute present places by selecting spatial narratives that reinforce their claims to a particular past, to power in the present and to constrain place-making processes in the future.

As the Northern Irish society struggles to put the past behind it, the abstract notion of peace must move from the realm of ideas to the reality on the ground. The negotiated peace has to be transformed into everyday practices and embedded in place. One way to 'emplace' peace was to establish an International Centre for Conflict Transformation (ICCT) at the MLK. The idea was proposed by the all-party Maze Consultation Panel[6] in the report *A New Future for Long Kesh/Maze*. According to the report, the ICCT was to be emplaced in, and thereby transform, a contested material legacy of the conflict – the MLK prison.[7] A guiding notion was that the transformation of the MLK 'provides a physical expression of the on-going transformation from conflict to peace' (The Maze/Long Kesh: Master Plan and Implementation Strategy, 2006: 2, 5). According to the proposal, the ICCT would provide a place for visitors from around the world to exchange views on conflict transformation, a focus for education and research about the troubles, together with exhibition space and an archive. Furthermore, lessons were to be learned from the Northern Irish experience of transitioning from conflict towards peace. It was envisioned that there would be input from ex-prisoners, prison officers and victims. The Centre would sit alongside a preserved H block and other buildings, including the chapel and the hospital where the hunger strikers died. The peace centre was to be built with an £18 million EU grant through the PEACE III programme (Urban scholar, authors' interview, Belfast, 2014). It was envisioned that 'the International Centre for Conflict Transformation would play an important role in the transformation of the region in the period of post-conflict normalisation through promoting a shared society and the ICCT would give new meaning to the old prison (Maze/Long Kesh Master Plan and Implementation Strategy, 2006: 2, 5).

Transitions from conflict to peace happen in part through the transformation of material places, particularly those that host the legacy of the conflict. The MLK is part of the legacy of the Troubles yet as a place it can be given different meanings and it can be transformed to host peace rather than the conflict and its legacy. Such transformation may occur when peacebuilding agents ascribe certain qualities to the place: a place of shared heritage where peace can be embedded; a home for peace education; and where lessons learned from the Troubles can be taught. Thus, The MLK can be seen as a place filled with people, things, practices and representations (Gieryn, 2000: 465). The MLK as a legacy of conflict can be given a new sense of place through the attribution of meaning to it as a place of peace (Rotenberg & McDonogh, 1993). Thus, the MLK heritage is part of peacebuilding processes.

The transformation of the MLK was spurred by a coalition of peacebuilding agents. However, the ICCT was not established at the MLK due to lack of agreement among the political parties. New consultations took place, new ideas were floated and new negotiations have started, of which the MLK is part. The idea was reformulated and the prison was to be transformed by hosting what was now called the Peacebuilding and Conflict Resolution Centre (PbCRC). Also supposed to be funded by the EU through PEACE III, the PbCRC was to be designed by star-architect Daniel Libeskind (BBC, 2013). The Peace Centre was to be placed in a new, separate building at the site, though physically linked to the prison building. The centre would also take on responsibilities for education and be relevant to Northern Irish schools, in terms of overcoming conflict-generated cleavages in society. It has been argued that the centre should be reflective of what happened at the MLK but not a rewrite of the past. Thus, it remains uncertain whether the prison will emplace peace in terms of providing the place for a centre for peacebuilding and conflict resolution. The discussion reveals the tensions that emerge between managing authenticity and performing reconstruction, and the importance of ownership and the ability and right to interpret and present the narrative of the past and the present as the place-making process is initiated.

When reading peace and conflict through a spatial lens, the analysis is tightly bound to the material legacy of conflict such as the MLK, and one risks losing sight of the different ways in which agency actually produces place and space. By focusing in on the ideational realm, we can read agency from the process of place-making during the course of which actors are able to give physical presence to an ideational space as in the case of the MLK. Aforementioned, places do not emerge 'like that', but they are the result of an on-going process of creative and transformative agency. Thus, place-making involves a transformation of the physical place into an imagined space.

Conclusion

The division in Belfast persists regardless of the GFA, which was negotiated at the state level and brought the Troubles to a successful end. This is an indication that the conventional focus of peacebuilding on the state-level at times may have counterproductive effects at sub-state levels. The peace agreement was not well suited for addressing the divisive material and immaterial legacy of the Troubles and in fact, the divides in the city were frozen by the agreement. To overcome such obstacles to peace, peacebuilding agents need to be able to address the physical fabric of separation, the violent past, its influences on actions in the present and its determination of attitudes in the future. Peacebuilding agents work to overcome segregation and cemented divisions and to transform spatial expressions of the Troubles to make sure that the peace dividend materialises and that peace will be emplaced in the everyday.

The peacebuilding efforts in Belfast highlight the complexity, diversity, contestation and contradictions involved in the reconstruction of symbolic urban spaces after violent conflict. The limited success of the GFA to address these spatial issues indicates an inability to understand these complexities and contestations and to acknowledge the material and immaterial legacy of the conflict as a major obstacle to building sustainable peace. The fact that peacebuilding agents need to be able to capture the specificities of the urban landscape as an arena for peacebuilding and that spatial planning is a key means to address issues of ethnic co-existence, tolerance and democracy in the everyday. By paying attention to the urban and its dynamics, peace-building agents could uncover the workings of power relations and how these relations are reproduced in the cityspace. As Belfast illustrates, peacebuilding strategies may either fragment or integrate a conflict-affected city socially, by suppressing or dominating cultural identities or by re-imagining identities in ways that may nurture diversity within unity. Peacebuilding may reconstruct spaces and places that either reinforce or seek to transcend community identities (Bollens, 2007: 248).

Notes

1 The Good Friday Agreement is also known as the Belfast Agreement.
2 Recognising that British Protestant/Unionists/Loyalist are not homogenous groups and that there are differences between being Unionist and Loyalist, the term Loyalist will be used through out to describe this community. In a similar manner, the terminology of the Irish Catholic/Nationalists/Republicans also represents different views, attitudes, politics, etc., but throughout the chapter Republicans will be used to describe this community.
3 This chapter will apply the term 'Long Kesh/Maze Prison' to cover both the internment camps at Long Kesh and the later H Blocks of the Maze. This convoluted term acknowledges the two separate narratives, and regimes, within the one prison site and that not everyone used the same term for the prison site. It has been widely accepted that the change of name from 'Long Kesh' to 'HMP, the Maze' was part of the struggle by the authorities to change the prisoners' status from political prisoners to criminals.
4 The Northern Ireland mural tradition dates back to 1908 and evolved through the Troubles to the present period of the peace process.
5 The Loyalist paramilitaries were mainly from the Ulster Volunteer Force (UVF) and Ulster Defence Association (UDA) and Republican ones were from the Irish Republican Army (IRA) and Irish National Liberation Army (INLA).
6 The Maze Consultation Panel which comprised an Ulster Unionist Chair, a Social Demoratic and Labour Party Vice Chair and nominees from the Democratic Unionist Party and Sinn Fein was established and had its inaugural meeting on 10th March 2003.
7 After cumbersome and contentious consultations with various community representatives, the Maze Consultation Panel published a number of proposals detailing how the site should be redeveloped, and the ICCT was not the only idea. Among the other ideas were a Rural Excellence and Equestrian Zone including an International Exhibition Centre and showgrounds; offices, hotel and leisure village; Employment Zone; Community Zone all of which would add new and very different meanings to the MLK site (Graff-McRae, 2009).

Bibliography

Abdelmonem, M. G. & McWhinney, R., 2015. In Search for Common Grounds: Stitching the Divided Landscape of Urban Parks in Belfast. *Cities* 44(1), pp. 40–49.

BBC, 2013. Architect Daniel Libeskind says Maze peace centre will go ahead. [Online] Available at: http://www.bbc.com/news/uk-northern-ireland-24289701 [Accessed 2 October 2016].

Belfast Interface Project, 2011. *Belfast Interfaces: Security Barriers and Defence Use of Space.* [Online] Available at: http://www.belfastinterfaceproject.org/sites/default/files/publications/Belfast%20Interfaces%20%20Security%20barriers%20and%20defensive%20use%20of%20space.pdf [Accessed 2 October 2016].

Belfast Telegraph, 2010. Belfast's Murals: Off the Wall?. [Online] Available at: http://www.belfasttelegraph.co.uk/life/features/belfasts-murals-off-the-wall-28530297.htm [Accessed 1 September 2016].

Belfast Telegraph, 2013a. The Maze: DUP's Jimmy Spratt also Ends up Full of Regret for Calling Plan's Opponents 'Nutters'. Available at: http://www.belfasttelegraph.co.uk/news/northern-ireland/the-maze-dups-jimmy-spratt-also-ends-up-full-of-regret-for-calling-plans-opponents-nutters-29378828.html [Accessed 4 November 2016].

Belfast Telegraph, 2013b. Maze Peace Centre Plans Approved. Available at: http://www.belfasttelegraph.co.uk/news/northern-ireland/maze-peace-centre-plans-app roved-29205585.html [Accessed 4 November 2016].

Belfast Telegraph, 2016. Peace Wall is Demolished in Northern Belfast. [Online] Available at: http://www.belfasttelegraph.co.uk/news/northern-ireland/video-pea ce-wall-is-demolished-in-north-belfast-34485846.html [Accessed 4 July 2016]

Belloni, R. & Deane, S., 2005. From Belfast to Bosnia: Piecemeal Peacemaking and the Role of Institutional Learning. *Civil Wars* 7(3), pp. 219–243.

Bollens, S. 2007. *Cities, Nationalism and Democratization*, London, New York: Routledge.

Brand, R., 2011. Polarisation Takes Place. *Shared Space* 5(11), pp. 17–27.

Brand, R. & Fregonese, S., 2013. *The Radicals' City: Urban Environment, Polarisation, Cohesion*. Surrey: Ashgate.

Byrne, J., 2011. *The Belfast Peace Walls: Problems, Politics and Policies of the Troubles Architecture*. (PhD Thesis). s.l.: Ulster University.

Byrne, J. & Gormely-Heenan, C., 2014. Belfast's Peace Walls: Can you remove the conflict architecture? Available at: http://blogs.lse.ac.uk/politicsandpolicy/belfasts-p eace-walls-can-you-remove-the-conflict-architecture/ [Accessed 4 July 2016].

Byrne, J., Gormley-Heenan, C. & Robinson, G., 2012. *Attitudes to Peace Walls: Research Report to Office of First Minister and Deputy First Minister*. [Online] Available at: http://www.ark.ac.uk/peacewalls2012/peacewalls2012.pdf [Accessed 4 July 2016].

Byrne, J., Gormley-Hennan, C., Morrow, D. & Sturgeon, B., 2015. *Public Attitudes to Peace Walls: Survey Results*. [Online] Available at: http://www.socsci.ulster.ac.uk/p ws.pdf [Accessed 4 July 2016].

Campbell, D., 1998. *National Deconstruction: Violence, Identity and Justice in Bosnia*. Minneapolis, MN: University of Minneapolis Press.

Clarke, B., 2012. Personally Endorse the Principles of Conflict Transformation! [Online] Available at: http://www.transconflict.com/2012/06/draw-down-the-wa lls-296/ [Accessed 1 September 2016].

Dixon, P., 2008. *Northern Ireland: The Politics of War and Peace*. 2nd ed. Basingstoke, New York: Palgrave Macmillan.

Finlay, A., 2011. *Governing Ethnic Conflict: Consociation, Identity and the Price of Peace*. New York: Routledge.

Flynn, M., 2011. Decision-making and Contest v Heritage in Northern Ireland: The Former Maze Prison/Long Kesh. *Irish Political Studies* 26(3), pp. 383–401.

Gaffikin, F. & Morrissey, M., 2011. *Planning in Divided Cities*. Hoboken, N.J.: Wiley-Blackwell Pub.

Gieryn, T. F., 2000. A Space for Place in Sociology. *Annual Review of Sociology* 26, pp. 463–496.

Goldie, R. & Ruddy, B., 2010. *Crossing the Line: Key Features of Effective Practices in the Development of Shared Space in Areas Close to an Interface*. Lisburn: Belfast Interface Project.

Graff-McRae, R. L., 2009. Popular Memory in Northern Ireland. In: M. Keren & H. H. Herwig, eds. *War Memory and Popular Culture: Essays on Modes of Remembrance and Commemoration*. Jefferson, NC: McFarlan and Company Inc., pp. 41–56.

Graham, B. & McDowell, S., 2007. Meaning in the Maze: The Heritage of Long Kesh. *Cultural Geographies* 14(3), pp. 343–368.

Hill, A. & White, A., 2012. Painting Peace? Murals and the Northern Ireland Peace Process. *Irish Political Studies* 27(1), pp. 71–88.

Hocking, B. T., 2013. Beautiful Barriers: Art and Identity along a Belfast 'Peace' Wall. *Anthropology Matters Journal* 14(1), pp. 1–12.

Hocking, B. T., 2015. *The Great Re-imagining: Public Art and Urban Space and the Symbolic Landscapes of a 'New' Northern Ireland*. New York and Oxford: Berghahn Books Ltd..

Horgan, J. & Morrison, J. F., 2011. Here to Stay? The Rising Threat of Violent Dissident Republicanism in Northern Ireland. *Terrorism and Political Violence* 23 (4), pp. 642–669.

Jarman, N., 2005. Changing Places, Moving Boundaries: The Development of New Interface Areas. *Shared Space* 1, pp. 9–19.

Kliot, N. & Mansfield, Y., 1997. The Political Landscape of Partition: The Case of Cyprus. *Political Geography* 16(6), pp. 495–521.

Komarova, M. & O'Dowd, L., 2016. Belfast, 'The Shared City'? Spatial Narratives of Conflict Transformation. In: Björkdahl, A., & Buckley-Zistel, S., *Spatialising Peace and Conflict: Mapping the Production of Places, Sites and Scales of Violence*. Hampshire: Palgrave Macmillan, pp. 265–285.

Kostovicova, D., 2004. Republika Srpska and its Boundaries in Bosnian Serb Geographical Narratives in the Post-Dayton Period. *Space and Polity* 8(3), pp. 267–287.

Leerssen, J., 2001. Monument and Trauma: Varieties of Remembrance. In: I. McBride, ed. *History and Memory in Modern Ireland*. Cambridge: Cambridge University Press, pp. 204–222.

Lefebvre, H., 1991. *The Production of Space*. Oxford: Blackwell.

Leonard, M., 2011. A Tale of Two Cities: Authentic Tourism in Belfast. *Irish Journal of Sociology* 19(2), pp. 111–126.

Mac Ginty, R., 1999. 'Biting the Bullet': Decommissioning in the Transition from War to Peace in Northern Ireland. *Irish Studies in International Affairs* 10, pp. 237–247.

McAtackney, L., 2014. *An Archaeology of the Troubles: The Dark Heritage of Long Kesh/Maze Prison*. Oxford: Oxford University Press.

McDowell, S., 2009. Negotiating Places of Pain in Northern Ireland: Debating the Future of the Maze Prison/Long Kesh. In: W. Logan & K. Reeves, eds. *Places of Pain and Shame: Dealing with a 'Difficult Heritage'*. London and New York: Routledge, pp. 215–230.

McDowell, S. & Shirlow, P., 2011. Geographies of Conflict and Post-Conflict in Northern Ireland. *Geography Compass* 5(9), pp. 700–709.

McEvoy, S., 2009. Loyalist Women Paramilitaries in Northern Ireland: Beginning a Feminist Conversation about Conflict Resolution. *Security Studies* 18(2), pp. 262–286.

McGarry, J. & O'Leary, B., 2006. Consociational Theory, Northern Ireland's Conflict, and its Agreement. Part 1: What Consociationalists Can Learn from Northern Ireland. *Government and Opposition* 41(1), pp. 43–63.

Meager, K., 2016. Brexit is the Beginning of the End for Northern Ireland. [Online] Available at: http://www.newstatesman.com/politics/staggers/2016/07/brexit-beginning-end-northern-ireland [Accessed 2 October 2016].

Michael, L., Murtagh, B. & Price, L., 2016. Where Conflict and Peace Take Place: Memorialization, Sacralization and Post-Conflict Space. In: A. Björkdahl & S. Buckley-Zistel, eds. *Spatialising Peace and Conflict: Mapping the Production of Places, Sites and Scales of Violence*. Hampshire: Palgrave Macmillan, pp. 221–241.

Murtagh, B., 2002. *The Politics of Territory*. Basingstoke: Palgrave.

Murtagh, B. & Keaveney, K., 2006. Policy and Conflict Transformation in the Ethnocratic City. *Space and Polity* 10(2), pp. 187–202.

Nagle, J., 2009. Sites of Social Centrality and Segregation: Lefebvre in Belfast, a 'Divided City'. *Antipode* 41(2), pp. 326–347.

Nagle, J., 2013. 'Unity in Diversity': Non-sectarian Social Movement Challenges to the Politics of Ethnic Antagonism in Violently Divided Cities. *International Journal of Urban and Regional Research* 37(1), pp. 78–92.

Nolan, P., 2014. *Northern Ireland Peace Monitoring Report No. 3*, Belfast: Community Relations Council.

Purbrick, L., 2004. *The Maze*. London: Granta,.

Rotenberg, R. & McDonogh, G., 1993. *The Cultural Meaning of Urban Space*. Westport CN, London: Bergin & Garvey.

Schramm, K., 2011. Landscapes of Violence: Memory and Sacred Space. *History and Memory* 23(1), pp. 1–5.

Shirlow, P., 2006. Belfast: The 'Post-conflict' City. *Space and Polity* 10(2), pp. 99–107.

Shirlow, P. & Murtagh, B., 2004. Capacity-building, Representation and Intracommunity Conflict. *Urban Studies* 41(1), pp. 57–70.

Smith, L., 2006. *Uses of Heritage*. New York: Routledge.

The Maze/Long Kesh: Master Plan and Implementation Strategy, 2006. Available at: http://cain.ulst.ac.uk/issues/sport/docs/mazeplan/ofmdfm300506.pdf (Accessed 3 November 2016).

The Executive Office, 2013. Together: Building a United Community. Available at: https://www.executiveoffice-ni.gov.uk/articles/together-building-united-community (Accessed: 3 November 2016).

Wiedenhoft Murphy, W. A., 2010. Touring the Troubles in West Belfast: Building Peace or Reproducing Conflict?. *Peace and Change* 35(4), pp. 537–560.

Young, J. & Bell, J., 2013. A Model of Consultation? Transformation and Regeneration at the Interface, Unpublished paper: Institute of Conflict Resolution.

Interviews

John O'Donnel, Belfast Interface Project, authors' interview Belfast, 13 March 2013.

Breandán Clarke, North Belfast Interface Network, authors' interview, Belfast, 14 March 2013.

Curator at Golden Thread Gallery, authors' interview, Belfast, 13 April 2013.

Housing executive, authors' interview, Belfast, 16 January 2014.

Confidential source, authors' interview, Stormont, 17 January 2014.

Urban scholar, Queens University, authors' interview, Belfast, 16 January 2014.

6 South Africa: Perpetuating Spatial Apartheid?

Introduction

South Africa is a particular case in that the transition towards peace in the South African context was and still is primarily a national, rather than an internationally-led exercise. The 1991 National Peace Accord was largely domestically driven and included a variety of social and political actors in the country. Yet, although this peace process, linked with the work of the Truth and Reconciliation Commission, has come far in terms of the development of more inclusive governance structures in the country, the spatial legibility of conflict is still striking. Indeed, we would argue that one main dimension of conflict in South Africa can be considered a spatial one, with dividing lines shaping the cityscapes of the major urban metropoles in the country. In that respect, although South Africa is often cited as a role model for democracy, its spatial exclusion mechanisms remain powerful in terms of the political organisation and (lack of) mobilisation of the population. The racially segregated areas, the presence of gated communities and the absence of public transport, particularly in suburban areas, continue to have substantial impacts on people's everyday lives, from all strata of society. These pre-set spatial structures severely inhibit individuals' agency to transgress them and they impede social mobility across the categories of race and class. It therefore requires a high degree of creativity for social actors, whether they be individuals or groups, to find ways of mobilising excluded communities to let them participate in political decision-making processes. It can therefore be said that in South Africa the use and transformation of space cannot be separated from the underlying issues of inequality, social and spatial immobility and therefore the political economy of the transition process. Indeed, while this is an important issue in all our case studies, South Africa stands out as particularly spatially constrained in the way in which its people are segregated not only racially, but also based on socio-economic status in terms of gated communities, townships and continuing eviction processes of the poorest parts of the population. This has crucially affected the ways in which the country has been struggling to find a way towards democracy, peace and social justice.

This chapter will therefore investigate the powerful spatial structures at play in South Africa and key actors who have resisted, or even been able to transgress such mobility limitations. It becomes clear that one of the biggest spatial issues that the country faces is the issue of relocation and spatial exclusion. The chapter therefore investigates spatial politics and we focus on Abahlali baseMjondolo, an organisation that is now established in several townships around the country, and which advocates improved access to resources as well as encouraging political mobilisation. It has mobilised local people's agency in townships, both in place-making (resisting to pressures to leave a place physically) and space-making (centring on the rights of the most marginalised in the country). The movement has to be understood in the context of the increasing marginalisation of the poorest sections of the population as regards access to political power and resources, which has led to tense conflicts about the use and distribution of land, in specific terms, but also in relation to South Africa as a whole.

Then, with a particular focus on Cape Town, the chapter highlights practices of place-making, quoting the example of the District Six Museum and its associated Homecoming Centre. They represent processes of 'place-making' in that they give a material home to the abstract idea of reconciliation. Situated in an area shaped by discussions about (formerly expelled) returnees, they are a powerful materialisation of social activists' efforts to make reconciliation a practical project in the District Six area of Cape Town. We then go on to analyse the process of 'space-making', as exemplified by Robben Island. We investigate the different meanings developed for this former prison island and the emergence of the dominant narrative of reconciliation over competing narratives.

These examples make it clear that a spatial analysis always has to take into account the contextual power relations at play. The creation of a place, or a space, always depends on the agents involved, who in South Africa include political elites, social activists, international donors, domestic and international tourists and local political communities. Yet, as this chapter shows, spatial agency is also always faced with structural constraints, including race, gender, class and social status, amongst others. The development of diverse forms of agency in spatial practice over time therefore must include an acknowledgement of such wider structural constraints that make a reversal of prevailing power structures extremely difficult for the actors challenging them. At the same time, even small-scale attempts to challenge spatial power can make a considerable impact on people's everyday lives, as our examples will show. In fact, fieldwork in South Africa makes the researcher feel the power of spatial infrastructures. When moving around Cape Town it becomes obvious that social mobility is so far very limited and that people tend to move in restricted areas. For us as researchers, transgressing the invisible, but powerful boundaries between gated communities and townships, between town centres and peripheries, between mixed and racially segregated areas, has been eye-opening, given that many South Africans do not enjoy the freedom of movement that we have.

Transitions from apartheid

South Africa has indeed a long contested history of spatial politics. The politics of place can be seen as having constituted a particular problem during the era of apartheid, which focused on disempowering the black and, to a lesser extent, coloured people in terms of removing them from the centres of power. Apartheid in South Africa can therefore be considered as having relied on a spatial technology of separation (Robinson, 1996: 1). The power of the white minority was not only politically, but also spatially engrained through policies of relocation and eviction.[1]

However, this is not to say that spatial politics was an issue only during apartheid. One could go back to Dutch, German and British colonialism in the country and investigate the spatial practices of domination during this time. In fact, the use of space was for the colonial powers an important way of controlling the natives (cf. Noyes, 2012; Darian-Smith *et al.*, 2005). Noyes (2012) suggests that spatial politics was a crucial element for the colonisers, in maintaining an efficient system of control. In that sense, colonial spatial politics left a legacy in a number of colonies, and specifically in South Africa, shaped as it was by Dutch, German and British colonial practices. The dynamics of transition between the different colonisers as well as the end of colonialism are often neglected when people speak of transition in the South African context as they mainly relate to the end of apartheid and the role of Nelson Mandela in this process (cf. Coombes, 2003). At the same time, we need to acknowledge the importance of the late 19th-century Anglo-Boer Wars between the Dutch and British colonisers in the context of spatial politics, not least in so far as they concerned the long battle over access to the gold mines based in Witwatersrand. Access to resources can therefore be considered an important question in South Africa that has deeply shaped the contestations around access to and control over space.

The notion of apartheid had existed during the early period of colonialism, with the colonisers establishing categories of superiority and inferiority based on people's racial identities. It was formally introduced as a policy in 1948 and, from then on, continued to shape the state's policies in terms of land, education and public access to resources. The dynamic of maintaining control through spatial politics was mirrored during the formal apartheid regime, in the course of which the relocation of the most marginalised sections of society outside the city centres into isolated townships reflects the attempt not only to cleanse space, but also to disempower those sections of society, by means of the transformation of space and place. The apartheid regime indeed used spatial politics for its purposes of control. One point in case is the Natives (Urban Areas) Act No 21 of 1923 aiming to restrict the freedom of movement and particularly targeting blacks who would then not be able to travel easily into cities. In the same vein, even before apartheid, suburbs such as Langa outside Cape Town were created to act as a buffer in a situation of restricted movement and mainly to prevent the black population from entering spaces foreseen for white South Africans. As Besteman (2008: 50) suggests, apartheid policy made use of a 'self-sustaining geography' by normalising residential segregation. Relocations of blacks outside city centres into distant suburbs, often not accessible by public transport, continued to serve as a popular strategy to undermine resistance against the politics decided upon in the political power centres. The latter represented centres not only symbolically, but also geographically. Such policies led to large-scale evictions of blacks from central urban areas, with District Six (in Cape Town) being one example. It had had a history as a mixed, colourful area of Cape Town but its character was massively changed by the loss of the major part of its population as the result of the evictions. This was not a consequence of state planning alone, but it was also linked with the desire of multi-national companies to occupy the district, which led to a 'Hands Off District 6' campaign in 1989 as part of an ongoing period of political activism (Crischene Julius, Tina Smith, Mandy Sanger, authors' interview, Cape Town, 2012). Indeed, the district is rich in its ability to mobilise resistance, which, as we will show below, has been an important feature in terms of reclaiming the area after the end of apartheid.

In the context of apartheid, transformation in South Africa has long been associated with its end as well as the associated transition to democracy in and after 1994. This step has often been celebrated as a huge leap for the country (cf. Waldmeir, 1997). Indeed, South Africa's transition looked promising to begin with, not only for the country itself, but also for the wider region. The empowerment of black people through the success of the African National Congress (ANC), led by Nelson Mandela, was indicative of the considerable change that the country was prepared to undergo after decades of oppression and racial segregation. Particularly the Truth and Reconciliation Commission (TRC) in its attempt to give voice to the victims and to deal with the past in a constructive way is still being used as a model for other post-conflict cases in seeking to deal with a history of injustice and violence (cf. Boraine, 2010). At the same time, the TRC and its associated process has faced criticism due to a variety of issues. Critics have remarked that the findings of the commission lacked clarity (Pigou, 2006) and were limited in their wider impact across society (Cole, 2007: 174). Others remarked that the commission made ambiguous use of the notion of reconciliation (Borer, 2004), whilst privileging white and powerful people (Chapman & Ball, 2001: 8–9) and failing to provide reparations to the poorest and most vulnerable sections of the population (Shirley Gunn, authors' interview, Cape Town, 2012).

At the same time, the post-1994 future turned out to bring a set of its own problems in its train. Guelke (1998), for instance, calls the South African situation a 'misunderstood miracle', warning that the transition was perhaps not a success story as first envisaged since it brought along a number of economic and social problems. Such a conceptualisation does not view transformation as a necessary and automatic outcome of the period of transition, but views the process on a temporal continuum during the course of which certain problems wane, while others persist or emerge. This issue has been ascribed in part to the key role played by the neo-liberalisation of the political economy. Taylor explains that that process was driven by a 'change industry' within civil society, representing a 'complex convergence of interests between the established political elites, domestic and transnational capital, and crucially, aspiring elites espousing, initially perhaps, an alternative vision for the country' (Taylor, 2002: 36). This also means that big businesses became drivers of change (Taylor, 2002: 40), both economically and politically, and cemented a particular neo-liberal economic approach. In that sense, transition became a set of processes increasingly driven by elites and the corporate sector (Bond, 2000). This situation has not improved, indeed it has even exacerbated the degree of inequality in the country (World Bank, 2012). We can argue that the transformation process may have put an end to formal racial inequality, but has in parallel cemented a situation of economically engrained class apartheid. In this context, Hart (2007: 95) points to 'the obscene inequalities cutting across race lines that have intensified with the (further) unleashing of neoliberal forms of capitalism in the post-apartheid era.' These inequalities persist in terms of class, but cut across race and even gender. The actual process of transition is indicative of this problematique as it largely excluded women from a number of the associated official processes (de la Rey & McKay, 2002). This problem has equally been recognised by the World Bank in their 2012 report on the inequality of opportunity that persists in South Africa and limits the social mobility of the most disadvantaged sections of the population (World Bank, 2012).

And indeed, dynamics of exclusion and inequality still permeate the entire social, political and economic life to the present date. This has, not least, resulted in the formation of a large number of protest movements, often working in collaboration with community-based organisations to shed light on the adverse effects of neo-liberalism, particularly on the poor (Dawson & Sinwell, 2012: 3). Alexander (2012: 63) suggests that 'South Africa probably has the highest level of ongoing urban revolt in the world'. This has sometimes resulted in violent confrontations between the state and the protesters (Alexander, 2012: 65) as well as a number of violent incidents, such as the 'xenophobic attacks' of 2015. The latter reflect on the fragility of the nation up to this day as well as underlying social and economic grievances which have not been addressed in the transitional process of the country. Against the background of the continuing high poverty levels, it comes perhaps as no surprise that the dividing lines between racial groups have gradually transformed into economic or class-based segregation.

These dynamics are replicated spatially: they extend from gated communities within which wealth is protected, to the creation of townships for the poor (and mostly black) citizens. They include mass eviction campaigns from populated areas (cf. Runiman, 2012: 178) and the relocation of the poorer citizens from city centres (Kappler, 2015). Indeed, Besteman (2008: 50) points to the increasing cleavages visible in Cape Town's cityscape, which are by no means unique to this city, but can be found throughout the country. In that sense, it is doubtful as to whether the transition from apartheid to democracy has in fact resulted in a clear transition from conflict to peace, or whether conflicts of segregation and distribution are carried on into the democratic period by other means. This is in line with Robinson's suggestion that the 'location strategy' of the pre-apartheid government translated into apartheid politics in terms of elites governing the country through the use of space on the one hand (Robinson, 1996: 58), while on the other hand, the end of apartheid did not put a stop to spatial control mechanisms. As early as 1996, Robinson (1996: 219) even argued that '[t]he spatial dimensions of race, privilege and wealth in the apartheid city have been translated into the interim local government legislation, in ways which could once again affect the outcomes of state actions.' In that sense, large sections of the population, and mainly the poorer ones, continue to feel excluded from access to political power and wealth and tend to find themselves on the fringes of large urban areas.

In fact, spatial politics have continued to play a major role in South Africa's power struggles around the ownership and use of land and has been mirrored in heated discussion about the right to return for citizens evicted earlier. The latter has not always been supported politically and institutionally and continues to divide cities, as the example of District Six shows (a formerly mixed area that was 'racially cleansed' during apartheid and is now preparing for the return of the evicted people) (Geschier, 2007: 38). Such ongoing political debates reflect the extent to which South Africa is still shaped by divisions and the distinction between conflict and peace, or apartheid and democracy, becomes less obvious than one might first have thought. It also means that South African cities are predominantly physically structured by those inequalities. Poor, mostly black, people are unlikely to inhabit city centres, whereas one can find almost no white, let alone rich, people in the marginalised townships around the big cities. Gated communities inhibit movement physically, just as much as the fear of the other side means that people tend not to move outside their spatial comfort zones and are hardly likely to visit the townships outside the bigger cities. Kids from the townships outside Cape Town will often never have seen the very nearby beaches, as that is neither financially viable for them, nor is it a space where they would be naturally travelling and feeling welcome (Confidential source 1, authors' interview, Cape Town, 2012). In that respect, transition has not really taken place for these children who are confined to the environment in which they were brought up, both physically as well as symbolically in terms of lacking the equality of opportunity to move out of it, thanks to either education or a professional career. Some school visits that we undertook in the area around Cape Town indeed demonstrated the fact that, in many cases, the children attending the same school can be considered to have similar backgrounds, at least in economic terms.

Spatial politics: mechanisms of exclusion and relocation

As outlined above, South Africa has a long history of spatial exclusion, with the latter being used as a common strategy to marginalise black people from politics during the era of apartheid. Perhaps surprisingly, this phenomenon has not, however, ended with the end of apartheid. Spatial politics of exclusion and control continue and demonstrate the strong concentration of power and agency in the governing authorities. At the same time, resistance against such politics of exclusion is high, and people still spatially excluded from access to political power, resources or public transport have mobilised to protest against their exclusion. One could argue that almost any of the larger cities of South Africa represent case studies through which dynamics of exclusion can be studied in similar terms. Cape Town is certainly no exception to this rule and will therefore act as a primary case-study for this chapter.

In fact, the Western Cape Anti-Eviction Campaign is just one example in which people have mobilised to advocate their right to land in the light of the repeated eviction campaigns of the government (Mzonke Poni, authors' interview, Cape Town, 2012). Khayelitsha, the largest suburb outside Cape Town, was particularly affected by an eviction campaign in 2005, which was, however, prevented through advocacy on the part of the organisation Abahlali baseMjondolo (Mzonke Poni, authors' interview, Cape Town, 2012). The organisation campaigns not only for the use of land, but with related issues, such as sanitation, electricity and housing. The organisation states:

> Life is always difficult in the shacks. If you are poor and black you can be killed with impunity. […] We live in life threatening conditions every day. We die in the fires, from disease, drugs and crime. Our children die from diarrhoea. Our neighbours die because the roads next to the settlements are not made safe for pedestrians. The economy excludes us. The development of the cities excludes us. We are denied access to land, electricity, water, housing, education and work. We are also denied the right to participate in the discussions about the future of our society and in decision making about our lives and communities.
>
> Abahlali baseMjondolo, 2016

It becomes clear in this quote how profoundly spatial exclusion affects the everyday lives of the poor and particularly those living in badly sanitised townships. In fact, this concerns not only one, but almost all, central aspects of daily life, including education and work, as Abahlali baseMjondolo states. These remain pressing issues even after more than 20 years since the transition to democracy, and exclusive politics, traditionally known to be caused by the apartheid system, continue and there has been no neat rupture between the past and the present. In that sense, the work of social activists remains a key aspect of advocacy for the South African poor and it is often their only way of making their voices heard vis-à-vis powerful governmental structures.

In a different context, but with similar results, Abahlali baseMjondolo was also active during the Football World Cup in 2010, which had led to evictions, the breakup of pre-existing social links within townships due to relocations as well as increasing levels of poverty (Mzonke Poni, authors' interview, Cape Town, 2012). Tensions around the use of land, the role of the state, the police and multinational corporations (MNCs), as well as their attempts to access profitable land, can be seen as the extension of such spatial politics during the course of which contestations around the ownership of land become an indicator of political power. In fact, Abahlali baseMjondolo explicitly names 'members of the [South African Police Services], the City Police, private security companies and sometimes also structures of the ruling party' as the main perpetrators of eviction campaigns (*The New Independent*, 2015). As early as 2015, the organisation therefore had already warned of similar effects connected with the 2022 Commonwealth Games, including the construction of a sports village without consulting the inhabitants of the Cornubia development outside Durban, which was affected (Sosibo, 2015).

This example reflects the extent to which physical place ('land') has become extremely significant as far as political conflict in South Africa is concerned to this day. At the same time, although places have officially been racially desegregated since the end of apartheid, cityscapes are increasingly becoming divided along class lines. As Lemanski (2006) shows, the presence of 'gated communities' is but another indicator of the striking degrees of inequality affecting the country (World Bank, 2012), playing out spatially. Indeed, areas of wealthy housing are protected with walls and security guards, whereas poorer areas are located outside city centres, often inaccessible by public transport and economically disadvantaged as far as access to work places is concerned. This situation affects not only the poor, but equally the rich, who feel they have to shield themselves, sustained by a continuous feeling of insecurity. Jürgens & Gnad (2002: 339) term this as strong as 'a "paranoia" of personal insecurity and political uncertainty', with origins dating back to the 1970s and the context of increasing unrest within the black population against the apartheid regime. Interestingly, the demand for gated communities increased *after* the 1994 elections (Roberts, 1996 cited Jürgens & Gnad, 2002: 341), not least as a result of fears of crime. Given that the rent and additional monthly charges preselect who can afford to live there (Jürgens & Gnad, 2002: 347), these gated communities effectively establish material boundaries between the rich and the poor, desired and erected by the former to defend themselves against the latter. This eventually results in what Lemanski (2004) terms an 'architecture of fear' and continues to divide the South African population.

At the same time, spaces and places have not only been used in the context of political conflict, but also as a tool to achieve peacebuilding. The often-praised 'peace parks' all over Southern Africa, for instance, have been said to represent an 'African approach' to peacebuilding in terms of serving as a venue of cooperation and encounter, whilst, on the other hand, being criticised for still being shaped by national politics and interests (van Amerom & Büscher, 2005). The presence of peace parks can therefore be read as an attempt to create common spaces, even if they are politically contentious. Social movements like Abahlali baseMjondolo are using their campaigns to reclaim community space or prevent it from being taken away. This clearly plays a community-strengthening role in terms of addressing questions of social justice and cohesion. Similarly, the District 6 Museum, a very socially active and engaged museum focusing on the reintegration of formerly expelled district inhabitants, has taken an interest in the restitution of land and the political contestations around it. It is indeed becoming increasingly important for museums (amongst others) also to cater for those spatially marginalised from cities. To quote but one example, the Iziko Museum in Cape Town has connected to the Khayelitsha Museum, which portrays life in a township outside a major metropolitan area. This can certainly be viewed as considerable progress, given that township life has long been side-lined from political and cultural action as devised by the political centres (cf. Kappler, 2015). Iziko has, in addition, a museum bus that goes out to rural and harder-to-reach areas (Confidential source 2, authors' interview, Cape Town, 2012). Similarly, many NGOs engaged in trauma work, arts and curating as well as political work are starting also to address the areas outside city centres as there seems to be an increasing acknowledgement of the importance of physical location and the disadvantages linked to residing outside city centres and other easily accessible areas. The Cape Town-based Trauma Centre, for instance, became very active in Manenberg, a township in the 'Cape Flats', after the 2013 rise in gang violence to provide both counselling and crime-prevention services to a deprived community. It is indeed often such communities that receive least political attention, whilst being most dependent on such support. This is not dissimilar to the above-mentioned case of the suburb Khayelitsha, where high levels of poverty co-exist with political mobilisation and resistance against the formal political system.

What these examples show is the centrality of space in the political discourse. It is a question of living and surviving on the one hand, but also a matter of financial, economic and political participation as well as a key issue in terms of community building and cohesion. Peacebuilding can thus not occur without addressing the issue of place and space as well as the manifestations of agency that unfold within it. If we take for granted that spaces are inherently infused with political power, then the case of South Africa makes it obvious how spaces are not only being used to control and govern, but also to emancipate and resist. The control of space can thus be read as a political strategy and is thus highly contested – not least as livelihoods depend on place and space. Place-making and space-making, as we outline below, are therefore key processes in the negotiation of social and political agency. In that vein, an analysis of the transformation of urban landscapes can give us important insights into the ways in which agents are conditioned by powerful spatial structures, whilst at the same time continuously renegotiating the latter.

Place-making

Place-making refers to the ongoing process of transforming abstract, symbolic ideas of space into material reality. It requires a commitment of physical place to abstract notions such as segregation or unification. Indeed, while in South Africa, land and places in general have long been shaped by tendencies of segregation – starting with colonialism, and then moving into the apartheid era – the idea of reconciliation and shared space have become key markers of the transition process since 1994. Yet to what extent have initiatives to engrain these notions into material places been successful? To what extent have they become a physical reality? The District Six Museum and its Homecoming Centre in Cape Town can give us important insights into a case-study of place-making.

The District Six Museum

To investigate practices of place-making in South Africa let us turn our attention to Cape Town and, more specifically, to District Six, a residential area in the inner city of Cape Town. District Six has long had a reputation of being multicultural, cosmopolitan and hosting a mix of different ethnic groups. However, in the late 1960s the area was declared 'whites only' and all non-whites were forcibly evicted from it (Geschier, 2007: 38). This has resulted in the transformation of the district, from a relatively mixed and cosmopolitan place, into a mainly white space with an increasing number of attempts to return by those formerly evicted.

At the same time, this narration of District Six as a historically cosmopolitan area is still contested today. Geschier (2007: 40) even suggests that District Six only came to be an important signifier of multicultural life due to its destruction. In that sense, the place can be said to have come into existence because of its loss, a narrative which currently strengthens the community of returnees to the district. What this shows is the extent to which the narrative and symbolic meaning of a space – almost independently of its realities – impacts upon the physicality of its creation and re-creation. District Six is currently being re-created, based on the narratives of its past and the ways in which actors relate to it.

This is also the capital on which the District Six Museum, launched in 1994, builds its narrative.[2] The museum emerged from the activism of a few individuals who envisaged it as a social hub in District Six and as a way of expressing resistance against relocations through the creation of a physical venue which welcomes returnees rather than rejecting them. The idea of re-creating a space which is welcoming to those formerly evicted from the area was implemented in practice through the opening of the museum as a venue in which the idea of return could be made manifest and celebrated. The museum considers itself a 'living memorial' (District Six Museum, 2016) and hosts a mix of life stories (written and audio), photographs, spatial markers (street signs) and arts material linked to the multi-cultural identity of the district as well as to the questions of relocation and return of those earlier expelled. When visiting the museum, we realised that, perhaps unlike the Apartheid Museum in Johannesburg or the tours on Robben Island, as we outline below, the District Six Museum attracts former and current residents of the district itself and can therefore be considered as a museum for its own community.

The museum is therefore not only an exhibition space symbolising the district as an area, but is also actively involved in supporting people returning to District Six. In fact, this is one of the key ambitions of the museum staff. It is in this frame that the museum has evolved from a history of activism, not least through a campaign called 'Hands off District 6'. This campaign was launched in 1989 to stop multi-national corporations from occupying the district and at the same time paved the way for restitution of the land to those formerly expelled. It becomes obvious that this museum does not limit itself to the exhibition of artefacts, but places emphasis on maintaining close links with the surrounding communities as well as on a social justice agenda that clearly emerges from their activism.

One of the aims in this context is to reconnect different generations, in order to establish a memory in dialogue between older generations (still remembering the pre-eviction life in the area) and children who have no personal memories of District Six. This is particularly crucial in a context in which young people tend to grow up with seemingly natural divisions and have not experienced the feeling of being mixed and part of a racially diverse community, as District Six used to be. In that vein, the museum represents a venue in which inter-ethnic cohabitation is imagined and made apparent in the place of the museum. It relies on an intergenerational memory narrative where the past can serve as an inspiration for the present. Photographs of what the district used to be when it was still cosmopolitan and mixed therefore constitute a key aspect of the exhibition space and make the visitor feel as if transported back in time. In that sense, the idea of a 'common venue' in which people can meet irrespective of race has materialised in the museum, that is, a place where this idea can be put into practice and be given material presence, inspired by narratives of the past of the district. However, whilst the museum represents such a highly localised place with a narrative tied to the very community it is surrounded by, it increasingly aims to reach out to an international audience. It is now possible to look at the museum's artefacts online and even go on a 'virtual tour' through the exhibition. In addition, the museum also regularly hosts international exhibitions that are connected with its own mission and vision. In that respect, the museum fulfils a dual purpose, that is, the creation of a place of remembrance for the local community and also the connection of this place to a more global audience. Both strategies support a core mechanism of the museum in its ambition to provide a 'home' for the idea of return to a local and international community. It is the result of a place-making process that situates ideas of return, social justice and cosmopolitanism in materiality and represents an important go-to place for people hoping to return, or having done so.

The Homecoming Centre

The idea of becoming a community venue is further reinforced by the Homecoming Centre, located next to the Museum and affiliated with it. The centre serves as a venue for different kinds of events such as book launches and concerts, usually with a socially engaged character to them. It is also a venue where the museum staff organise soup kitchens and high tea for elderly people, all of which are rather popular in the community and are well-attended. In that sense, the Homecoming Centre can be considered as an arena for meetings as well as a platform on which people can exchange their stories of relocation and, in addition, their potential opportunities to return to District Six. The deep nostalgia that relocated people and returnees seem to have for the district makes the Homecoming Centre a popular location. It indeed hosts a regular series of events, often funded by sporadic international donations and grants, and has developed into a place where people from different racial and economic backgrounds can meet, all in the spirit of how District Six is remembered. It is exactly the notion of returning 'home' and feeling welcome which are at the origin of the District Six Museum and the accordingly labelled Homecoming Centre. Through the agency of the museum curators and activists, the notion of returning has become more than just a wish, but instead a real possibility as returnees are given a social arena in which they can discuss the conditions and challenges of their return. The enthusiasm of the museum staff is not least responsible for the relative success of this project, alongside the input of a variety of community members. This also means that the Homecoming Centre has become an important place of encounter and meeting as well as political discussions. In this spirit, we witnessed a book launch in the centre in 2012, the speakers at which were prominent figures such as Archbishop Desmond Tutu and the Mayor of Cape Town on the one hand, while on the other hand the audience represented a societal cross-section of both wealthy and influential actors as well as ordinary people from the surrounding community.

Indeed, the museum places emphasis on its participatory approach, which is visible in the collections and inscriptions, many of which are contributions from returnees to the district. This is equally visible in the Homecoming Centre where the curators have placed exhibitions of community work, amongst others. The transformation of the idea of a space of return is therefore not only due to the agency of the museum curators and organisers alone, but has to be situated in the light of the agency of a whole community that is eager to recreate a 'better' District Six and give spatial meaning to this idea.

In that vein, the narratives collected in the museum space and implemented through the work of the Homecoming Centre reflect the creation of a community on cosmopolitan values as celebrated in the district's past. It is this process which is given material presence through the museum as well as the Homecoming Centre. It can certainly be argued that it has become one of the socio-political centres of gravity around which narratives of returnees have been centred and organised. The Homecoming Centre is becoming a key location in which people from different backgrounds can meet and interact in order to reconstitute a District Six that returns their agency rather than depriving them of it. It is the materialisation of an imaginary past as people imagine it in connection with District Six. It is this very past that shapes people's notion of a future that connects back rather than starting on a blank canvas. In that respect, the museum and Homecoming Centre offer a chance for its visitors to move back to the past and find inspiration for community-building in the present and future. The place can thus be considered a different temporality and a reversion to the past, by hosting material based on ideas of community, cosmopolitanism and diversity.

Space-making

Space-making denotes the process during the course of which material places are equipped with meanings and symbolism – either to close down the narratives around the place, or to open it up to competing meanings. A particularly interesting place, the meanings of which can tell us more about the underlying political agency as well as spatial politics, is Robben Island where Nelson Mandela was kept prisoner during apartheid. Following Deacon (2004: 310), the island can be considered as 'intangible heritage' (referring to the non-material values and emotions connected with heritage), but at the same time holds a material counterpart, what Deacon refers to as 'tangible heritage'. Both these different manifestations of heritage are inherently political and point to the actors involved in the decisions and interpretations made. In that sense, Robben Island is a place at which multiple meanings come together, whilst the government as well as tourist agencies have managed to put a very specific imprint on it in the process of space-making, or intangible heritage in Deacon's words, as we show below.

Robben Island

In the case of South Africa, Robben Island can be said to represent a frequently visited tourist attraction. Situated a 30-minute ferry ride from Cape Town, the island became known for hosting the high-security prison in which anti-apartheid activists, famously including Nelson Mandela and Walter Sisulu, were detained before the transition to democracy in 1994.

In the light of space-making, that is, the process of imbuing a space with a particular set of meanings, it is particularly interesting to see that the physical space has a complex and diverse history. Not only did it host the world-famous prison, but there are also interesting traces of the Khoi (the indigenous people of South Africa), the British occupation of the country, the Second World War as well as a rich and diverse wildlife. To a small extent, lobby groups for the Khoi have used the island to point to the colonial oppression of the people since the 17th century due to the imprisonment of a Khoi leader on Robben Island (Deacon, 2004: 314). However, this interpretation of the island has largely been side-lined in the way in which the island is currently narrated to tourists, not least as a result of the dominance of the apartheid prison narrative. There was indeed prior debate on what should be highlighted on the island, but the brand of the island ultimately came to focus on its role in and importance for democracy (Deacon, 2004: 314–315). This was by no means an automatic choice, but rather a political one that considers the transition to democracy as the key aspect that merits representation on the island. Robben Island could indeed have been used to commemorate the suffering of the Khoi through colonialism, or alternatively as a reminder of the fact that the island was used as a military base for the South African defence troops in World War II, pointing to the role that the militarisation of the island played in the construction of a high-security prison by the apartheid government. However, there is only a small paragraph on South Africa's marketing web page on the continuity of oppression on the island:

> Those who fought against Dutch colonisation in southern and eastern Africa, religious Muslim leaders, opponents of British empire building in Africa, prisoners of war, criminals, leprosy sufferers, mentally ill patients, and more recently opponents of the apartheid government, were all packed off to Robben Island.
>
> (SouthAfrica.info, 2016)

Yet, despite the richness of meanings that all mark the island as well as the different forms of violence that have shaped its past, it is really only one master narrative that is now presented to the outside world, namely the struggle for democracy and reconciliation. In that vein, the island has deliberately been created as a space of memorialisation of the apartheid era and was turned into 'Robben Island Museum' in 1997. Having acquired UNESCO World Heritage Site status, the museum is currently staffed by former prisoners who now offer guided tours for visitors to it. A visit to the island made clear that the main visitors are tourists, and it is almost impossible to find a South African among them – apart from the tour guides of course.

The overall approach is to present Robben Island as a symbol of reconciliation (Strange & Kempa, 2003: 394), situated in the wider history of the transformation of South Africa as a whole. The museum has even been said to be aligned with a larger political message, not only of reconciliation, but also of human rights (Deacon, 2004: 312, 313), thus reinforcing a message about the country that the current government is also keen to send. In a way, we could argue, the place of the island has been transformed into a space of political significance, not least pointing to the model role that South Africa claims to play in its efforts to deal with the past as well as the success story tied to this narrative. In this context, Shearing and Kempa (2004: 65) suggest that the government can rely on the educational function that the museum fulfils and thus use it as a political tool. At the same time, the visitor will not encounter the narratives tied to the other aspects of the island's past, such as its military history or its function in the context of colonialism. It seems that those narratives have been side-lined to give heavier weight to the ideas of democracy, reconciliation and human rights and, thereby, to the success of the current government in achieving them.

At the same time, we must not forget that there are economic considerations underlying the use of the island as a museum. It is not unimportant to note that it offers employment to the former prisoners who now run the tours. The site receives overseas funding as well as private sector revenues and the income generated by visitor services (Shackley, 2001: 356). The latter, however, also mean that 'ordinary people' (including ex-prisoners) usually cannot afford the ticket (Shackley, 2001: 359), and in consequence the island mainly addresses itself an international audience rather than a domestic one. This certainly raises questions about the commodification of history as well as the extent to which this is legitimate or not. Therefore the meanings that Robben Island holds are created for an international audience. This helps to raise important revenues and create jobs on the one hand, but also lends a certain degree of legitimacy to the government that is thus seen as dealing with its past and taking the lessons of South African history seriously.

However, the victory of the apartheid narrative over other narratives also comes at a price. There is certainly the question around the issue of psychological distress for the guides, who potentially relive their traumas every time they guide a tour (Shackley, 2001: 361). This remains to be addressed by the museum organisers as some guides do several tours every day. The meaning of Robben Island is hence necessarily linked to the traumas of the former prisoners – an experience certainly sought by the visitors, but at the same time raising ethical issues in relation to the extent to which trauma can or should be used in practices of memory and commemoration (cf. Dawson, 2005).

On the other hand, there has been debate about the extent to which the guides should be able to deliver their own narrative freely, as opposed to a scripted tour on behalf of the museum. Strange and Kempa (2003: 388) confirm that '[i]n spite of official interpretation guidelines [...], onsite heritage interpreters and external pressure groups have lobbied to introduce alternative and in some cases discordant strains into site interpretation.' In fact, the tours are marked by a rather personalised approach, with the guides telling their own stories and experiences in the prison. This certainly helps instil a certain degree of diversity in the use of the place and the creation of multiple meanings. Yet the narratives (necessarily) centre on and connect with the official and dominant narrative of Robben Island's representation as a site of democracy, reconciliation and human rights. As a result, the diversity of meanings is limited through the nature of the tours and the associated tourist interest in the site. At the same time, it becomes clear that there is a particularly strong visitor interest in the story of Nelson Mandela, which the guides are aware of and respond to in their narration of events. As a result, the interpretation of the space is focused on Mandela's life in prison, in connection with the educational activities the prisoners were involved in through his initiative as well as their ad hoc university studies at the 'University of Robben Island'. Again, this process tends to narrow down the diversity of meanings that the island incorporates.

The politics of heritage on Robben Island

What this example reflects is the extent to which the space of the island is (at least partially) scripted to serve wider political and social goals. The use of the place has largely been narrowed down to represent the apartheid prison story, and, more specifically, the life story of Nelson Mandela, with the guides' personal experiences serving as a contextualisation and point of reference. These debates are certainly in flux, for instance with an earlier proposal for the development of a Centre for Conflict Resolution and Education on Robben Island. Not completely dissimilar to the plans put forward at the Maze Long Kesh in Northern Ireland, this centre would have led to the institutionalisation of a particular idea of space (e.g. a space of progress). Shackley (2001: 362) had warned, however, that '[t]he cynical might see this is a thinly disguised means of allowing private developers to make a great deal of money from the provision of overnight hotel facilities, including luxury accommodation for VIPs.' This example illustrates the extent to which the identity of the island is both political and economic in nature and is shaped not least by financial concerns.

The space of the island and its interpretation are therefore created from diverse dynamics, ranging from the goals of the museum organisers, the tour guides, private funders, government and political actors as well as tourism and the visitors to the site more generally. This is coupled with a political economy in which this space is situated and the ways in which it contributes to the self-understanding of South Africa as a nation that is facing and dealing with its past in a constructive way. Robben Island therefore reflects the agency of this variety of actors and their varying influences in the power jigsaw which determines the use and interpretation of the island. It is, in this context, particularly interesting to note the extent to which the international visitors and their funds as well as interests play a key role in this space-making process. The meanings of the island are thus shaped by a highly internationalised as well as nationalised discourse and reach way beyond the immediate geographical location. The place of Robben Island can thus be read as a space of memorialisation of apartheid as well as a symbol of reconciliation – a logical, but by no means automatic, choice, underpinned by a range of political and economic choices. The spatial meanings and logic of Robben Island therefore reflect powerful interests and agents, overcoming the

Figure 6.1 Robben Island, photo taken by authors, 2012.

past on the one hand, but also using it as a tool to legitimise the present political situation on the other hand.

Conclusion

As the examples above reflect, the sites in question collectively illustrate the conundrum for actors in constructing the meaning as well as the materiality of the places and spaces in question. This is particularly politicised in the context of South Africa as a country in which there are firm boundaries between the rich and the poor, as well as the political elites and the marginalised sections of the population. This division plays out spatially and tends to have the effect of political dominance being manifested spatially. In that sense, those powerfully controlling key political spaces are in the position to build networks facilitating the emergence of spaces and places that further disenfranchise the already marginalised. This is certainly not without resistance, as initiatives, such as Abahlali baseMjondolo, show in their attempts to reclaim township spaces and oppose frequent eviction campaigns, albeit with only limited success. Yet this is not to downplay the possibilities that both place-making and space-making processes offer. In fact, the materialisation of the idea of 'homecoming' as illustrated in the District Six Museum and the associated Homecoming Centre are powerful reminders of the agency of social activists to resist dominant political narratives and to create a place in which even potentially difficult and contested ideas can find a material presence. Given that the museum and centre are now present and clearly visible in the community, they stand good chances of permanently transforming the place of District Six and sustainably impacting the narrative of return. Interestingly, the same sustainability seems to have been achieved through the space-making process on Robben Island. The deep stratification of the democracy and reconciliation narrative, throughout different social, political and economic layers, has successfully rooted this dominant narrative deep in the island's identity. Coupled with the strong national and international interest in it, the picture that emerges is one of a fairly stable and powerful narrative, though its legitimacy seems to be grounded chiefly in its predominantly international audience rather than in the communities surrounding it.

What these examples show is the extent to which the interaction between local, national and international actors matters in the feasibility and sustainability of the processes of place- and space-making. It is only through an interplay between a set of actors that a space can be materialised, or a place can acquire stable meanings over time. And even so, places and spaces are open to (re-)negotiation in terms of their political and social function as well as the extent to which they are used as platforms of social activism and political resistance. We can therefore conclude that the example of South Africa is telling when it comes to spatial politics. Every space, whether in a neighbourhood, township, city, tourist attraction or the country as a whole, is an illustration of underlying power dynamics. The persistence of gated communities, the lack of political inclusion of the poor, the commercialisation of memory in an increasingly neo-liberal environment are but few examples highlighting the power that spatial politics hold in the country, both in the past and in the present. The importance of spatial politics and spatial planning has also gained increasing traction and has in 2016 resulted in a bill allowing for state-led land distributions to make up for racial inequalities in land distribution (CNBC Africa, 2016). Hence, overcoming political divisions means overcoming spatial divisions, and maintaining control through space means facing political resistance. 'Peace' is thus inextricably linked to spatial politics and the awareness of those at the centre of political power that the exclusion of certain parts of the population will inevitably provoke further social unrest.

Notes

1 For a more comprehensive account on South Africa's transition to democracy, see Bond (2000).
2 The insights about the District Six Museum and Homecoming Centre are based on museum visits, an event in the Homecoming Centre as well as two meetings with organisers and curators of the museum. Crischene Julius, Tina Smith and Mandy

Sanger, authors' interview, Cape Town, 19 August 2012; Crischene Julius and Tina Smith, authors' interview, Cape Town, 06 December 2012.

Bibliography

Abahlali baseMjondolo, 2016. The Struggle for Human Dignity Continues in the Shadow of Death. [Online] Available at: http://abahlali.org/node/15155/ [Accessed 12 May 2016].

Alexander, P., 2012. Barricades, Ballots and Experimentation: Making Sense of the 2011 Local Government Elections with a Social Movement Lens. In: M. C. Dawson & L. Sinwell, eds. *Contesting Transformation: Popular Resistance in Twenty-First Century South Africa*. London and New York: Pluto Press, pp. 63–79.

Besteman, C., 2008. *Transforming Cape Town*. Berkeley and Los Angeles: University of California Press.

Bond, P., 2000. *Elite Transition: From Apartheid to Neoliberalism in South Africa*. London and Sterling, VA: Pluto Press.

Boraine, A., 2010. South Africa's Truth and Reconciliation Commission from a Global Perspective. In: L. C. Sriram & S. Pillay, eds. *Peace versus Justice? The Dilemma of Transitional Justice in Africa*. Scottsville: University of KwaZulu-Natal Press, pp. 137–152.

Borer, T. A., 2004. Reconciling South Africa or South Africans? Cautionary Notes from the TRC. *African Studies Quarterly* 8(1), pp. 19–38.

Chapman, A. R. & Ball, P., 2001. The Truth of Truth Commissions: Comparative Lessons from Haiti, South Africa, and Guatemala. *Human Rights Quarterly* 23(1), pp. 1–43.

CNBC Africa, 2016. South Africa's Parliament Approves Land Expropriation Bill. [Online] Available at: http://www.cnbcafrica.com/news/southern-africa/2016/05/26/south-africas-parliament-approves-land-expropriation-bill/ [Accessed 4 July 2016].

Cole, C. M., 2007. Performance, Transitional Justice, and the Law: South Africa's Truth and Reconciliation Commission. *Theatre Journal* 59, pp. 167–187.

Coombes, A. E., 2003. *History after Apartheid: Visual Culture and Public Memory in a Democratic South Africa*. Durham and London: Duke University Press.

Darian-Smith, K., Gunner, L. & Nuttall, S., 2005. *Test, Theory, Space: Land, Literature and History in South African and Australia*. London and New York: Routledge.

Dawson, G., 2005. Trama, Place and the Politics of Memory: Bloody Sunday, Derry, 1972–2004. *History Workshop Journal* 59, pp. 151–178.

Dawson, M. C. & Sinwell, L., 2012. Transforming Scholarship: Soberly Reflecting on the Politics of Resistance. In: M. C. Dawson & L. Sinwell, eds. *Contesting Transformation: Popular Resistance in Twenty-First Century South Africa*. London and New York: Pluto Press, pp. 1–22.

de la Rey, C. & McKay, S., 2002. Peace as a Gendered Process: Perspectives of Women Doing Peacebuilding in South Africa. *International Journal of Peace Studies* 7(1), pp. 91–101.

Deacon, H., 2004. Intangible Heritage in Conservation Management Planning: The Case of Robben Island. *International Journal of Heritage Studies* 10(3), pp. 309–319.

District Six Museum, 2016. Permanent Exhibitions. [Online] Available at: http://www.districtsix.co.za/Content/Exhibitions/Permanent/index.php [Accessed 17 May 2016].

Geschier, S. M., 2007. So There I Sit in a Catch-22 Situation: Remembering and Imagining Trauma in the District Six Museum. In: S. Field, R. Meyer & F. Swanson, eds. *Imagining the City: Memories and Cultures in Cape Town*. Cape Town: Human Sciences Research Council, pp. 37–56.

Guelke, A., 1998. *South Africa in Transition: The Misunderstood Miracle*. London: I. B. Tauris.

Hart, G., 2007. Changing Concepts of Articulation: Political Stakes in South Africa Today. *Review of African Political Economy* 34(111), pp. 85–101.

Jürgens, U. & Gnad, M., 2002. Gated Communities in South Africa: Experiences from Johannesburg. *Environment and Planning B: Planning and Design* 29, pp. 337–353.

Kappler, S., 2015. Retelling the City: Competing Spaces of Social Engagement in Cape Town. In: A. Björkdahl & L. Strömbom, eds. *Divided Cities: Governing Diversity*. Lund: Nordic Press, pp. 131–150.

Lemanski, C., 2004. A New Apartheid? The Spatial Implications of Fear of Crime in Cape Town, South Africa. *Environment and Urbanization* 16(2), pp. 101–112.

Lemanski, C., 2006. Spaces of Exclusivity or Connection? Linkages Between a Gated Community and its Poorer Neighbour in a Cape Town Master Plan Development. *Urban Studies* 43(2), pp. 397–420.

Noyes, J., 2012. *Colonial Space: Spatiality in the Discourse of German South West Africa 1884–1915*. London and New York: Routledge.

Pigou, P., 2006. There are More Truths to be Uncovered Before we can Achieve Reconciliation. *Sunday Independent*, 23 April.

Robinson, J., 1996. *The Power of Apartheid: State, Power, and Space in South African Cities*. Oxford: Butterworth Heinemann.

Runiman, C., 2012. Resisting Privatisation: Exploring Contradictory Consciousness and Activism in the Anti-Privatisation Forum. In: M. C. Dawson & L. Sinwell, eds. *Contesting Transformation: Popular Resistance in Twenty-First Century South Africa*. London and New York: Pluto Press, pp. 166–182.

Shackley, M., 2001. Potential Futures for Robben Island: Shrine, Museum or Theme Park?. *International Journal of Heritage Studies* 7(4), pp. 355–363.

Shearing, C. & Kempa, M., 2004. A Museum of Hope: A Story of Robben Island. *The Annals of the American Academy of Political and Social Science* 592, pp. 62–78.

Sosibo, K., 2015. Costly Sports Events Ruin the Poor, Again. [Online] Available at: http://mg.co.za/article/2015-09-10-costly-sports-events-ruin-the-poor-again [Accessed 12 May 2016].

SouthAfrica.info, 2016. Robben Island Remembers. [Online] Available at: http://www.southafrica.info/about/history/robbenisland.htm#.Vzru9_mDGkq#ixzz48uHjr52v [Accessed 17 May 2016].

Strange, C. & Kempa, M., 2003. Shades of Dark Tourism: Alcatraz and Robben Island. *Annals of Tourism Research* 30(2), pp. 386–405.

Taylor, I., 2002. South Africa's Transition to Democracy and the 'Change Industry': A Case Study of IDASA. *Politikon: South African Journal of Political Studies* 29(1), pp. 31–48.

The New Independent, 2015. Shack Dwellers Take on the State in South Africa. [Online] Available at: https://newint.org/features/web-exclusive/2015/06/03/south-africa-shack-dwellers/ [Accessed 25 September 2015].

van Amerom, M. & Büscher, B., 2005. Peace Parks in Southern Africa: Bringers of an African Renaissance?. *The Journal of Modern African Studies* 43(2), pp. 159–182.

Waldmeir, P., 1997. *Anatomy of a Miracle: The End of Apartheid and the Birth of the New South Africa*. Harmondsworth: Penguin.

World Bank, 2012. *South Africa, Economic Update, Focus on Inequality and Opportunity*. [Online] Available at: http://siteresources.worldbank.org/INTAFRICA/Resources/257994-1342195607215/SAEU-July_2012_Full_Report.pdf [Accessed 23 November 2015].

Interviews

Confidential source 1, children's organisation, authors' interview, Cape Town, 28 August 2012.

Confidential source 2, Iziko Museum, authors' interview, Cape Town, 3 September 2012.

Crischene Julius and Tina Smith, authors' interview, Cape Town, 6 December 2012.

Crischene Julius, Tina Smith, Mandy Sanger, authors' interview, Cape Town, 19 August 2012.

Mzonke Poni, authors' interview, Cape Town, 30 August 2012.

Shirley Gunn, authors' interview, Human Rights Media Centre, Cape Town, 7 December 2012.

Conclusion: Reading the Politics of Peace and Conflict Spatially

The spatial turn

This book contributes to the spatial turn in peace research by investigating where and how peace comes about. Our analysis of space and place as vehicles through which transitions from war to peace can be explored has revealed how agency can be captured spatially. We have investigated sites in transformation in post-conflict environments as a way of reading spatial politics and expressions of agency. That way, sites and the transformation that takes place at and around them act as catalysts for both the building of peace as well as the continuation of conflict in a grounded, everyday context of peace and conflict. At the same time, we are cautious of romanticising spatial agency as an act of resistance or leading to progress. We can suggest that agency and structure are constituted by spatial practices. A spatial lens of analysis therefore allows for a nuanced understanding of the interplay of structures of war and peace, as well as the role of individual and collective actors either to engrain them, or to put them openly into question, as is often the case in contexts of transition. The combination of dynamics of space and time can provide a 'geo-story' or 'histo-graphy' as a way of understanding transition (Galtung, 2017: xii). The stories around space and place provide a nuanced understanding of their embeddedness in a geo-political and socio-economic context. This allows for a reconfiguration of space in time and opens up options for thinking about peacebuilding in new, multidimensional ways.

In this vein, we argue for a dynamic understanding of spatial agency in peacebuilding contexts, in that only the transformation of spaces and places, as well as their mutual interplay through practices of space-making and place-making, can help us understand the agency that surrounds them. Indeed, we often see a spatially engrained continuity of violence and oppression in that they are deeply embedded in place and space. On the other hand, the transformation of places and spaces points to the mobilisation of agency. Such transformations may or may not be permanent, but even the temporary reversal of spatial structures, such as, for instance, the Occupy Buffer Zone movement in Cyprus suggests that a particular set of actors can play a key role in the development of any given transition process. What is more, through such a reading of agency that centres around the mobilisation of different forms of agency as concentrated around a particular site, we can avoid the dichotomy of local-international, or top-down and bottom up in favour of a multidimensional approach to agency that reveals various forms of expressions of agency.

Findings

Against this background, we summarise and outline in the following sections eight key conclusions to be drawn from the analyses undertaken in this book.

1 Spatial practices blur the distinction between warscapes and peacescapes

First, we conclude that a spatial analysis tends to challenge our initial assumption that there are warscapes and peacescapes as two almost separate phenomena. Instead, what we have seen is that spaces of war can be transformed into spaces of peace – and vice versa. Places therefore always hold the possibility of hosting spaces that reinforce division or that challenge and overcome the latter. It is the forms of agency that develop around a particular place that determine its social meanings and functions. In that sense, the buffer zone in Cyprus that was originally intended to serve as a zone of separation is meanwhile being used by a large number of peace activists in different shapes and forms. Therefore, places are not fixed in meaning, but space-making offers different interpretations of place and its social functions, creating a multidimensional range of possibilities. The definition as to whether a place is a warscape or a peacescape can hence be said to depend on the observer, narrative and narrator and can change over time as well.

2 Peacebuilding, statebuilding and nationbuilding are spatially conditioned

Our second conclusion postulates that the processes of peacebuilding, statebuilding and nationbuilding necessarily contain a spatial dimension and must also be read in concrete, grounded terms, with respect to how they affect and are affected by the spatial landscape in which they take place. Particularly the example of Bosnia-Herzegovina illustrates the extent to which identity is expressed in spatial terms, for instance with respect to the question of belonging and return, which affects many formerly displaced Bosnians from all ethnic groups. This is somewhat similar to the statebuilding process in Kosovo in which urban landscapes are plastered with markers of belonging and where cityscapes tend to act as platforms on which contested statehood is expressed and spatially made visible. The power of the spatial expression of politics of the state, the nation, and peace more generally, can be linked to the bond that connects people and place. People do connect to places and make them their own, mark them and transform them constantly. Therefore the question of 'homecoming', as our South African example of District Six has shown, is certainly more than just a logistical question, but instead a symbolically-laden process taking place over time in the remaking of the South African nation. It is the reclaiming of a place of belonging that gives a sense of identity in a political community. Given that peacebuilding inevitably deals with questions of the political community and the cohesion that emerges from such forms of belonging, it has to engage with the spatial expressions of such dynamics. This also holds true for the opposite dynamic: if peace relies on spatiality and temporality, then so does war. Indeed, as all our cases have shown, conflict legacies can leave deep traces in spatial terms that make such structures extremely difficult to overcome. The continuous spatial perpetuation of an apartheid system is as illustrative of this process as the continued presence of the 'peace walls' in Northern Ireland that act as a reminder of the different communities inhabiting the cityscape. This goes hand in hand with the militarisation of space, often triggered by clashing statebuilding and nationbuilding processes, that impacts upon the avenues that transitions from war to peace can take. Transformation of the ghost town of Varosha (Cyprus) is hard to achieve, not least due to the continuing presence of the military safeguarding the status quo. Similarly, the buffer zone is still monitored and policed by UN peacekeepers, even decades after the end of violence in the Cypriot conflict. Robben Island's military history contributed to its being used as a prison island during and after the formal end of colonialism, and this is what it has now become known as. The colonial and apartheid use of the island has shaped its identity so much that it has left only limited scope for transforming the island into a different kind of place. We therefore suggest that the practices of building a state as much as a nation are spatially expressed and implemented. Long-standing power structures leave their traces in space as much as do the expressions of agency that challenges those structures.

3 Agency emplaced in time and space evolves through interactions with material and immaterial structures

As this reflexive comparison has shown, our conceptions of place and space engage both material and immaterial structures. We can see from our case analyses that it is the interplay between those two sides of the same coin that tells us about the types of agency that we can find at their intersection. One field which clearly makes visible the connection between the material and immaterial is the field of tourism. Particularly in the cases of Cyprus, Northern Ireland and South Africa, tourism reflects both the continuity and change in the narratives around particular sites. The contestations around the Maze/Long Kesh in Northern Ireland are indeed part of a wider prison tourism discourse and cast light on the connection between the prison as a site of the past and its significance in both economic and political terms in the present. Similar questions arise around the meaning of Robben Island for the Western Cape. Should it be used as a memorial to the past, a site of reconciliation, a tool for the government, or a means of generating economic income? Such questions tell us in depth about the politics that surround the discourses of transition and reflect the agency of those involved in shaping such discourses in relation to the physicality of the island. Yet not only tourism, but also social activism can be understood through a reading of the material and immaterial structures of transition. The Occupy Buffer Zone Movement in Cyprus, for instance, was not only inspired by the idea of unification, but actively used the material site of the buffer zone to make their point. In a similar vein, social movements coming from South African townships are shaped by their geographical location and physical exclusion from city centre politics (Kappler, 2015). In that sense, the spatial dimension of public protest and social activism must be acknowledged if we seek to understand how they work. The Sarajevo Roses are seen as citizen monuments, and can only make sense in the light of their spatial position as well as their transformation over time. They incorporate both the immaterial trauma of the violence of the past and the material presence in the urban landscape of Sarajevo. Eleftheria Square in Nicosia links the presence at the city walls as a connecting place with its social function as a protest place, and the Capetonian District Six Museum needs to be physically placed in the District in order to be able to promote its message of homecoming and return. Such contestations are equally at play around the bridge in Mitrovica that is being claimed and reclaimed by both sides to the conflict. It is the intersection between space and place that, in all of those cases, helps us understand the agency behind them as well as their social and political functions.

4 *The politics of transition and transformation can be read spatially*

In this book, we have looked at the forms of agency that emerge at and drive politics of transition and transformation. As our case studies have shown, such transitions have to be seen in the light of surrounding social dynamics, political contestation as well as their economic underpinnings. Particularly the examples of Northern Ireland and South Africa reflect the degree to which dynamics of (in)equality impact upon the success or failure of transitions to peace. In Northern Ireland, part of the reason of why debates around the past remain heated is the perceived lack of justice. Similarly, South African society continues to manifest high degrees of inequality, which have undermined possibilities of return, reconciliation and social integration. The spatial dynamics of inequality are obvious in both cases: gated communities, townships, walls and the separation of communities. It therefore does not come as a surprise that the forms of agency emerging at this transitional stage are driven by demands for peace and justice. The restoration of land is a key claim in South Africa, while the question of return remains an issue not only there, but also in Bosnia-Herzegovina and Kosovo. In Northern Ireland, resistance against the continued presence of the peace walls has taken various forms, one being the 'Draw Down The Walls' project that gives a face to a potential future without physical barriers between communities. This example reflects an attempt to transform contested space and sheds light on the agency of those involved in overcoming such barriers, at least symbolically. But even in the case of Varosha, the ghost town in Famagusta in the North of Cyprus, transformation is visible. Not only are plans being developed that could lead to the transformation of the place into an eco-zone, but it also plays an important part in the peace negotiations of the island. Varosha itself is a place laden with history and symbolism and must not be underestimated in its political functions. A spatial lens to investigate such processes of transition can therefore give us important clues about underlying dynamics as well as potential political options within such negotiations.

5 A self-sustaining geography can freeze the conflict and cement divisions

Our examples keep showing the power of spatial politics as a way for the state as well as other actors to maintain a system based on divisions. In that sense, we suggest that the power-holders are able to reinforce themselves spatially through the constant reproduction of places and spaces of division. This is what Lemanski (2004) terms the 'architecture of fear', that is, an infrastructure that limits possibly alternative expressions of agency in spatial terms. The constant relocation of the poorest section of the population in South African cities is but one example through which a system of control is maintained and through which political marginalisation takes place. This spatial technology of separation leads to an increasing cleavage between the wealthy and the poor and prevents the formation of a South African community that could reach across those spatial divides. In Bosnia-Herzegovina, the geography of the state as different (ethnic) entities is not only maintained on a national level, but further legitimised through the international community which helped to develop this system in the first place with the ethnic divisions of power and place cemented in the Dayton Peace Agreement. This means limited interaction between the two entities that make up the state of BiH, but also almost-impossible processes of minority return. Our example of Višegrad is telling in this respect. At the same time, this self-sustaining geography also reaches deep into the everyday life of city dwellers. The divided city of Mostar in the South West of Bosnia is a bleak example of spatial governmentality and the limits this imposes on those moving around in the city. This environment makes it not impossible, but hard for activists such as the Youth Cultural Centre Abrašević to act against this infrastructure of division. Instead, what we tend to see in this, but also in the context of Belfast or Mitrovica, is the normalisation of the respective division, given it becomes part of people's everyday lives. In order to deal with this infrastructure, they accept and reinforce such spatial cleavages in their everyday practices, and their normalisation renders divided spaces and places invisible.

6 Spaces and places connect the past, present and future in non-linear ways

Our selected localities have highlighted that spaces and places are never mono-dimensional, but always include a time dimension as well. At the same time, they do not carry forward the past in a linear way into the present and future, but a much more complex process opens up. Indeed, many of the sites we have investigated seem 'frozen in the past' and carry the legacy of the past right into the consciousness of inhabitants and visitors encountering the site. The ghost town of Varosha in Cyprus is a particularly obvious example of this, not least as no human beings are to be found using the site itself. However, this is not a unique process and quite comparable to Robben Island, the identity of which has been fixed as a prison island, continuously perpetuated by tourist visitors and the remarks that are made to them. In that sense, the island struggles to change its reputation as a prison island, in favour a different type of identity – just like the Maze/ Long Kesh prison in Northern Ireland. The latter could have been transformed into a conflict resolution centre but, due to the political contestations around that identity change, it is also frozen in time and so is its prison identity. Indeed, the prisons that we have outlined in our analyses carry a highly symbolic function. They are politically sensitive places, places of pain on the one hand, and at the same time an institutionalisation of memory space in relation to conflict. The contestations around their function in the present and future are therefore so fierce, as the sites in Northern Ireland and South Africa illustrate. This ties in with the wider question of the ownership of the past and the ability to use it in the present: who has the power to label places and spaces? Who has the right to transform the ghost city of Varosha into something new? How can we determine the function of the bridge in Mitrovica? Should the Sarajevo Roses be maintained and highlighted? These and other related questions emerge from the presence of the past in the landscapes of the present. In Pristina, the urban landscape and, specifically, the Mother Teresa Boulevard represent the battles around the ownership of the past and the authority to define what merits preservation. Particularly when it comes to the material legacy of conflict, these questions become political. The peace walls in Northern Ireland are just one example that reflects the extent to which communities can be divided over the need to keep these powerful reminders of the conflict in place, and, alternatively, the desire to transform the urban landscape into one that is less visibly divided.

Against this background, peacebuilding has to take into account not only a perspective geared towards the future, but equally one that ties in with the ways in which the past keeps playing a role in it. Spaces and places are able to sustain narratives of the past into the present and future and can therefore act as important markers of controversies as they emerge in post-conflict landscapes.

7 Shared places offer a platform for intergenerational narratives cutting across time

In the light of the temporal power of spaces and places, we also have to understand that they are able to connect and disconnect users across time. This also means that places and spaces shared across different user groups hold the potential to act as platforms for intergenerational narratives. In our examples, this was particularly evident with cultural spaces that act as inter-generational connectors. The District Six Museum in Cape Town, for instance, is based on sharing the memories of older generations with younger generations. By acting as microcosms of the pan-Yugoslav idea the Youth Cultural Centre Abrašević in Mostar connects Mostar's older generations with the younger. Murals in Belfast also reflect an intergenerational narrative as they communicate a legacy of the past to youth too young to have experi-enced the Troubles. The planning process and policies on cultural heritage in Kosovo negotiate between different generations of community members, some of whom are keen to preserve the past, and others who need to create economic opportunities from this process. In that sense, generational gaps can be overcome through shared spaces and competing narratives of the past can be discussed. The example of Robben Island reflects the needs of different generations and groups – for some it is to share the experiences of being imprisoned, for some it is about employment, and for others it is both at the same time. We can therefore read spaces and places as translators of intergenerational and intercommunity disputes and conflicts.

8 Spatial practices and mobilities can challenge material and immaterial borders and boundaries

We have emphasised that spatial practice is an important factor in cementing power and keeping unjust systems in place. Very often, this is reinforced through the construction of borders: examples include the inter-entity line in Bosnia-Herzegovina, the two-part division of Kosovo, gated communities in South Africa, the buffer zone in Cyprus or the peace walls in Northern Ire-land. However, such structures can be challenged on their own terms and countering spatial practices must not be overlooked. Our diverse examples have shown that spatial resistance can emerge from everyday practices. Borders are often contested and transgression as an act of resistance is no rarity. Crossing the bridge in Mitrovica does indeed have strong symbolical meaning, just as much as entering or crossing the buffer zone in Cyprus. Although the process of minorities returning in Bosnia-Herzegovina is almost a rarity, in the cases where it happens, it carries high symbolic significance and makes a lasting impact on the lives of the returnees as well as those in the communities they are returning to. The fact that the Occupy Buffer Zone Movement in Cyprus dared to cross the boundary and started camping in the buffer zone can be considered an important part of their political activism. This is also the context in which the Nicosia Master Plan, as an incentive to walk across the city despite the material and immaterial borders that have to be crossed, is a political statement that goes beyond a mere tourist attraction. Walking can therefore become a subversive act and can, in the long run, transform spaces and places in terms of connecting them to other places and spaces, as well as opening them up for new groups of users. And the ways in which space is used and activated are always political acts.

Implications of findings

We expect these findings to impact upon peacebuilding theory and practice alike. Theoretically as we have demonstrated above, spaces and places need to be seen as playing a key role in the understanding of transitional processes as well as reading the agency involved in peacebuilding. For the practice of peacebuilding, our findings mean that there needs to be an increased degree of attention to the spatial causes of conflict as well as to the possibilities that spatial politics open for grounded and contextualised peacebuilding. Conflict about space has to be taken seriously and the construction of shared spaces and places may become an important approach to building peace. In that sense, peacebuilding is partly linked to spatial planning as well. In some cases, the removal of physical and mental barriers to interaction is a first step towards connecting communities, and venues such as parks, bridges and walls can act as catalysts of both war and peace. Peacebuilding then becomes a question of societies claiming and designing such places jointly and in a shared way. It relates to the question of who can access and move across different spaces. The facilitation of mobility can, in this context, be of primary importance – in great contrast to the current almost global tendency that tends to close down spaces and borders rather than facilitating movement across them.

At the same time, peacebuilders need to shy away from tokenism in terms of constructing meaningless places just for the sake of creating a 'façade of peace' (cf. Bliesemann de Guevara & Kühn, 2010). Material places, without the counterpart of symbolic, meaningful space, will be limited in their ability to catalyse transformation. Similarly, a purely symbolic idea of space without any material underpinning also remains ideational and lacks sustainability. Therefore, in both peacebuilding practice and theory we have to acknowledge the interplay of space and place and the need always to look at them as two sides of the same coin.

Towards a future research agenda

There are more areas of research that this book opens up and that deserve attention in future research. Importantly, while we have emphasised the relationship between spaces and places and community relations, we have not been able to focus specifically on all possible dimension of this process.

First, it is therefore important to acknowledge that gender is a key platform for the expression and playing out of agency as well as dynamics of marginalisation, also in spatial terms. In that sense, a gender reading of where peace comes about can give important insights into the ways in which gender plays a role in the spatial development of structures of oppression and emancipation.

Second, and tying in with this first point, although, or because, gender studies have challenged the neat distinction between public and private, an analysis of which places and spaces are transformed from private spaces into public ones, and vice versa, helps us understand the policitisation of space and place. In line with that, we have already hinted at the distinction between visible and invisible spaces. Conflict often takes place across the visible and invisible, but tends to be captured in its visible dimensions only. Similarly, we need to acknowledge the hidden dynamics of peace. Whilst we have highlighted this in our different case studies in this book, a systematic analysis of the interplay between visible and invisible, between public and private spaces, would be welcome.

Third, what this book opens up is a rethinking of deeply engrained peacebuilding categories, and foremost the dichotomy of 'local' versus 'international'. As our spatial analysis shows, such categories cannot be upheld in a neat way as complex networks of actors come together around different places in spaces. In practice, this means that every place has its very own locals and internationals, and these categories are constantly being made and re-made, as places find themselves in constant transformation. A focused breakdown of the implications of such categorisations therefore necessitates an analysis of the networks of actors that interact around places and the fluidity of their engagement that cuts across categories. No normative judgement about the 'local' can be made without its spatial and temporal contextualisation.

Therefore, fifth and last, it is crucial that we pay tribute to the temporal aspect of agency. We have focused on a spatial reading of agency in this book, but acknowledge that without the focus on transformation over time, spatial agency remains mono-dimensional. Agency takes on spatial and temporal forms, and both dimensions need to be explored in the light of the insights they give us into the transitions from conflict to peace. In that sense, moving on from our spatial reading of agency in contexts of transition, an analysis of the ways in which spaces, places and time can be linked will open up new ways of understanding and configuring peacebuilding throughout history and geography.

Bibliography

Bliesemann de Guevara, B. and Kühn, F. P., 2010. *Illusion Statebuilding: Warum sich der westliche Staat so schwer exportieren lässt.* Hamburg: edition Körber-Stiftung.

Galtung, J., 2017. Foreword. In: A. Björkdahl, and S. Kappler, *Peacebuilding and Spatial Transformation. Peace, Space and Place.* Abingdon, New York: Routledge.

Kappler, S. (2015). Retelling the City: Competing Spaces of Social Engagement in Cape Town. In: A. Björkdahl & L. Strömbom, *Divided Cities. Governing Diversity.* Lund: Nordic Academic Press, pp. 131–150.

Lemanski, C., 2004. A New Apartheid? The Spatial Implications of Fear of Crime in Cape Town, South Africa. *Environment and Urbanization* 16(2), pp. 101–112.

Index

Taylor & Francis eBooks

Helping you to choose the right eBooks for your Library

Add Routledge titles to your library's digital collection today. Taylor and Francis ebooks contains over 50,000 titles in the Humanities, Social Sciences, Behavioural Sciences, Built Environment and Law.

Choose from a range of subject packages or create your own!

Benefits for you

>> Free MARC records
>> COUNTER-compliant usage statistics
>> Flexible purchase and pricing options
>> All titles DRM-free.

Benefits for your user

>> Off-site, anytime access via Athens or referring URL
>> Print or copy pages or chapters
>> Full content search
>> Bookmark, highlight and annotate text
>> Access to thousands of pages of quality research at the click of a button.

eCollections – Choose from over 30 subject eCollections, including:

Archaeology	Language Learning
Architecture	Law
Asian Studies	Literature
Business & Management	Media & Communication
Classical Studies	Middle East Studies
Construction	Music
Creative & Media Arts	Philosophy
Criminology & Criminal Justice	Planning
Economics	Politics
Education	Psychology & Mental Health
Energy	Religion
Engineering	Security
English Language & Linguistics	Social Work
Environment & Sustainability	Sociology
Geography	Sport
Health Studies	Theatre & Performance
History	Tourism, Hospitality & Events

For more information, pricing enquiries or to order a free trial, please contact your local sales team: www.tandfebooks.com/page/sales

Printed in Great
Britain
by Amazon